The Roots of Modern English

The Roots of Modern English

The Roots of Modern English

L. M. Myers, *Arizona State University*

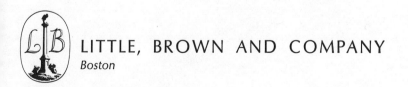

LITTLE, BROWN AND COMPANY
Boston

Preface

Our profession is deeply committed to the idea that every English teacher (and preferably every citizen) should take a course in the history of the language, but our opinions of what material should be covered vary enormously. A generation ago it could be comfortably, if not always accurately, assumed that a student taking such a course had at least a fair knowledge of Latin and of either French or German; that he had a firm grasp of the principles of traditional grammar; and that he and his instructor were in agreement about both the validity and the importance of those principles. None of these assumptions can reasonably be made today. If a student has any foreign-language training at all it is likely to be a couple of years of Spanish, which is a very fine language, but less useful than some others as preparation for the history of English. Many students admit that they have only the vaguest notions about English grammar. And if one does show up with an old-fashioned mastery of that subject he may encounter an instructor who advises him to forget all he has learned and start again from an entirely different approach. I think it is fair to say that in no other area of our discipline do so many competent students struggle so hard to memorize material that they do not really understand, in the pious hope that it will all make sense some day — or at least that it will get them through the required examinations.

In attempting to meet this situation I have left out a good deal of detail, particularly on phonology, and I have treated some apparently simple matters with what may seem like painful elaboration. My judgment is of course open to question. Perhaps the best defense I can offer is that I have not tried to supersede the many admirable books already available in this area, but to prepare students to read them with better understanding.

Since it has seemed advisable to keep the documentation light, my great debt to contemporary and earlier scholarship is very imperfectly indicated. Aside from the borrowings specifically acknowledged I have drawn heavily on A. C. Baugh's *A History of the English Language,* particularly for developments in the vocabulary; and on G. L. Brooks' work of the same title for the dating of sound-changes. Most of the examples of Early Modern English are taken from J. L. Moore's *Tudor-Stuart Views of the Growth, Status, and Destiny of the English Language.* Rolf Kaiser has very kindly allowed me to select specimens of Old and Middle English from his *Medieval English* (an admirable collection which deserves to be better known in this country).

Professors Jack Conner of Stanford University, Robert Daniel of Kenyon College, and Kenneth G. Wilson of the University of Connecticut have read considerable parts of the manuscript, and Professor Samuel R. Levin of Hunter College has corrected the proofs with a scholarly as well as an editorial eye. These gentlemen are responsible for many improvements, though quite free from blame. To all of them I offer my hearty thanks.

L. M. MYERS

Table of Contents

CHAPTER ONE   *What Is a Language?*   1

1. Some Confusion About Language, *1*.   2. Some Theories of
the Origin of Language, *3*.   3. The Structural Levels of Language, *4*.   4. Speech and Writing, *5*.   5. Some Writing to Look
Through, *6*.   6. The Variations of Language, *8*.   7. The Chicken
or the Egg? *9*.   8. Langue and Parole, *10*.   9. The True-
Language Theory, *11*.   10. The Sum-of-Parts Theory, *14*.   11. A
Suggested Compromise, *17*.

CHAPTER TWO   *The Sounds We Talk With*   19

12. The Selection of Sounds, *19*.   13. Phonetics, *20*.   14. Phonemes, *22*.   15. Origin and Distortion of the Ordinary Alphabet, *24*.   16. The IPA, *26*.   17. The Two Extremes of Our
Sound System, *29*.   18. The Consonant Phonemes, *29*.   19. The
Vowel Phonemes, *33*.   20. The Short Vowels, *34*.   21. Short
and Long Vowels and Diphthongs, *35*.   22. Long Vowel and
Diphthong Symbols, *36*.   23. Diphthongs in "*r*-less dialects," *36*.
24. Phonemic Transcription, *37*.

CHAPTER THREE   *The Pre-History of English*   40

25. Reconstructing Languages, *40*.   26. Some Romance Languages, *40*.   27. Mechanics of Sound Change, *43*.   28. English and German, *45*.   29. The Great Language Families, *45*.
30. Origin of the Indo-European Family, *46*.   31. The Branches
of Indo-European, *48*.   32. The Modern Discovery of Indo-
European, *50*.   33. The Germanic Group and Grimm's Law, *52*.

34. The Heavy Germanic Stress, 57.   35. The Three Branches of Germanic, 58.   36. The Genealogy of English, 59.

CHAPTER FOUR   *Old English*   61

37. The Beginnings of English, 61.   38. Pre-Christian England, 63.   39. Historical Background of the Old English Period, 65. 40. Alfred and English Prose, 68.   41. The Sounds of Old English, 69.   42. The Structure of Old English, 71.   43. Nouns, 73.   44. Pronouns, 76.   45. The Personal Pronouns, 76.   46. Demonstrative and Interrogative Pronouns, 78.   47. Adjectives, 80.   48. Verbs, 81.   49. Strong and Weak Verbs, 81.   50. The Strong Verbs, 82.   51. Classes of Strong Verbs, 84.   52. The Weak Verbs, 85.   53. Changes in Classification, 86.   54. Adverbs, 87.   55. Prepositions, Conjunctions, and Interjections, 88.   56. Summary of Old English Inflections, 88.   57. Specimen of Old English, 88.   58. "The Creation," 96.   59. Analyzing "The Creation," 97.   60. Vocabulary Replacements, 102.   61. The Romans in Britain, 103.   62. The Latin Element in Old English, 104.   63. The Scandinavian Element, 107.

CHAPTER FIVE   *The Middle English Period*   113

64. The Norman Conquest, 113.   65. The Feudal System, 115. 66. The Organization of the Country, 117.   67. The Submergence of English, 119.   68. The Diversity of Middle English, 120. 69. Some Peculiarities of Middle English Manuscripts, 122. 70. Sound-Changes in Middle English, 125. 71. Diphthongs, 126. 72. Consonants, 126.   73. Loss of Inflections, 127.   74. Borrowings from the French Vocabulary, 128.   75. Characteristics of Norman-French Words, 130.   76. Learned and Popular Words, 130.   77. Indirect Influence of French, 131.   78. Other Foreign Influences on Middle English, 132.   79. Loss of Native Words and Word-Elements, 132.   80. Middle English Spelling, 133.   81. "The Orrmulum," 135.   82. "Alysoun," 139. 83. The London Dialect, 140.   84. The Text of Chaucer, 141.   85. Specimen of Chaucer, 142.   86. Chaucer's Phonemes: Consonants, 143.   87. Short Vowels, 144.   88. Long Vowels, 144. 89. Pronunciation, 144.   90. Vocabulary, 147.   91. Grammatical Structure, 151.   92. Nouns, 151.   93. Pronouns, 152. 94. Adjectives, 152.   95. Verbs, 153.   96. Negatives, 154. 97. Impersonal Constructions, 155.   98. The Morte Darthur, 159.

CHAPTER SIX *The English Renaissance* 166

99. Early Modern English, *166*. 100. The Great Vowel Shift, *168*. 101. The Short Vowels, *170*. 102. Consonants, *170*. 103. Changes in Inflection, *170*. 104. The Spread of Education, *173*. 105. Weakening of Class Distinctions, *174*. 106. Introduction of Printing, *175*. 107. Development of Spelling Conventions, *177*. 108. English and Latin in the Renaissance, *179*. 109. The Debatable Importance of Authors, *181*. 110. Increase in Vocabulary, *183*. 111. The Conservatives, *184*. 112. The Enthusiasts for Native Resources, *189*. 113. The Travelers: Oversea Language, *192*. 114. Scholarly Innovators: Inkhorn Terms — and Others, *192*. 115. Copiousness, *195*. 116. Compendiousness, *196*. 117. Other Reasons for Borrowing, *198*. 118. Renaissance Neglect of Grammar, *201*. 119. Development of Sentence Structure, *202*. 120. The Status of Local Dialects, *205*. 121. The Quality of Renaissance English, *205*.

CHAPTER SEVEN *The Authorities Step In* 207

122. The Desire to Regulate the Language, *207*. 123. "Universal Grammar," *210*. 124. The Idea of an Academy, *211*. 125. The Incubating Period, *212*. 126. The Earliest English Dictionaries, *213*. 127. Johnson's Dictionary, *216*. 128. The Beginnings of Our Traditional Grammar, *221*. 129. The Lowth Tradition, *222*. 130. Lowth's Preface, *223*. 131. Lowth's Grammar, *226*. 132. Sound Changes, *228*. 133. Development of Progressive and "Emphatic" Constructions, *229*.

CHAPTER EIGHT *English Spreads Out* 231

134. The Double Expansion of English, *231*. 135. Trade and the British Empire, *232*. 136. The Influence of American English, *233*. 137. The Expansion of Knowledge, *236*. 138. The Making of Compounds, *236*. 139. Shortenings, *238*. 140. Other Sources, *239*. 141. What Is a Word? The Size of the Current Vocabulary, *239*. 142. When Is a Word in the Language? *241*. 143. Advantages and Disadvantages of a Great Vocabulary, *243*. 144. Changes in Meaning, *245*. 145. Varieties of English, *249*. 146. "Formal English," *251*. 147. Changes in the Verb System, *253*.

CHAPTER NINE   *The Background of Traditional Grammar*
255

148. Some General Remarks About Grammar, *255.*   149. Structural Patterns, *258.*   150. Variations in Traditional Grammar, *260.* 151. Nouns and Adjectives, *261.*   152. Number, *264.*   153. Gender, *265.*   154. Case, *267.*   155. Pronouns, *270.*   156. Verbs, *272.*   157. Person and Number, *273.*   158. Tense, *273.*   159. Mood, *274.*   160. Voice, *274.*   161. The Latin and English Systems Compared, *275.*   162. Adverbs, *277.*   163. Prepositions and Conjunctions, *278.*   164. Interjections, *279.*   165. A Few Roman Ghosts, *279.*

CHAPTER TEN   *Contemporary Developments in America*
282

166. The Language Still Changing, *282.*   167. "Functional Grammar," *283.*   168. The Doctrine of Usage Reappears, *285.* 169. Structural Linguistics, *288.*   170. Three Approaches to the Parts of Speech, *290.*   171. A New View of Standard English, *293.* 172. Fries's *Structure of English, 294.*   173. Phonological Grammar, *299.*   174. Another Phonemic Notation, *300.*   175. The Suprasegmental Phonemes, *301.*   176. Pitch, *302.*   177. Stress, *303.*   178. Juncture, *303.*   179. The Importance of Intonation, *304.*   180. The "New Grammar" in Schools and Colleges, *306.* 181. Generative-Transformational Grammar, *307.*   182. Phrase Structure, *310.*   183. Transformations, *311.*   184. Morphophonemics, *311.*   185. Some Guesses About Future Developments, *312.*

Select Bibliography   316

Index   319

The Roots of Modern English

CHAPTER ONE

What Is a Language?

1. SOME CONFUSION ABOUT LANGUAGE. It is quite possible to spend years studying or even teaching various languages without ever having a very firm or useful notion of what a language is. But to proceed in this way naturally involves a good deal of waste motion and makes the learning of a language much more difficult than it need be. This is probably the principal reason why so many Americans say: "Of course I don't really know any French — I just had it in college." This casual pessimism is bad enough when applied to a foreign language. When extended, as it often is, to the native tongue, it can cause very serious worry and outright suffering. Our confusion about the nature of languages is such that many people who speak excellent English never have the satisfaction of knowing that they do, but go through life with recurrent feelings of guilt about their supposed inadequacy.

It would be pleasant to avoid such dangers by agreeing on a nice, efficient definition, but unfortunately no such convenient solution will work. A language is much too complicated an affair to be effectively summarized in any sacred set of words. If we adopted one we should continually find that we were either stretching the definition to cover some aspect we had not pre-

1

viously considered or narrowing our ideas of language to fit the definition. Such stretching and narrowing are quite legitimate when they are done explicitly and for specified purposes by qualified scholars; but they are dangerously misleading when offered to the general public. What most people need is not a definition of language, but some information about how a few languages have developed and how they work; some discussion of what we actually know about languages and what we can only guess at; and (perhaps most of all) a demonstration that some of our most widely cherished beliefs about language are inaccurate to the point of superstition.

To begin with the obvious, language is what human beings talk with. Anybody who wants to may of course define the word *language* so as to include the noises made by crows or the wing-signals made by bees, but I am simply not using the word that way. Without language the human race would hardly be human in any very important sense. We couldn't even think as we now use the term, because most of our thinking is done in language and couldn't be done without it; and it seems most unlikely that we could have developed even the simplest kind of stone-age culture.

I have just mentioned the wing-signals of bees, and we all know that some of the social life of dogs seems to be carried on by sniffing. The fact that our main system of signals is composed of sounds is therefore a matter of choice rather than of necessity, but there is little doubt that our ancestors made a wise choice. If we consider each of the five senses we can see at once that a really extensive set of symbols based on smell or taste would be rather hard to organize and transmit. We might use touch, but not at a distance, and sight has various disadvantages as a *basic* system. It won't work in the dark or in thick brush or under many other conditions; there is no generally satisfactory way of attracting the attention of the one you want to communicate with; and it interferes too much with other activities. On the whole hearing seems to be the most promising sense to receive with, and that is the one our ancestors somehow selected. Maybe they tried all five and that one simply worked out best.

2. SOME THEORIES OF THE ORIGIN OF LANGUAGE. Of course there are many ways of making sound. Crickets rub their legs together and ruffed grouse drum on hollow logs, but neither method seems to permit of much variety. By using their mouths and some nearby organs our ancestors developed a much more flexible system. Nobody knows how the first steps were made. One very old theory is that some sounds just naturally represent some things, and man somehow made the connection. This has been expressed metaphorically by saying that when early man for the first time saw a cow, somehow "a bell rang" in his brain, and he said *cow*. People who do not care for the explanation have called this the *"ding-dong theory."* Another guess is that language began by imitation of natural sounds. According to this the first words were the ancient equivalents of *bow-wow, meow, gurgle, swish,* etc. There certainly are words of this sort, which may be called "echoic" or "onomatopoetic"; but there is no proof that they are among the earliest words, and there are not enough of them to make a very satisfactory basis for all language. Unbelievers have accordingly called this the *"bow-wow theory."*

A third theory is that vocal sounds were at first merely an accidental accompaniment of gestures. A man who was disgusted, for instance, might make a face to indicate his disgust, perhaps rounding and pushing out his lips. If he did this forcefully enough some breath might escape and he would make a noise. At first it was the face that had the meaning; then the sound which accompanied the face began to have a share of the meaning; and finally, since the sound was more convenient, it took over the job of conveying the meaning all by itself. If you try to make such a face and noise you may guess that people who don't accept it call this the *"pooh-pooh theory."*

There is also the *yo-he-ho* theory which argues that men engaged in heavy shared labor automatically made grunts, which gradually became symbols of the activities that called them forth; and there are various others. But no one of them really explains very much, and certainly no one is now generally accepted as satisfactory. We just don't know how language began, and there is no sound reason to suppose that we ever shall.

3. THE STRUCTURAL LEVELS OF LANGUAGE. However they began, the early speakers of a language had to make the following steps, though presumably not in such a clearcut and logical order as here indicated:

1. Select, from innumerable possibilities, a few dozen sounds to serve as the building blocks of their speech. No two of them could possibly pronounce the sounds exactly alike, but the variations had to lie within recognizable limits. These sounds, or rather sound-classes, are called *phonemes.* They are not pronunciations of letters; letters are indications, often very ambiguous, of phonemes.

2. Arrange these phonemes into some thousands of meaningful units, which may be either complete words or significant parts of words, called *morphemes.* For instance, *fire* contains only one morpheme; *fireman* contains two, each of which could occur alone; and *fireman's* contains three, one of which occurs only in combinations. Though the morpheme indicated by *'s* is not a word, it is an important unit in the structure of the language.

3. Develop a *syntax,* consisting of some habitual patterns for arranging the morphemes into longer utterances, such as sentences. The three most obvious elements in the patterns are:

a. word-order

b. "inflectional" morphemes, such as those found in *walk, walks, walked, walking,* or *big, bigger, biggest.*

c. "function words," such as prepositions and auxiliary verbs, which are often more important as structural elements in sentences than for any exact meanings of their own.

Just as real, though not so clearly indicated in writing, are the elements of pitch, stress, and transition between sounds, which can often give different ways of saying the "same" sentence entirely different meanings.

This is obviously the barest outline of the sort of thing that happened. The actual process must have been incredibly complicated, and it is not surprising that no group ever managed to make these steps with complete uniformity. There is no reason to believe that even two people can either speak exactly alike or understand each other perfectly and consistently, or that one person can speak at seventy exactly as he did at twenty. When the communicating group consists of hundreds of millions of people spread over millions of square miles and developing through fifteen centuries of an ever-changing world, a complete and tidy analysis of their language is an obvious impossibility. It is, however, entirely feasible to discuss some of the forces at work in language, and some of the events which directed the particular course that these forces should take as Modern English evolved from its earliest discoverable sources.

4. SPEECH AND WRITING. Language developed for a good many thousand years, and apparently became as complicated as it ever got to be, before any way of writing it down was invented. The old and apparently logical idea that uncivilized and illiterate people must speak a very simple kind of language has been completely destroyed by modern investigation. Linguists have found that African Bushmen and Amazonian Indians speak languages of a grammatical complexity that would make most of us shudder. The spoken form of language is therefore primary, and the written form, however important it may be, is secondary. Most of us realize this — in a way, and part of the time. It seems perfectly obvious when we think of history. But when it comes to our everyday use of language we often think of the written form as the true one, and of speech as an often very imperfect reflection. For instance, our usual pronunciations are often considered careless or sloppy when they do not contain all the sounds that seem to be indicated by the established spelling. It seldom

occurs to most people that when writing and speech differ, the simplest explanation is that writing is falling down on its job of reflecting speech.

Of course the simplest explanation may be a little too simple to be entirely accurate. Writing began simply as a secondary representation of speech, but for many purposes it has obvious advantages, especially in its comparative permanence; and among literate people it always develops some independent characteristics of its own, and exerts some influence on the original spoken form. Even the English spoken by a man who personally is illiterate is very different from what it would have been if our society had no tradition of literacy. It is therefore natural — as most things that happen consistently are — that the comparative importance of the written form should often be exaggerated in schools. When the teacher writes a sentence on the blackboard or calls attention to one in a textbook, it is there for all to consider uniformly and at leisure. It seems both more real and more important than a spoken sentence which disappears as soon as it is uttered; and it is certainly more convenient to consider and discuss. So the teacher uses it as a model for rather than a record of speech, and says things like, "Danny, don't say *ol' knight*, say *old knight*. Can't you see the *d*? You must learn to pronounce words the way they are written." The fact that even the teacher does not pronounce the *k*, the *g*, or the *h* in *knight* is seldom considered at this point.

The importance given to the written form of language, in schools and in many other situations, is an undeniable fact, and not necessarily a shameful one; but we will find it very useful to remember that the spoken form is not only the earlier, but for most purposes still the primary one.

5. SOME WRITING TO LOOK THROUGH. This last point is easy enough to accept in theory, but quite hard to grasp firmly as a working principle; and the better educated we are, and the more our education has concentrated on English, the more likely we are to feel that the language really lives in books and is only im-

perfectly reflected in speech. Perhaps the best way to illustrate this tendency is to examine a passage that was printed before our conventions of writing had become comparatively uniform:

> And certaynly our langage now vsed varyeth ferre from that whiche was vsed and spoken whan I was borne; for we Englysshe men ben borne vnder the domynacyon of the mone, whiche is neuer stedfaste, but euer wauerynge, wexynge one season, and waneth and dyscreaseth another season. And that comyn Englysshe that is spoken in one shyre varyeth from a-nother in so moche, that in my dayes happened that certayn marchauntes were in a shippe in Tamyse, for to haue sayled ouer the see into Zelande; and for lacke of wynde thei taryed atte forlond, and wente to lande for to refreshe them. And one of theym, named Sheffelde, a mercer, cam in-to an hows, and axed for mete; and specyally he axed after eggys. And the goode wyf answerde, that she coude speke no Frenshe. And the marchaunt was angry, for he also coude speke no Frenshe, but wolde haue hadde egges, and she vnderstode hym not. And thenne at laste a-nother sayd that he wolde haue eyren. Then the good wyf sayd that she vnderstod hym wel! Loo, what sholde a man in thyse dayes now wryte, egges or eyren? Certaynly it is harde to playse euery man by cause of dyuersite and chaunge of langage.[1]

[From Caxton's Preface to his *Eneydos*, 1490.]

It is really quite amazing how differently people of approximately equal intelligence will react to such a passage as this. One man will read it almost at sight, possibly pausing for a second or so at *vsed* and *wauerynge*, but adapting himself almost immediately, and quickly recognizing every word except perhaps *forlond* and *mercer*. Another will find it almost unintelligible at first glance, and almost intolerable even after a good deal of study. For anybody who finds it difficult the following steps are suggested:

1. Make up your mind that there is not a misspelled word in the passage. Never mind whether this statement is true — it is

---

[1] Rolf Kaiser, *Medieval English* (Berlin-Wilmersdorf, 1961), p. 567, lines 195–211.

useful. The man who wrote the passage was simply using the letters he knew to indicate the sounds of the words he used, and he is fairly, though far from perfectly, consistent. If he happened to spell a word two different ways — for instance *eggys* and *egges* — there was no way he could find out which was right, because there was no dictionary of the language in existence, and he could find plenty of practice on both sides.

2. Notice that he tends to use some conventions quite different from ours. If we reversed his *u*'s and *v*'s the passage would look far more normal, and if we reversed his *i*'s and *y*'s we should gain about as much as we lost.

3. Use your ears to help your eyes. A number of words which seem strange to the sight are immediately clear to the ear, especially if they are pronounced in context and with no excess of precision. For instance, *comyn* alone might suggest nothing, but if you read aloud and rather casually "that comyn Englysshe" it could hardly be anything but "that common English."

What we have, in other words, is a spoken language represented somewhat inadequately, but not hopelessly, in print; and the way to understand this language is to look through the groups of letters for the sounds that lie behind them. (Semi-literate people sometimes seem to understand this better than the thoroughly educated.) In studying Modern English it is possible, if not reasonable, to think of a word as a group of letters which should be pronounced in a certain way; but in studying the earlier stages it is absolutely necessary to remember that a word is a group of sounds, which the spelling suggests but does not control.

6. THE VARIATIONS OF LANGUAGE. This particular passage of Caxton's is also interesting for another reason. Nearly five hundred years ago the man who introduced printing into English was considerably worried by the "dyuersite & chaunge of langage." He would have had just as much reason for worry if he had lived five hundred or a thousand years earlier; and he has

successors who are just as much worried now. Uniformity and stability in language would certainly have their advantages, but before we yearn for them too passionately perhaps we should consider whether they are even theoretically possible.

To begin with, nobody talks simply language — we have to talk English or Spanish or German. Several hundred millions of us talk English, in one way or another. The Americans don't talk just like the British, and the Americans in South Carolina don't talk just like the Americans in Cleveland. In fact, nobody talks simply English — we have to talk one dialect or another. Of course there are snobbish people who think that what they talk is pure English, and anything different is a dialect; and there are humble people who realize that they talk a dialect, but credit other more fortunate people with talking the language pure. However, all qualified students of the subject now seem to agree that the language is composed exclusively of dialects. They also agree that we are on pretty slippery ground if we argue that some dialects are *intrinsically* better than others, though of course it is obvious that some have more prestige, and may therefore be worth learning.

If we go one step further we will realize that no two speakers of a given dialect talk exactly alike. Each has his own *idiolect,* or individual language, which differs at least a little from all others. And if we consider our own idiolects we realize that no one of us talks exactly the same way all the time. So language is really languages, which are really collections of dialects, which are really collections of idiolects — and even these aren't quite uniform and dependable.

7. THE CHICKEN OR THE EGG? We are now faced with a very difficult question. Are the dialects and idiolects merely group and individual departures from the true language? Or is a language simply the sum total of what the idiolects that compose its dialects happen to add up to? Unfortunately, each answer looks quite reasonable from one point of view, but entirely impossible from another. We are then reminded of the ancient

puzzle of which came first, the chicken or the egg; the situation seems to be completely paradoxical. No solution so far proposed squares with all the evidence, or satisfies all competent linguists. Probably the best way to approach the question is to remove the word *merely* from the second sentence of this paragraph, and the word *simply* from the third. Anybody who wants to keep either word in and answer *yes* to the question in which it occurs is interested in defending a dogma rather than forming an opinion. And anybody who really wants to learn anything about the subject will find it profitable to devote most of his effort to understanding the point of view he finds least attractive. There really is important evidence on both sides.

8. LANGUE AND PAROLE. About sixty years ago the great Swiss linguist, Saussure,[2] attempted to clarify the problem by dividing human speech into two components — *langue*, an impersonal set of conventions to which all members of a speech community must (subconsciously) subscribe in order to understand and make themselves understood; and *parole*, a collective term for individual acts of speaking. *Parole* would be utterly meaningless if it were not based on *langue;* but it never reflects *langue* quite perfectly, and it inevitably involves certain physical phenomena which are no more a part of *langue* than the chalk mark with which a circle may be represented on a blackboard is part of the circle which it represents. Saussure says that *langue* is "the social side of speech, outside the individual who can never create or modify it by himself; it exists only by virtue of a sort of contract

[2] Ferdinand de Saussure, *Cours de Linguistique Générale* (Paris, 1916). Unfortunately, this book was not actually written by Saussure, but was compiled by two of his students from notes on his three series of lectures, delivered between 1906 and 1911. It is impossible to determine whether certain contradictions which mar an exceedingly valuable book are due to changes in his thinking or to inaccurate reporting and editing. The book has been translated into English by Wade Baskin as *Course in General Linguistics* (New York, 1959). The quotations and references in this chapter are all from pages 14 to 20 of the English version.

signed by the members of a community." A little later he adds that it "exists in the form of a sum of impressions deposited in the brain of each member of a community, almost like a dictionary of which identical copies have been distributed to each individual."[3]

Saussure says that one might, if really necessary, apply the term "linguistics" to each of the two branches, and speak of a linguistics of *parole;* but that such a science must not be confused with linguistics proper, whose sole object is *langue.* Since his time most European linguists have followed his lead, while American linguists have emphasized *parole,* denying with considerable vigor his statement that it was no part of "linguistics proper." During the past decade many American linguists have adopted the Saussurean attitude, but discussion of this development will be postponed to Chapter 10.

9. THE TRUE-LANGUAGE THEORY. To a non-linguist the Saussurean emphasis on *langue* is likely to seem merely a more precise statement of a theory that all sensible people have always (if rather vaguely) taken for granted. According to this theory a language is a set of conventions, an agreement that certain combinations of sounds (or letters) stand for certain things and activities and ideas; and that these combinations must be arranged in a limited number of grammatical patterns. Whether

[3] *Langue* is often translated as *language,* and some of Saussure's more zealous followers seem to think that this settles the question of what language really is. It seems unlikely that he would have agreed with them, since he says:

> Note that I have defined things rather than words; these definitions are not endangered by certain ambiguous words that do not have identical meanings in various languages. . . . No word corresponds exactly to any of the notions specified above; that is why all definitions of words are made in vain; starting from words in defining things is a bad procedure.

Since *language* is used here (and in many other books) to include both components, I use the French terms to avoid confusion.

we believe that these conventions are ultimately based on logic or are purely arbitrary makes, for the moment, little difference. At any rate our ancestors have somehow decided, for instance, that Rags is to be called a *dog*, and not a *chien* or a *cane* or a *perro* (as other sets of ancestors have decided elsewhere). They have likewise decided that we should say *a black dog*, and not *a dog black*, which would be the normal word-order in some other languages. This is not merely a matter of style, but an important signalling device. We recognize at once the difference between *business college* and *college business;* but a Frenchman, whose language has the opposite conventions, would be likely to get the two reversed. Countless other decisions of the same general nature were made before we were born, and as children we could neither understand nor talk to our elders until we somehow began to be aware of their conventions, and to imitate them — at first pretty crudely. After a few years of steady effort, imitation, practice, and correction much of the crudeness disappeared, and we eventually learned to reflect the conventions in our own speaking with some degree of accuracy. Whenever we failed we simply made a mistake; the language was already in existence, and we had neither the right nor the power to modify it. The mistake might be a purely personal one, or it might be one picked up from our parents and other elders who had already departed from the true path, and thus spoke a dialect rather than the pure language.

Obviously, the more closely we adhere to the established conventions, the more dependable our communication will be. Every conceivable effort should therefore be made to encourage uniformity, and to discourage any departures in pronunciation, word-forms, patterns of arrangement, meanings assigned to each word, or any other variations from the established system. And whenever any group of people, whether from geographical isolation, social submergence, foreign influence, or any other reason, develops a system noticeably different from the pure and original one, their kind of language should be considered an inferior dialect, and they should be penalized (not nastily, of course, but firmly) for speaking it.

The trouble with this theory is that there is no such thing in nature as that intrinsically pure, good, or correct English that we would like so much to teach; and there never has been. Neither can we find a uniquely pure form of French, German, or Latin, though it is easy enough to talk as if we could. There is nothing to prevent Harris from talking about "pure, Parisian French" if he wants to; but there is likewise nothing to prevent Clarke from replying, "What do you mean, pure Parisian? They speak with a horrible twang in Paris. If you want to hear really good French you should go to Tours." Meanwhile Reade is thinking how silly they both are, since he has known for years that the only *really* good French is spoken in Geneva, the entire French nation having lost the true way some generations back. And of course if we actually went to Paris (or Tours or Geneva) we should find that its inhabitants spoke with much variety and argued about certain points, that the older ones accused the younger ones of corrupting the language, and so forth.

A linguist — even one who concentrates on *langue* — knows all this, and has no theories at all about how people ought to use a language. His approach is purely descriptive; and what he wants to describe is not the infinitely varied acts of *parole,* but the underlying system of conventions which these acts imperfectly reflect. His basic theory is that all members of a speech community must have the same "set of impressions deposited in the brain" in order to communicate. Their performance may vary enormously, but their "competence" — their mastery of the system — is identical.

This is a very useful hypothesis, since it frees him from having to take account of all the physical irregularities of *parole,* and it has resulted in some important advances in our knowledge. Its chief defect is that there is no precise way of determining the exact membership of a speech community sharing an identical set of conventions. Probably no two adults anywhere in the

world know exactly the same list of words, and certainly no two
people know exactly the same things about them, or pronounce,
arrange, and react to them identically. Some of the differences
can be dismissed as matters of *parole,* but others seem to be
based on a difference in the *langue* itself. This certainly varies
from one dialect to another; and there is satisfactory evidence
that it varies in a smaller degree within each dialect. Language,
like everything else, is always and necessarily changing. No
speaker ever reflects his underlying conventions (whatever they
are) quite perfectly, and of course speakers are influenced to
some extent by each other. With each act of speech there is at
least the possibility of a tiny modification in the conventions of
a group, and a good many of these possibilities eventually take
obvious effect, so that in time the whole set of conventions
changes beyond easy recognition.

10. THE SUM-OF-PARTS THEORY. Until very recently most American linguists paid little attention to the theories of Saussure, but
followed what is called the structural approach of Leonard
Bloomfield.[4] They started with the basic assumption that language is simply people talking, and that if we want to study it
scientifically we should not (at least in the beginning) try to
look *behind* the talking for some system assumed to underlie it.
We should look directly *at* the talking, and try to describe it as
accurately and completely as possible. Like other scientists we
should begin by observing the phenomena, and we should do
this with absolute impartiality. When we have made enough
observations we may try to arrange them into a system; but our
procedure must be purely inductive, and we can neither make
value judgments nor discard inconvenient evidence in order to
do this. We cannot, for instance, say that *ellum* is a mispronunciation of *elm,* but only that two different pronunciations of this
word occur. Similarly, we must record the fact that some people
say "He don't like them apples" where others would say "He

---

[4] *Language* (New York, 1933).

doesn't like those apples" without permitting ourselves to make any prejudiced comment about "bad grammar."

This inductive, objective approach was developed in studying previously unwritten languages, such as those of American Indians, and proved extremely fruitful for this purpose. It reduced the temptation for an investigator to distort his description to make it fit any preconceived theory about how the language ought to be constructed. Anything a native speaker said had to be accepted as part of the data. A particular pronunciation, for instance, might be comparatively unusual, but it simply could not be wrong, any more than a pebble can be of a wrong shape.

Attempts to apply this approach to English immediately run into two difficulties. In my ignorance, I am perfectly willing to postulate that any three Papago Indians who consent to act as informants can give me a satisfactory sample of their language. After all, there are not very many of them, and they are a fairly homogeneous group. But English is spoken by hundreds of millions of people, and spoken with such variety that it is hard to find a sample small enough to study intensively, and at the same time widely acceptable as typical of the whole. Moreover, I have no reason to suppose that any Papago is dissatisfied with his own use of his language, or contemptuous of his neighbor's use. His *langue*, to the best of my knowledge, is completely subconscious. He knows what words and grammatical patterns mean, and uses them accordingly. But an American usually has two kinds of *langue*, one as subconscious as the Papago's, the other quite explicit, though perhaps not completely mastered. For instance, he knows perfectly well what *ain't* means, whether or not he himself uses it. But even if he does use it, he is conscious that it is often regarded as wrong. Whether he tries to conform or decides to go on living comfortably in a state of grammatical sin, he seldom quarrels with the idea that the explicit conventions are somehow right.

A few structural linguists want to treat English exactly like Papago, and take the stand that anything a native speaker says (except a slip that he would himself correct) must be right because he says it — a language is simply what its speakers talk, and all attempts to legislate about it are illegitimate. Most structuralists, however, are willing to admit that "standard English" has so much social importance that we are justified in teaching it in our schools. They insist only that such instruction should be based only on careful observation of how certain speakers do actually talk, and not on any theories about how they should. Such an attitude immediately arouses the fury of a good many people. To anybody who feels outraged I can only say that I am not advocating it as *the* true approach; but that I do most urgently suggest that the more it annoys him, the harder he should try to understand its possible value for some purposes, because it simply cannot be tossed aside as worthless. The pronunciation of English has changed a good deal since Anglo-Saxon times, and quite noticeably even since the time of Dr. Johnson, and the structure has changed along with it. It would probably be impossible to find a single correct sentence today that would not have been wrong once. Take such an innocent-looking one as "Those little girls are very nice." If the repeated mistakes of our ancestors had not somehow come to be sanctified as "good grammar," *those* should be *tho* — the *s* got in by mistaken analogy with other plurals; *little* should have a special ending to agree with the noun it modifies; *are* should be something else, though it is hard to say what, since this Scandinavian form drove out several perfectly good English ones; and *very,* having started life as an adjective, should not be permitted to modify another adjective without adding *-ly*. Perhaps we should add that *nice* meant "ignorant" before it meant "foolish," "foolishly precise," and "precise" on its way to its current meaning of something like "mildly admirable"; and that *girls* formerly meant something like "teenagers" — young people of either sex.

In short, all the evidence we have tells us that any language is always changing, and never quite uniform at any one time. It seems a little naive to assume that all the changes that took place up to about Aunt Emma's day were improvements, while all those that have been taking place since are calamities.

11. A SUGGESTED COMPROMISE. Since neither the "chicken first" nor the "egg first" theory is entirely satisfactory, some sort of compromise seems necessary. It would be ridiculous for me to pretend that I can offer a final solution to a question that divides the linguists of the world, but I feel bound to make a clear statement of where I stand so that readers who prefer a different approach can make appropriate allowances. We have already seen that no two people can possibly *use* a language in exactly the same way. The critical question is, do they differ merely in *performance* — the degree of accuracy with which their *parole* reflects the *langue* which has been built into their nervous systems and is identical for them all? Or is the *langue* itself a little different for each speaker? Saussure chose the first answer, which has an obvious advantage, since it allows us to investigate the underlying system without being distracted by insignificant physical differences. But it is of course an assumption, not a demonstrable fact; and its adherents are likely (in my experience) to shy away from the question of exactly how widely a particular *langue* is spread. They admit differences in dialects, but (like everybody else) have found it impossible to give the precise boundaries of a homogeneous dialect group.

It seems to me more reasonable to assume that all speakers differ somewhat in their *langue* as well as their *parole*. We can say then that each speaker of a language must somehow have in his mind a chart of that language which his acts of speech must approximately reflect, or they would have no meaning at all, even to him. And each of the neighbors with whom he talks must also have a chart, somewhat similar to his, or they could not interchange ideas; but not quite the same, because all men are different. In any group of speakers the various charts must overlap considerably to make some communication possible; but they are never quite identical, and the possibilities of variation in the degree of overlap are practically infinite. In other words, our idiolects do not differ from each other simply as imperfect reflections of one perfect chart. Rather, each is based on its own chart — imperfectly constructed in imitation of other charts already imperfect. When we speak of the chart for a whole language we are using a fiction, useful for some purposes, very troublesome for others. In this book, for instance, I shall sometimes use the term "standard English" because it will save an intolerable amount of qualification: but a reader should be careful not to take it for more than it is worth. I use it simply to mean the kinds of English that cultivated (and don't ask me how cultivated) speakers generally use or accept as satisfactory. Such speakers agree almost unanimously on some points, such as a preference for *I saw* rather than *I seen*. They differ rather casually on many others, and quite bitterly on a few. Some of the usages they condemn can be shown to be sounder, either historically or logically, than the ones they prefer; but these usages will remain non-standard unless and until enough standard speakers take them up.

So far we have been concentrating on one level of a language, the words which are its most obvious units. There is much more to be said about these, but much of it cannot be said intelligibly until we have looked both down and up — down at the particular assortment of sounds which the speakers of a language somehow manage to select as the building blocks with which they will make their words, and up at the structural patterns by means of which they combine the words into meaningful utterances.

Caxton's language is so close to our own that we can approach it without bothering much about these two levels. Once we learn to look through the spelling we can find recognizable words, and treat them almost as if they were our own. But in the earlier stages of the language we shall meet not only quite unrecognizable words but sounds and sound-combinations which may at first seem impossible; and we shall sometimes find, as we do with foreign languages, that even after we have looked up the meaning of every word in a sentence we are unable to read it because we do not understand its structure.

CHAPTER TWO

The Sounds We Talk With

12. THE SELECTION OF SOUNDS. The human voice can make hundreds, perhaps thousands, of recognizably different sounds, but no language uses more than a few dozen of these, and probably no two languages make exactly the same selection. If you listen to a Frenchman or a German talking his own language you will hear sounds that native Americans do not make in speaking English, and cannot make at all without long and careful practice or special training. If you listen to certain more remote languages you may feel at first that the sounds you hear are scarcely human. This is a natural reaction, because we are almost inevitably inclined to take our own familiar habits as normal, and to consider all conflicting habits as inferior, if not downright ridiculous. But like many natural reactions this one is worse than inaccurate, it is expensive. As long as we keep it we will be handicapping ourselves in learning any foreign language, and even in learning many important things about our own. It is a big step forward to decide firmly that the sounds we happen to be accustomed to are neither better nor more natural than those we encounter in other languages or dialects. Then we can consider both old and new sounds with the idea of seeing just what they are and how they are made and used.

19

13. PHONETICS. Many students have a strong resistance to phonetics because they don't see beyond the transcriptions, which they think of as being a sort of misguided spelling reform. Having already been forced to learn to spell English words in the conventional way they see little to gain by learning another system which they know is not generally much used, even if it is theoretically better. It must be conceded that the treatment of the subject in some language classes pretty well justifies such an attitude.

But transcription into phonetic symbols is an incidental technique, not an end in itself. The basic concerns of phonetics are the ways in which speech sounds are produced, the ways in which they influence each other as they fall into patterns, and the ways in which, under various circumstances, they change to other sounds. It is an extremely complicated study, and we cannot pretend to give even an outline of it here; but a few of its findings can be explained quite simply, and are useful even to beginners.

The sounds represented by any alphabet are traditionally divided into vowels and consonants. There is nothing wrong with this division, but it is so rough that it does not actually tell us much. Most of us probably have a vague idea that a vowel is a vowel because — well, because it has a vowel-like nature; and a consonant is a consonant because it is somehow consonantal. We may not even realize that some consonants have much more in common with vowels than others do. A slightly closer look at the situation may therefore be helpful.

Our vocal apparatus makes up a sort of complicated musical instrument. At the top of the windpipe are a pair of bands which serve the function of reeds in wind instruments. When they vibrate, our normally inaudible breath takes on the sound of speech. During the course of speech the vibrations may be briefly interrupted for certain consonant sounds, but without them we couldn't talk at all.

The inside of the mouth acts as a very flexible resonance chamber. Its shape can be modified by the position of the lips, and

especially by the movements of the tongue. Our vowel sounds
vary according to what part of the tongue is raised and how
close it comes to the roof of the mouth. There are other movements that can affect their quality, but in Modern English these
are incidental.

The air passage left for the pronunciation of different vowels
thus varies in size, but it must not be small enough to cause
audible friction, or the sound produced will be a consonant of
the type called *fricative* rather than a vowel. If the passage is,
for an instant, completely stopped, the resultant sound will be
a consonant of the type called *plosive* or *stop*. (This division
is rather rough, but it will do for the present.)

All English speech sounds are made as we are breathing out
— a limitation that is not true of some languages. Next (to re-
peat) they are made by definite muscular movements of the
various speech organs — vocal cords, tongue, lips, etc. For instance, the sound usually indicated by the letter *t* is made when
we stop the cords from vibrating and at the same time briefly
interrupt the breath stream by pressing the tip of the tongue just
behind the upper front teeth; and the sound indicated by *k* is
made by bringing some part of the tongue up hard against the
roof of the mouth, the exact location of the contact depending on
the neighboring vowels. We learned to make the movements
producing these sounds by a long-drawn-out process of trial and
error when we were very young, and most of us have very little
idea of how we do make them. This ignorance does not handicap
us in our normal speech, where we simply depend on habit, but
it interferes seriously when we want to learn something about
another language or about a different variety of our own. The
common belief that early childhood is the only time when the
pronunciation of a second language can be learned really well
is based on a half-truth. By the time we are twelve or fifteen
most of us have developed muscular habits of speech so strong
that we can no longer successfully modify them by simple imitation of strange sounds. But if we are shown what to do with
our mouths in order to make a French *u* or a German *ch,* and

then given an opportunity to listen and imitate intelligently, we can learn much faster than we could as children — assuming that our mental development did not stop completely before we got out of grade school. The same sort of knowledge will help us to understand how sound changes occurred in different areas and at different periods in the development of English. The new sound is always formed by a particular variation of the gymnastics used to produce the old one. Once we know what these gymnastics are we can see how some sound changes occur easily, while others are quite impossible.

14. PHONEMES. The statement made at the beginning of this chapter that no language uses more than a few dozen sounds now requires further explanation. Since no two of us have exactly the same pronunciation, the number of actually different sounds that millions of us can and do make is enormous, even though it is only a fraction of those we could make. But in order to communicate at all we have somehow come to an agreement to group all the sounds we make into a few dozen *contrasting classes* of sounds, technically called *phonemes*. When two sounds are recognized as significantly different, so that the substitution of one for another will change or destroy the identity of a word, they are said to belong to different phonemes. Thus the word *till* consists of the three phonemes /t/, /i/, and /l/ (the slashes — also called virgules — indicate that the symbols between them are used to indicate phonemes, rather than as ordinary letters). If you substitute a /p/ for the /t/ or an /e/ for the /i/, you get a different word; and if you substitute a /z/ for the /t/ you get no word at all. All these are therefore different phonemes. But differences in pronunciation which, though quite audible, do not change the identity of a word, are considered variations of the same phonemes. Even if we disregard personal and dialectal differences in pronunciation, there are certain variations which we all make under the influence of neighboring sounds, though most of us are entirely unconscious of them. For instance, the sounds represented by the letter *t* in the words *till* and *still* are

definitely different, because they are made in different ways. If you hold the palm of your hand about an inch in front of your mouth and pronounce the two words, you will find that *till* is uttered with strong puff of breath — strong enough to blow out a lighted match if you have one handy. *Still* is uttered with no such puff. The *t* in *till* is therefore said to be "aspirated" and the *t* in *still* to be "unaspirated." The difference in sound made by the aspiration is audible, but only to people who are used to listening for it.

In some languages the difference between an aspirated and an unaspirated *t* is distinctive — that is, sufficient to distinguish two words which are otherwise identical. If we used the symbol *t* for the unaspirated sound, and the special symbol *t'* for the aspirated one, we might have such pairs of words as *till* and *t'ill* or *still* and *st'ill*, with entirely different meanings. Native speakers of such languages, being trained to notice the difference, could tell *till* and *t'ill* quite as easily as we can tell *till* and *dill* apart (though these two words would sound alike to the speakers of some languages in which aspiration is significant but voicing is not). But most native speakers of English cannot readily hear the difference between *till* and *t'ill* even after it has been explained and demonstrated to them. This is not simply because they have not been trained to hear it. They have been very definitely (though informally and subconsciously) trained *not* to hear it. We can understand each other only by disregarding those differences in pronunciation that are not, in our language, significant, and concentrating on those that are. It is exactly as important not to notice some differences as it is to notice others. Only by doing both, for example, can we recognize that words pronounced quite differently by people from different regions are somehow the same.

When two sounds are demonstrably but not significantly different they are called *allophones* of the same phoneme. It may be helpful to compare nonsignificant differences in sound to differences in typefaces or in handwriting. Davis and Cassidy may make their capital *A*'s quite differently, or Davis may make an *r* that looks like Cassidy's *v*, but we soon learn to disregard these peculiarities. Both of them use exactly twenty-six letters that we interpret as being the same; and we read by identifying the intended letters through any irregularities that may occur in the handwriting. In other words, in order to be able to read a number of different handwritings, or kinds of type, we must look through certain physical differences in order to find the underlying similarities of intention; and the same thing is true in understanding various pronunciations. Spoken language is not composed of exact and invariable sounds any more than written language is composed of exact and invariable shapes. We recognize a spoken word when we (subconsciously) identify the phonemes of which it is composed, and to do this we must disregard many details of the actual sounds produced. It is rather like recognizing the same musical phrase when played on different instruments in different keys. The actual sounds heard are quite different, but the significant relations are identical.

15. ORIGIN AND DISTORTION OF THE ORDINARY ALPHABET. We must be careful not to push the analogy between letters and sounds too far, since there is by no means a one-to-one correspondence between the two in our erratic spelling. Presumably our ordinary alphabet was originally devised on what we now call phonemic principles, as an attempt to find a symbol to represent each significant and contrasting sound wherever it occurred. We have no way of knowing how accurately it did this in Phoenician (if it *was* the Phoenicians who invented it). It was probably not perfect, because it is hard to believe that the Phoenicians had solved all the problems that are still bothering us; but it was good enough to be reasonably effective, and it was certainly one of the most durable inventions of all time. The Greeks borrowed it, directly or indirectly, from the Phoenicians, but had to make a number of changes to fit their somewhat different sound system. The Romans borrowed it from the Greeks, making more adjustments; and hundreds of other languages have borrowed, adjusted, and modified it ever since. Many of the letters have changed form,

and letters of the same form may now indicate entirely different sounds in different languages. For instance, our *p* comes from the Greek *rho,* which was an *r* sound, as it still is in Russian; and our *x* comes from the Greek *chi,* which had the value of *ch* in German words like *nicht* and *doch.*

Considering how many different languages this alphabet has been stretched to fit, it is not surprising that it does not always work equally well. In Spanish the results are very good, for the spelling represents the pronunciation with a high degree of accuracy and efficiency. A Spaniard therefore seldom has trouble either in spelling correctly any word that he can pronounce or in pronouncing any unfamiliar word that he sees in print. But the relation between sound and symbol in English is notoriously irregular. Our alphabet contains a few characters that it could well spare, and lacks a number that it could well use, so that some must do at least double duty. But these deficiencies only partly account for the fact that more than half the letters can represent distinctively different sounds in different words, and that many sounds can be spelled in a bewildering number of different ways. Another reason is that our spelling conventions were crystallized some centuries ago, and therefore do not reflect some important sound changes that have occurred during the last few hundred years. A third, and probably the most important, is that these conventions were derived from a curious mixture of conflicting traditions, including those of French scribes and Dutch printers, and a wild assortment of odd bits of theories, often misguided.

All this is confusing enough when we are dealing only with Modern English, but when we try to trace the development of the language the difficulties are compounded. For instance, if we look at the two Old English words *cpic* and *leaf* and compare them to their modern derivatives *quick* and *leaf,* it seems that the first changed a good deal while the second has remained constant; but if we hear the words pronounced we get the opposite impression. *Cpic* sounds exactly like *quick,* but the Old English *leaf* sounds much more like *layoff* than the modern *leaf.*

Both sound and spelling changes are of course real; but as we saw in the first chapter, it is the sounds rather than the symbols for them that are our primary concern. The basic elements of our language are not the twenty-six letters of the alphabet, but the sounds that these letters rather inconsistently and ambiguously represent. In order to discuss them intelligibly on paper we therefore need a special alphabet.

16. THE IPA. The International Phonetic Alphabet, hereafter called the IPA, was devised, and is still being improved and expanded, in an attempt to indicate clearly and dependably all the speech sounds used in all known languages. It includes symbols for many sounds not used at all in English, and others for indicating many minor differences in sound (such as that between aspirated and unaspirated *t*) which do not happen to be phonemically significant in English, though they may be in other languages. An expert can therefore use the IPA not merely to show how a given sound "is pronounced" in English, but quite precisely just how a particular speaker pronounced it at a particular time. Such "narrow" transcriptions are valuable for certain purposes, but they require much skill and practice, and are of course intelligible only to other experts. We shall therefore be very little concerned with them here. When used, they are enclosed in square brackets ([ ]).

"Broad" transcriptions aim merely to indicate the phonemes of which words are composed, and omit all non-contrastive detail. They are enclosed in slashes (/ /). The symbol /t/, for instance, will do for either [t], [t'], or several other allophones of this phoneme which we haven't even mentioned. Such transcriptions can be made and understood by anyone who will devote a few hours of unemotional practice to them; and for some purposes — of course not all — they are more useful than the narrow ones. For instance, if you were not familiar with the words *heath* and *heather* you would want a transcription that showed that they rhymed with *wreath* and *weather* rather than with *breath* and *breather,* and you would probably not care much how or whether a particular speaker pronounced the final *r*. In the words of Daniel Jones:

> A *broad transcription* is a form of phonetic writing which uses the smallest number of letters and marks which will represent a given form of a language without ambiguity, and uses for this purpose familiar letter shapes as far as possible. It differentiates in writing all the words of a given language or dialect which are different in sound. The reduction of the number of symbols to a minimum is effected by applying certain conventions which have to be stated once for all.[1]

Whether broad transcriptions can properly be called phonemic is a question on which there are strong differences of opinion, based largely on disagreement about whether the term *phoneme* should be limited to vowel and consonant sounds or should be stretched to cover contrasting elements of pitch, stress, and "juncture" (roughly, the transition between two sounds or between sound and silence). A good many linguists are quite sure that these elements simply are phonemes, and that no transcription that does not include them can be called phonemic. Other linguists, without denying the importance of these elements, prefer to call them something else. Whichever side we take, we do not know enough about the use of the other elements in the earlier stages of English to justify trying to include them in a transcription. I call my broad transcriptions phonemic, and enclose them in slashes rather than brackets, simply to indicate that only phonemic differences are shown, and that a few of the symbols have slightly different values from those assigned to them in the IPA. Anyone who wants to can, of course, call them "semi-phonemic," or even something ruder.

For phonemic transcriptions of contemporary English most American linguists now use a special alphabet devised by Trager

[1] *The Pronunciation of English* (4th ed., Cambridge, England, 1958), p. 28.

and Smith.[2] Although the analysis on which this depends is open to (and has received) serious criticism, I should use it without argument if we were dealing only with the modern period. But the system is neither intended for nor suited to transcriptions of earlier stages of the language, with which we are principally concerned. Moreover, my own experience is that while students can easily learn in theory that /day/ indicates the pronunciation of *die* rather than *day*, and /pat/ the pronunciation of *pot* rather than *pat*, it takes more time than is usually available for their reactions to this system to become automatic and reliable. I have found that they respond much more quickly to Jones's modification of the IPA (with a few minor adjustments necessary for American pronunciation). For example, /u/ and /u:/ serve quite as well as the strict IPA /ʊ/ and /u/ to differentiate the vowel phonemes in *book* and *boot*, and it is much easier to remember which is which, since the colon always indicates greater length.

One difficulty for which there is no completely satisfactory solution is that the distribution of phonemes is not the same in all dialects. Thus some people pronounce *root* to rhyme with *boot*, others to rhyme with *foot;* and (whatever our personal feelings may be) both pronunciations are perfectly legitimate. If we confine ourselves to either group of people, we simply choose the appropriate symbol. But when I attempt a transcription broad enough to cover both groups (as I must in this book to keep it within bounds), I have to choose one symbol or the other, and not everybody will be happy with my choice. In this case I choose /ru:t/, but am of course willing to accept /rut/ from any student who uses the other pronunciation.

In the interest of sanity rather than logic we shall begin our phonemic analysis with the sounds of contemporary English, which most readers can make but have never examined systematically. We will then have some foundation for later treat-

[2] George L. Trager and Henry Lee Smith, Jr., *An Outline of English Structure* (Norman, Oklahoma, 1951. Later printings by American Council of Learned Societies, Washington, D.C., 1957 ff.). Their system is shown in Chapter 10.

ment of differences in the sound systems of the earlier stages of the language.

17. THE TWO EXTREMES OF OUR SOUND SYSTEM. We may begin by analyzing the simple word *pa,* which is composed of two phonemes and may be transcribed as /pɑ/. The one indicated by /ɑ/ is as complete a vowel as we can manage. We open our mouth as wide as we ever do, keep the tongue low, set our vocal cords to vibrating, and the result is /ɑ/. When a doctor wants to look down our throat he tells us to say "ah" just because we have to make a wide-open passage to say it. If we said "ee" we should not open our mouth so wide, the front part of the tongue would be close to the roof of the mouth, and the doctor would not get much of a view. And if the tongue got so close as to touch the roof of the mouth the breath would be interrupted, the vowel would slide into a neighboring consonant, and the result would be something like "eek!"

Furthest removed from /ɑ/ is the sound indicated by /p/, which might be called the extreme consonant. To make it we close our lips completely and do not allow the vocal cords to vibrate. This is as far as we can get from the sound of /ɑ/ and still be talking. The sounds indicated by all the other phonemic letters are somewhere between /ɑ/ and /p/, though not all in one straight line.

18. THE CONSONANT PHONEMES. Twenty-four consonant phonemes are generally recognized in Modern English. Since the symbols of the phonemic alphabet have no established order to correspond to the "a b c" order of the ordinary one, they are listed in a way which may at first seem peculiar, but which has the advantage of grouping together the symbols for sounds with certain features in common.

```
p  t  k    s  ʃ    tʃ      l  r    m  n  ŋ     j  w  h
b  d  g    z  ʒ    dʒ
f  θ
v  ð
```

The three phonemes /p/, /t/, and /k/ are pronounced as the letters of the same shape usually are. These are the only three *voiceless stops* in English. "Voiceless" means that the vocal cords do not vibrate, and "stop" refers to stopping the breath-stream. In /p/ the stopping is done by closing the lips, as we have already seen. In /t/ it is done by pushing the tip of the tongue so firmly against the gum-ridge behind the upper front teeth that no air can escape over it. In /k/ the stopping is done by raising some part of the tongue against the roof of the mouth, the exact position of contact depending on the neighboring vowel sounds. If you pronounce the two words /kik/ (*kick*) and /kuk/ (*cook*) slowly, you can feel that your tongue presses against the roof of your mouth much farther forward in /kik/ than in /kuk/, and if you practice long enough you will find that you can hear a difference between the resulting sounds. In some languages the difference is as important as that between /k/ and /t/, since it is sufficient to distinguish between otherwise identical words; but in English it is negligible, since these two sounds of /k/ are allophones of the same phoneme. That is, we automatically make one of them in one environment (when the vowel of the syllable is /i/), and the other in a different environment (when the vowel of the syllable is /u/).

The next three sounds, /b/, /d/, and /g/, are similar to /p/, /t/, and /k/ respectively except that they are "voiced" — that is, the vocal cords vibrate when they are pronounced. You can test this in two steps. First, grasp the very top of your Adam's apple between the thumb and forefinger of either hand and pronounce a prolonged "ahhh." When you get the right position you will feel the vibration that is characteristic of voicing. Then, retaining your grasp, pronounce the two words *gob* and *cop*. As you pronounce *gob* the vibration will continue throughout the word, because the consonants as well as the vowel are voiced; but when you pronounce *cop* the duration of the vibration is shorter, because both consonants are voiceless. Moreover, the presence or absence of voicing at beginning and end is the only reliably significant difference between the two words. It is possible that you put your tongue in very slightly different positions for /k/ and /g/; but if you voice a /k/ you get a /g/, and if you unvoice a /g/ you get a /k/.

   The next four sounds, indicated by /f/, /θ/, /v/, and /ð/, are not stops but *fricatives*. The passage of the breath is restricted but not entirely stopped. You breathe through a narrow opening, and the friction at that point makes a characteristic sound. To make /f/ and /v/ you press the lower lip, not against the upper lip as for /p/ and /b/, but against the upper front teeth. Without voicing this results in an /f/, with voicing in a /v/. These four phonemes are known as *labials* from a Latin word for *lip*. (More precisely, the stops are bilabial and the fricatives are labio-dental.) To make /θ/ and /ð/ you put the tip of your tongue into a position near that used for /t/ and /d/, but not quite so high. Instead of pressing firmly against the gum-ridge and blocking the air, the tip presses more lightly against the bottom of the upper front teeth, allowing some air to escape. Unvoiced, the result is /θ/ (*theta*) as in *thin*. Voiced, it is an /ð/ (*eth* or *edh*), as in *this*. The phonemes /t/, /d/, /θ/, and /ð/ are often referred to as *dentals*, though the two stops are more precisely called *alveolar*, from the anatomical term for the gum-ridge. You will notice that there is the same sort of relation between the four dental as between the four labial consonants — voiced and voiceless stop, voiced and voiceless fricative.

   In Modern English there are no fricatives to correspond to the /k/ and /g/ stops, though there were in earlier English. The group name for these four sounds is *palatal* or *velar*.

   The next two pairs of fricatives are formed by placing the tip of the tongue farther back in the mouth than for /θ/ and /ð/. Voiceless /s/ and voiced /z/ are made by forming a very narrow passage between the tip of the tongue and the gum-ridge. Voiceless /ʃ/ and voiced /ʒ/ are made by forming a passage still farther back. The closeness of these three positions accounts for the difficulties some people have with these sounds. If you attempt to make an /s/ with the tongue just too far forward, you will lisp and make a /θ/. On the other hand, a foreigner who keeps his tongue too far back in attempting a /θ/ will make an /s/. And anybody who attempts an /s/ with his tongue still farther back will make an /ʃ/. The two sounds indicated by /tʃ/ and /dʒ/ are known as *affricates*. As the symbols indicate, an affricate may be regarded as composed of two successive sounds — a stop and its corresponding fricative. Some phoneticians do so regard them; but it is convenient (and usual) to consider them as single phonemes. At any rate, these sounds are pronounced as indicated below, and you are advised to notice carefully the position your tongue takes when you do pronounce them.

/s/ as in *sit* (/sit/) or *hiss* (/his/)
/z/ as in *zip* (/zip/) or *his* (/hiz/)
/ʃ/ as in *ship* (/ʃip/) or *fish* (/fiʃ/)
/ʒ/ as in *vision* (/viʒən/)
/tʃ/ as in *chip* (/tʃip/) or *pitch* (/pitʃ/)
/dʒ/ as in *gem* (/dʒem/) or *edge* (/edʒ/)

The sounds indicated by /l/ and /r/ are impossible to describe simply, because they vary so much, both among speakers of different dialects and as they occur in different phonetic environments. Moreover, there is a good deal of similarity between some ways of making the two. The difference between the two phonemes is usually clear to native speakers of English, who have been trained to react to it, but not to speakers of some other languages. It is well known, for instance, that a Chinese tends to pronounce *very* as /veli/, while a Japanese is likely to go the other way and pronounce *hello* as /hero/.

It is worth special mention that English has three, not two, nasal sounds, and that these are related to the three pairs of stops. That is, /m/ is pronounced with the lips in the same position as for /b/, /n/ with the tongue in the same position as for /d/, and /ŋ/ (called *eng*) with the tongue in the same posi-

tion as for /g/. What distinguishes the nasals from the corresponding stops is that the passage from the mouth to the nose,
which is closed by the uvula when the stops are pronounced, is
left open so that air escapes by the alternate route and the sounds
can be continued. (You may have noticed that when a head cold
closes the nasal passage an attempted /m/ sounds very much
like a /b/, and so forth.) That /ŋ/ really does indicate a single
sound rather than a combination can be shown by contrasting the
pronunciation of *singer* (/siŋər/) with that of *finger* (/fiŋgər/).
Such a pronunciation as that indicated by the spelling *fishin'* is
not therefore a matter of "dropping a g," but of substituting /n/
for /ŋ/.

The phoneme /j/ does not resemble the English letter of the
same shape, but has the value of *y* in *yet* (/jet/). The phonemes
/w/ and /h/ do have the normal values of the corresponding
letters.

To master this part of the phonemic alphabet it is necessary to
learn five special symbols: /θ/ (theta), /ð/ (eth), /ʃ/ (esh),
/ʒ/ (ezh), and /ŋ/ (eng); two special combinations of these:
/tʃ/ and /dʒ/; and the fact that /j/ is used in a different way from
the letter of the same shape. The other symbols have the most
usual value of the corresponding letters.

19. THE VOWEL PHONEMES. Since vowel sounds depend largely
on the positions taken by the extremely flexible tongue, a very
large number can be made. The number that can be distinguished varies with the acuteness and training of our ears. Even
the number that are used phonemically, to distinguish one word
from another, varies considerably more among different speakers
than does the number of consonants. As a result there is some
difference of opinion as to how many different vowel phonemes must be recognized in English, and a greater difference
about how they should be symbolized. The system used here
is offered as adequate, but with no argument as to its superiority.

20. THE SHORT VOWELS.

	Front		Central	Back	
High	i	*pit* /pit/	(ɨ)	u	*put* /put/
Mid	e	*pet* /pet/	ə *putt* /pət/	o	*pony* /poni/
Low	æ	*pat* /pæt/	ɑ *pot* /pɑt/	ɔ	*pot* /pɔt/
			(in most areas)		(in Boston area)

The terms *high, mid,* and *low* refer to the height of the tongue
in pronouncing these sounds, and the terms *front, central,* and
back to the part of the tongue that is highest. It may not be
graceful, but it is very instructive to sit in front of a mirror with
your mouth wide open and pronounce the various vowel sounds
so that you can see that these terms have a phonetic reality.

The illustrative words should make most of the pronunciations
clear, but a few need further explanation.

a. The word *pot* is pronounced in most parts of the country
with a short version of the vowel sound in the first syllable of
father (/ɑ/). In eastern New England it is pronounced with a
short version of the vowel in *paw* (/ɔ/). Since most people use
one or the other of these sounds, but not both, it is impossible to
find two different words that differentiate them clearly for everybody.

b. The high central vowel ɨ (called *barred i*) has a clearcut
phonetic existence, but its phonemic status is both complicated
and debatable. You probably use it if you pronounce *pen* in such
a way that ignorant strangers accuse you of saying *pin,* or if you
pronounce *pretty* so that it does not quite rhyme with *pity, petty,*
or anything else; and many people use it in the unstressed syllables of such words as *depend* and *senate,* where others use /ə/
or /i/. On the other hand, you are probably not conscious of it
as a phoneme — a sound sufficiently distinct to contrast one word
with another. Most people who say /pɨn/, for instance, firmly believe that they are saying /pen/. The sound is therefore real, and
the symbol is useful in comparing dialects or idiolects, but it is
not needed in transcriptions as broad as those used in this
chapter, and there is no evidence that it was phonemic in earlier

English. We need not, therefore, give it any more attention for the present.

21. SHORT AND LONG VOWELS AND DIPHTHONGS. The usual schoolroom way of using the terms "short vowels," "long vowels," and "diphthongs" may be useful in spelling rules about when to double consonants, but is inaccurate and misleading in the description of sounds. In discussing phonemes it is necessary to use these terms in a very different way.

When a vowel-sound is prolonged without movement of the tongue (and consequently without change in quality) the result is a long vowel. Though any number of gradations in length are possible, only two — short and long — are considered significant. But if the tongue changes position during the prolongation, the result is not a long vowel but a diphthong. It must be emphasized that a diphthong is a sequence of two vowel-sounds, not of two letters. You cannot pronounce the word *I* while holding your tongue in the same position throughout. You begin by saying /ɑ/, and then move your tongue up and forward to the position required for /i/. The word is therefore physically a diphthong, as indicated by the transcription /ɑi/. The fact that it is conventionally spelled with a single letter is an unfortunate and deceptive historical accident. On the other hand, the word *bread* contains a single short vowel and can be transcribed /bred/. The *ea* combination used to spell the simple sound is a digraph, not a diphthong.

It is generally believed (though it cannot be definitely proved) that in Old and Middle English the difference between short and long vowels was simply a matter of length. But in Modern English there is usually some difference besides length between contrasting pairs of vowels. Either there is a different quality throughout or the tongue changes position during the pronunciation of the so-called long vowel, so that it is actually a diphthong. Almost anybody can recognize that the "long *i*" discussed in the preceding paragraph is composed of two elements. We can prolong one and say something like "ahhhh-ee," or we can prolong

the other and say something like "ah-eeee"; but we cannot prolong the whole complex sound. It is not quite so easy to hear that
the "long *a*" and "long *o*" are also diphthongs; but if you will
pronounce them you will notice that in pronouncing *a* the front
of the tongue rises from an /e/ to an /i/ position, so that the
sound can be indicated as /ei/; and in pronouncing *o* the back
of the tongue rises from an /o/ to an /u/ position, so that the
sound can be indicated as /ou/. But in the older stages of the
language (we believe) there was no such raising of the tongue.
The first element was simply prolonged, and the length can be
indicated by putting a colon after the vowel.

The vowel sounds in such words as *boot* and *beet* are also
considered diphthongs by Trager and Smith, and transcribed
accordingly; but the evidence is less convincing. Accordingly,
boot is here transcribed as /buːt/ and *beet* as /biːt/, in contrast
to /fut/ (*foot*) and /bit/ (*bit*). In both these pairs of short and
long vowels there is certainly some difference in quality as well
as length; but since the two go together, only one feature need
be indicated to make the phonemic distinction. The standard
IPA practice of transcribing the shorter and more open vowels
with small capitals is just as defensible, but a little harder to
remember. The following symbols are therefore used:

22. Long Vowel and Diphthong Symbols. The long vowels are:

iː	as in *peat*	/piːt/	uː: as in *pool*	/puːl/
ɑː	*palm*	/pɑːm/	ɔː: *pawn*	/pɔːn/

The diphthongs in general use are:

ei	as in *pate*	/peit/	ɔi as in *point*	/pɔint/
ɑi	*pike*	/pɑik/	ou *pose*	/pouz/
ɑu	*pout*	/pɑut/	ju *puke*	/pjuk/

No colon is needed after diphthongs, which are necessarily long.

23. Diphthongs in "*r*-less dialects." In British Received Pronunciation, and in some varieties of American English (includ-

ing my own) the phoneme /r/ does not occur in some positions. Words spelled with the letter *r* in final position (*tour*), before a silent *e* (*here*), or before another consonant (*fort*) are pronounced with no /r/ sound, but with the preceding vowel either lengthened or diphthongized. British linguists therefore normally use such transcriptions as /tuə/, /hiə/, /fɔət/, rather than /tur/, /hir/, and /fɔrt/. If I were transcribing my own dialect I would do the same; but in this book I use /r/ in my transcriptions, not to imply that everybody should pronounce it, but simply because it is easier for a Georgia student to recognize /pɔrtər/ than for an Iowa student to recognize /pɔətə/. Anybody who wants to emphasize his freedom from *r*'s may use the following symbols:

iə as in *here* /hiə/		ɔə as in *fort*	/fɔət/
eə	*there* /ðeə/	uə	*tour* /tuə/

The phoneme /ɑ:/ is merely lengthened, not diphthongized; thus *part* is transcribed /pɑːt/. Even when the /r/ is pronounced it modifies the quality of the preceding vowel; but since this effect is automatic, it need not be indicated in a *phonemic* transcription, though it would have to be in a phonetic one.

24. PHONEMIC TRANSCRIPTION. Before studying the following transcription you should get two things firmly in mind:

1. It is *necessarily* arbitrary in some of its details. I do not argue that transcribing *sit* and *seat* as /sit/ and /si:t/ is more accurate than transcribing them as /sɪt/ and /sit/ or /sit/ and /siyt/. Any of these three methods will indicate the difference between the two words, once you get used to it. I choose (perhaps unwisely) the one that my students seem to find it easiest to get used to.

2. It is not an attempt to indicate "correct" pronunciation, but only what seems to me the most usual one. Though no two of us pronounce exactly alike, we are pretty uniform in the use of all the consonant phonemes except /r/ in certain positions; but we vary a good deal in the use of the vowel phonemes, especially

when they are not stressed. If you pronounce *not* as /nɔt/ rather than /nɑt/, or *sounds* as /sæundz/ rather than /sɑundz/, you may transcribe accordingly if you wish to. And it is not worth worrying about whether the best way of transcribing *senate* is /senət/, /senit/, or /senᵻt/. All three pronunciations are widely used, and it would take a good deal more counting than I have time for to decide which is actually the most frequent among educated people.

After studying the interlinear transcription you should be able to decipher the unaccompanied one with a moderate effort. It will then be useful to make a few of your own until you can do it without too much trouble. If you are already familiar with some other method of transcription you may not find it necessary to make active use of this one. I don't feel very strongly about alphabets, and if any one were in general use I would gladly conform to it, whether I liked it or not. Unfortunately, anybody who reads many books on the language must at present be prepared to encounter a large number of variations. However, as long as he realizes this, and is in firm control of one system into which he can translate the others, he can manage to get along.

There are certain limitations on this transcription. In
/ðer   ɑr   sɔrtən   limiteiʃənz   ɔn   ðis   trænskripʃən   in

the first place, it gives only the "alphabetical" sounds.
ðə   fɔrst   pleis   it   givz   onli   ði   ælfəbetikəl   sɑundz

Stresses, pitches, and junctures are not marked, simply
stresiz   pitʃiz   ænd   dʒəŋkʃərz   ɑr   nɑt   mɑrkt   simpli

because it seems advisable not to bring up too many
bikɔ:z   it   si:mz   ædvɑizəbəl   nɑt   tu   briŋ   əp   tu: meni

difficulties at once. In the second place, each word is
difikəlti:z   æt   wəns   in   ðə   sekənd   pleis   i:tʃ   wərd   iz

transcribed in what is called its *citation form* — that is,
trænskrɑibd   in   hwɑt   iz   kɔ:ld   its   sɑiteiʃən   fɔrm   ðæt   iz

as if it were pronounced rather carefully by itself, and
æz if it wər   pronɑunst   ræðər   kerfəli   bɑi   itself   ænd

not as it would be pronounced in natural, connected
nat æz it wud   bi: pronaunst   in næt∫ərəl kənektid

speech, where it would often be affected by the
spi:t∫   hwer   it   wud   ɔfən   bi: æfektid   bɑi ðə

neighboring words in the sentence. For instance, if you
neibəriŋ   wərdz in ðə sentəns   fɔr instəns   if ju:

say "*And* is a conjunction," you pronounce *and* distinctly;
sei   ænd iz ə kəndʒəŋk∫ən ju: pronauns   ænd distiŋktli

but if you talk of "ham and eggs" your *and* probably
bət if ju: tɔ:k əv hæm n   egz   jɔr   ænd prɑbəbli

shrinks to "n." This is not, as some of us used to be
∫riŋks tu n   ðis   iz nɑt æz səm   əv əs ju:st tu bi:

taught in school, a vicious habit — it is something that
tɔ:t   in sku:l   ə vi∫əs   hæbit   it iz səmθiŋ   ðæt

occurs naturally and inevitably in many, if not all,
əkərz   næt∫ərəli   ænd inevitəbli   in meni   if nɑt ɔ:l

languages.
læŋgwidʒiz/

(When the French run their words together we speak admiringly
of their *elision* and *liaison,* and carefully try to imitate them.
When we do the same thing in our own language we are often
accused of "sloppy English." Of course the blending of sounds
can be overdone.)

/ðis trænskrip∫ən lɑik ðə wən əbəv iz nɑt intendid æz
i:ðər ə ful ɔr ə riəli akjərit rendi∫ən əv nɔrməl spi:t∫ bət æz
æn egzæmpəl əv hɑu veriəs siləbəlz kæn bi: indikeitid leitər
ɔ:n wi: ∫æl egzæmin ə mɔr kəmpli:t foni:mik trænskrip∫ən
əv mɑdərn iŋli∫ ænd bifɔr ðæt wi: ∫æl si: ðæt in its ərliər
steidʒiz ðə læŋgwidʒ hæd səm foni:mz hwit∫ wi: hæv nɑu
lɔ:st ænd feild tu meik səm foni:mik distiŋk∫ənz ɔ:n hwit∫
wi: nɑu regjulərli dipend ði eim əv ðis t∫æptər iz simpli tu
provaid æn ænælisis əv fəmiljər mətiriəl səfi∫ənt tu sərv æz
ə faundei∫ən fɔr stədi:iŋ ði ərliər steidʒiz əv ðə læŋgwidʒ/

CHAPTER THREE

The Pre-History of English

25. RECONSTRUCTING LANGUAGES. Scholars have been able to reconstruct a good deal of the pre-history of English and some other languages, in spite of the inconvenient absence of written records, complete with reliable dates. Like other searchers into the distant past they have had to depend heavily on various kinds of circumstantial evidence, and some of their conclusions may be mistaken — in fact some of them must be, because there are some conflicting theories. Nevertheless, the general picture of what must have happened is on the whole reasonably clear. The processes by which this picture was constructed are too complicated to be explained completely here, but some simple examples will give a general idea of the methods.

26. SOME ROMANCE LANGUAGES. We can begin with a development that took place late enough to be supported by a good deal of written evidence, though there are a number of sizable gaps. It is well known that the Romance languages, including French, Spanish, and Italian (as well as some others), developed from Latin. If we didn't know it already, we could prove it by comparisons. Let's look at the numbers from one to ten in each of the four.

Latin	French	Spanish	Italian
unum	un	uno	uno
duo	deux	dos	due
tres	trois	tres	tre
quattuor	quatre	cuatro	quattro
quinque	cinq	cinco	cinque
sex	six	seis	sei
septem	sept	siete	sette
octo	huit	ocho	otto
novem	neuf	nueve	nove
decem	dix	diez	diece

Whenever two languages have similar words with the same or closely related meanings, there are three possible explanations:

1. *Pure coincidence.* This certainly happens occasionally. For instance, there is no connection between the Latin *dies* and the English *day*. But we cannot accept too many coincidences, especially in a consistent pattern. When the same sort of resemblance occurs between many pairs of words in two languages there must be some other explanation.

2. *Direct borrowing.* This can occur whenever two languages are in contact with each other, and it often does happen on a very large scale. English has borrowed great numbers of words from Latin, Scandinavian, French, and Greek, and smaller numbers from a great many other languages; and other languages are now borrowing many words from English. Moreover, borrowing may be quite systematic in some ways. For instance, English has borrowed many musical terms from Italian — *adagio, allegro, alto, aria,* etc. This is understandable. At a certain period the Italians were the recognized leaders in developing musical theory, and when we began to learn from them it was natural to take their technical terms along with their technical knowledge. But it would have been amazing if we had borrowed their words for *one, two, three,* for *hand* and *foot,* for *brother* and *sister.* We simply had to have our own words for these before

we ever encountered the Italians, and we were very unlikely to give up ours for theirs.

3. *Common descent.* This is the obvious explanation for the resemblances in the sets of numbers listed above. In this instance we have all sorts of evidence that the obvious explanation is the true one. But even if we knew nothing of the history of these languages we could see that the resemblances were far too great to be accidental; and it would strain our imaginations to believe that three peoples had had to borrow the same set of such essential words from a fourth. Moreover, if we extend the list of words to be compared, we can see that the resemblances are not haphazard. Eventually we should be forced to conclude that Latin changed in rather different ways in France, Spain, and Italy, but that its changes in each country were amazingly regular.

It must be emphasized that it was the *sounds* in which the changes originally occurred. The three Romance languages were scarcely written at all until they had been spoken for centuries and had become quite distinct. And even the Latin from which they developed was not the literary language of Cicero and Vergil, but the spoken language of soldiers, peddlers, workmen, and so forth, mostly illiterate. The speech of these people differed from Classical Latin about as much as the speech of some of Al Capp's characters differs from standard English. If you heard the four lists instead of seeing them the resemblances would not be quite so obvious; but they would be there, and they would become clearer and clearer with further study. For instance, the French *cinq* is pronounced approximately /sæŋk/, and the Italian *cinque* approximately /tʃiŋkwe/. No reasonable man, hearing these two words in isolation, would suspect that they were related. The spelling, of course, gives us an immediate hint that they are; but even without this hint we might eventually discover the relation by studying other pairs of French and Italian words. If we did this carefully enough we would eventually find two important principles.

27. MECHANICS OF SOUND CHANGE. 1. A sound change is always from one sound to another that is phonetically similar in at least one way, but different in another. Thus a /b/ may change to a /v/ because both are labials and both are voiced, though one is a stop and the other a fricative. Or a /θ/ may change to an /f/ because both are voiceless fricatives, though one is dental and the other labial. In both cases a comparatively slight variation in the muscular movements of the speech organs results in the new sound. But a /b/ cannot suddenly change to a /θ/, because the motions required to produce these two phonemes are so different that one could not possibly slide into the other.

2. When any sound change occurs in a language it occurs with great regularity *in the same phonetic environment;* that is, when the sound affected is in the same position relative to neighboring sounds. But this regularity may not appear on the surface, since some words may be affected by more sound changes than others.

Let's look first at some very simple examples. In Spain, where *octo* became *ocho, noctem* (night) became *noche;* but in Italy, where *octo* became *otto, noctem* became *notte.*[1] In other words, the *ct* (/kt/) combination regularly changed to *ch* (/tʃ/) in Spanish, but to *tt* (/tt/) in Italian (in which language double consonants are a phonetic reality, not merely a spelling convention). We should therefore expect Latin *lactem* (milk) to develop into Spanish *lache* and Italian *latte;* but here the first complication sets in. The Italian word is in fact *latte,* but the Spanish one is *leche* instead of *lache.* If we happen to know such Latin-Spanish pairs as *sanctum-santo* (saint) or *mare-mar* (sea) we are at first surprised at the vowel change in *leche,* but perhaps it occurs only in the neighborhood of certain consonants. We first try another pair beginning with *l,* but *latronem-*

---

[1] For students familiar with Latin who may be puzzled by the choice of this form, it should be explained that nouns in the Romance languages were regularly derived from the accusative, not the nominative, case of their Latin originals. Often this makes no difference, but for many nouns it does. *Notte,* for example, could not possibly have come from *nox.*

ladrón (thief) shows no such change. If we then think of *lacum-lago* (lake) we seem to have come to a blind alley. But there is one more chance; what follows *a* in *lactem* is not simply *c*, but the combination *ct*. If this is the influence at work, then Latin *factum*, which becomes *fatto* in Italian, should become *feche* in Spanish.

Now we have another complication, for the Spanish word turns out to be not *fecho* but *hecho*. However, at least part of our expectation has been fulfilled, so we now wonder if the shift from Latin *f* to Spanish *h* can also be a regular occurrence. A search for additional examples turns up such pairs as *facere-hacer* (make), *famem-hambre* (hunger), *formoso-hermoso* (beautiful), and *filium-hijo* (son). The shift does seem to be regular, and if we pronounce such a pair of English words as *fit* and *hit*, exaggerating the initial consonants, we can see that it is phonetically quite a possible one. Of course the *br* in *hambre*, the *e* in *hermoso*, and the *j* in *hijo* leave still further questions to be resolved, but we shall not go into them here, since we are merely giving a few examples of the sort of evidence linguists use in finding relations between various languages. The process does get a little complicated, and it is easy to sympathize with Voltaire's complaint that "philology is the science where the vowels count for nothing and the consonants for very little." Nevertheless, the forces at work are quite regular, and scholars who know enough about them can get very dependable results.

Nobody really knows why Latin changed in such different ways in the different countries, and the various guesses are too complicated to go into now. But it seems to have been an invariable rule in the past that when the speakers of any language split into groups that lost contact with each other the changes that took place were never quite parallel, and the languages of the groups grew further and further apart. During recent times more and more unifying forces, from the printing press and public school to the radio, movie, and television, have to some extent counteracted this tendency, though they have by no means entirely stopped it.

28. ENGLISH AND GERMAN. English is not, like the Romance languages, descended from Latin. It belongs to another group, called Germanic, discussed on pp. 52–60. If we compare the same set of numbers in German and English we again find a relation between them.

German	English
eins	one
zwei	two
drei	three
vier	four
fünf	five
sechs	six
sieben	seven
acht	eight
neun	nine
zehn	ten

There is clearly enough resemblance to indicate a relation, and the evidence becomes much stronger if we notice that many other words that begin with *t* in English begin with *z* in German (*to, zu; twig, zweig,* etc.); and many that begin with *th* in English begin with *d* in German (*then, dann; think, denken,* etc.).

29. THE GREAT LANGUAGE FAMILIES. Now suppose we compare the English and German numbers with the Latin ones. There are still some obvious resemblances, but others are well hidden. It takes a rather elaborate demonstration to show that *quinque* and *five* are regular developments from a common original form, and I won't go into it here, but it can be shown quite conclusively; and altogether there is no doubt at all that the Germanic languages are related to the Romance ones, though much more distantly than these are to each other.

It is now time to step back a few hundred thousand years. We have already said that we do not know how language began. We do not even know whether it began just once and spread all

over the world, or began independently in a number of different
places at different times. In other words, we don't know whether
or not all languages are related to each other, but we do know
that some of them are. It is therefore usual to speak of various
families of languages; and this metaphor is convenient if not
taken too seriously. Strictly speaking, Italian is not a descendant
of Latin, but simply a late and localized form; and the enthusiastic statement that any language is "a living, breathing organism
with a life of its own" is not one of the happier misapplications
of the theory of biological evolution. All the same, the metaphor
is useful as a concise way of indicating relations. We can therefore say that French, Spanish, and Italian are sister languages,
born of spoken Latin. English and German are cousins, descended
from sister branches of a lost language which we may call primitive Germanic or Teutonic. This was never written, but we have
enough evidence to reconstruct a good deal of it, though of
course some guesswork is involved. Latin and English are something like third cousins twice removed; and all the languages
mentioned in this paragraph, along with a number of others,
make up what is now usually called the Indo-European family.

Choosing other areas, we can show that Hebrew and Arabic
and some others are related to each other as members of the
Semitic family; that certain American Indian languages are related in the Algonquian family, and so forth. But whether the
Indo-European and the Semitic and the Algonquian families are
ultimately related to each other we simply do not know. If they
are they have changed so much that the proof of their common
origin has been lost. There are occasional resemblances, which
some scholars take as evidence of common ancestry; but others
consider them as either late borrowings or pure coincidence. At
any rate, we shall not go beyond the Indo-European family in
this book.

30. ORIGIN OF THE INDO-EUROPEAN FAMILY. About five thousand
years ago our Indo-European ancestors were living more or less
together somewhere in Europe or western Asia, or maybe both.

Since they had not developed writing, and did not leave much for archaeologists to dig up and investigate, we have very little definite and direct evidence about them, and the indirect evidence we do have can often be interpreted in different ways. Without going into various learned arguments, we can say that they seem to have been a nomadic people, depending more on their herds and on game than on settled farming. Some scholars are quite sure that their homeland was as far west as Lithuania; others think it was way over across the Ural Mountains in Asia. Quite possibly both theories are partly true. Since the Indo-Europeans were occupying an enormous territory not very long after they were first heard of, it isn't necessary to assume that they all came from one small district in the beginning. We do not really know either that they all came from the same stock or that they spoke a "pure" and original language. Maybe both they and their speech were already mixtures. What we do know is that a lot of things can be traced back to them and no further.

There is good reason for thinking that on the whole they were tall, blond, fertile, and energetic, because within a few hundred years after 2000 B.C. different groups of them went out in various directions and took over most of what they found, all the way from India and Persia to the Scandinavian Peninsula. It obviously required both fertility and energy to do this, and in many places the earlier inhabitants (some of whom were much more civilized) referred to them as the tall, blond invaders. However, we don't know how accurate this generalization was. Some Germans still like to think of themselves as a tall, blond race, and consider the millions of short, dark Germans as exceptions who shouldn't be counted.

At any rate, each wave that went out soon lost touch with the others and began a new development of its own. Some of the waves, especially in northern Europe, seem to have driven out or killed off most of the earlier inhabitants of the areas they settled. Other waves conquered but did not eliminate. Beginning as ruling minorities, they soon mingled and intermarried with the native inhabitants, and eventually lost their distinctive physical traits. Their languages were also modified, some more and some less, by the native ones. Sometimes the modification was so great that it is debatable whether the result of the mixture can reasonably be called Indo-European.

While we cannot pinpoint the area from which all these waves went out, there are good reasons for thinking that it was inland and not too far south. In the various languages we find related words for such animals as wolves and bears, but no such related words for lions, tigers, or camels. In the same way we find common words for trees of the temperate zone, but not for tropical ones. And there are no common words for the sea or anything closely connected with it. It therefore seems very nearly certain that the area was well inland and too far north for subtropical flora and fauna.

Many scholars have tried to locate the area more specifically, but they run into conflicting evidence. For instance, so many languages have words related to our *beech* that it seems on the surface that the homeland must have been in the limited area where beech trees grew. Unluckily, it turns out that although all these words have a common origin, they do not all refer to the same kind of tree — and we can't be sure which of their quite different meanings was the original one — beech, oak, elm, or elder. In a very similar way a good many American trees have been given names once applied to quite different trees in Europe. People like to use the words they have grown up with; and if they move to an area where the objects to which they originally applied are not found, they are likely to use them for the nearest equivalents — which are not always very near. When trout fishermen moved to Alabama they went right on catching trout, even though they had to rechristen the large-mouthed black bass to do it. In the same way, quail hunters keep on shooting quail, though the birds they call by this name vary remarkably.

31. THE BRANCHES OF INDO-EUROPEAN. On page 49 is a chart of the Indo-European family of languages. Many of the details of this are open to argument, but fortunately they do not have much

The Indo-European Family of Languages

INDO – EUROPEAN

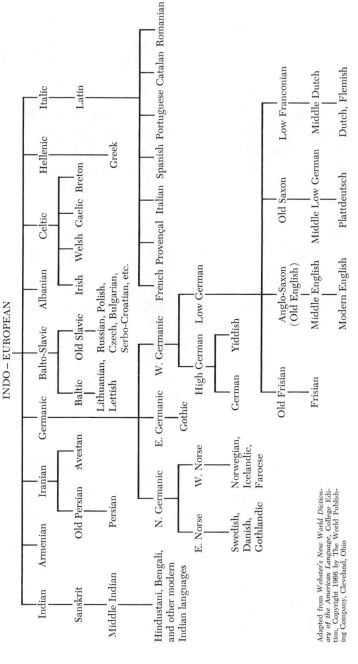

Adapted from *Webster's New World Dictionary of the American Language*, College Edition. Copyright 1966 by The World Publishing Company, Cleveland, Ohio

49

to do with the history of English. Of the Asiatic branches only Sanskrit concerns us, and that for scholarly rather than organic reasons. It is the language of ancient Hindu religious texts, and was analyzed and codified long before any other branch. Consequently it has been preserved in a form apparently much closer to the original Indo-European than anything else that has survived. The ordinary spoken languages of India have changed about as much as those elsewhere, but Sanskrit has been frozen in an early form — like classical Latin, but for a much longer time.

Persian, Armenian, and Albanian have little importance for English. Neither has Balto-Slavic, with which English had very little contact before the twentieth century. More surprisingly, neither has the Celtic (or Keltic) branch, with which English has been in contact throughout its whole existence.

The three branches of most importance in the development of English are, in ascending order, Hellenic (Greek); Italic, which includes Latin and its Romance descendants; and Germanic. From the first two we derive well over half of the total English vocabulary. From the third we get most of our everyday words and almost all of the structural devices by which we combine them into sentences.

32. THE MODERN DISCOVERY OF INDO-EUROPEAN. In discussing the words for the first ten numbers we have already seen that, though the Germanic forms are related to Latin ones, the relation is sometimes not at all obvious on the surface. Such closer resemblances as those between English and German, between the various Romance languages, and even between Latin and Greek had been noticed for centuries, but it was less than two hundred years ago that a comprehensive theory on a much larger scale was first developed. The decisive clue was the discovery by Sir William Jones, an English official in India, that Sanskrit, the classical language of the Hindus, contained such extensive and systematic similarities to Greek, Latin, and various other Euro-

pean languages that it was obviously related to them; and that it was preserved in a much earlier form than any of the others. The result was that many words, which had developed so differently in various languages that they no longer bore a recognizable resemblance to each other, were found to resemble, each in its own way, a form nearer to the original source.

To take one example, the Old English word for *am* is *eom*, and the Latin word is *sum*. They share only one phoneme, and neither look nor sound any closer together than, say, *eat* and *dot*. There is absolutely no reason to suspect a common origin. If we add the Greek equivalent, *eimi*, we can see that it might be related to the English word; however, the resemblance might be a pure coincidence, and there is still no sign of relation with Latin. But the Sanskrit equivalent, *asmi*, changes the whole picture. We know from such pairs as *prism* and *prismatic* that when a combination like /zm/ or /sm/ occurs at the end of a word it is necessary to insert a vowel sound in order to pronounce it. If the ancestors of the Romans happened to drop the /i/ ending, they would get /ásm/, with two syllables. If they shifted the stress to the second syllable they'd get /asúm/. Then if they dropped the unstressed syllable, they'd get /sum/. A little complicated, but all perfectly natural — and apparently exactly what happened.

On the other hand, anybody who knows much about French realizes that at one stage the speakers of that language found the combination of /s/ plus any following consonant hard to pronounce, and simply dropped the /s/, so that they have *bête* compared to our *beast*, *châtiment* compared to our *chastisement*, etc. (plain laziness is the obvious explanation of many sound changes). So the Greek *eimi* might have developed by dropping the /s/, and the Old English *eom* by dropping both the /s/ and the /i/ ending. We have already learned that we have to be broadminded (unless we want to work very hard) about early vowel changes.

This still looks pretty wild, but when we turn to the words

for *is* we get some strong confirmation — Old English *is,* Latin *est,* Greek *esti,* and Sanskrit *asti.* Three of these are very close, and the absence of the *t* in *is* needn't bother us — we have all heard *best* and *last* pronounced as *bes'* and *las'.* Moreover, the Modern German form is *ist,* and we know English and German are related. Now if we look at the two sets together, we see something else. If *eom* originally had an /s/ in it, it was closer to *is* than it now looks. In Sanskrit the forms are *asmi* and *asti.* The only difference is the /m/ in the first person and the /t/ in the third. Could that be related to the *me* and *tu* in Latin and the *me* and *thou* in English? Maybe these "personal endings" were originally pronouns of a sort.

If we had time we could examine many other sets of related words, but here we need only say that the evidence for a "family" of languages is overwhelming. For a while it was believed that Sanskrit was the parent of all the others. This theory soon had to be given up, but there has been no reason to change the belief that it is the earliest recorded form. It was described in precise detail about 500 B.C., and the description was based on religious texts that had carefully preserved the forms of a thousand years earlier. As we might expect under the circumstances, the inflectional system is more fully preserved than elsewhere. For instance, nouns have eight cases, all quite distinct in form. It is highly probable that the sound system had changed somewhat since the migration to India; but when we trace back the other related languages, which had diverged in various directions, we find by a sort of triangulation that their common source cannot have been very different from Sanskrit.

33. The Germanic Group and Grimm's Law. The Germanic group seems to have been one of the last to push out from the Indo-European homeland, probably somewhere about 600 B.C. During the next two thousand years or so it multiplied in size, divided into various subgroups, and spread out over an enormous territory. The Burgundians, Franks, Goths, Lombards, and Van-

dals were only a few of the better known tribes whose languages have now died out. The most important modern languages that can be traced to this group are English, German, Yiddish, Dutch, Flemish, and the Scandinavian tongues.

Either before or shortly after the migration, but before the various tribes had separated, the Germanic branch of the language developed several important characteristics which set it apart from the other Indo-European branches, and obscured its relation to them. The most remarkable was a displacement of a number of the consonant phonemes. Even before the western discovery of Sanskrit it was obvious that some Germanic words bore some resemblance to Latin and Greek ones. If we compare English *mother, father,* and *brother* to Latin *mater, pater,* and *frater,* for instance, it seems clear that the two sets have something in common, but it is not easy to see exactly what it is; and the discovery of Sanskrit did not immediately clarify the matter. However, in the early nineteenth century the German Jacob Grimm and the Dane Rasmus Rask succeeded independently in finding a regular pattern. Since Rask wrote in Danish, Grimm got most of the credit; and though his statement has been considerably modified since, it is still known as Grimm's Law.

The uncovering of a whole set of systematic resemblances which had escaped notice for centuries was naturally a very complicated process. In considering the development of certain Spanish-Italian pairs of words we have seen a bare hint of how involved the tracing of relations between even two closely related languages can be, and Grimm and Rask were attempting to cover an enormously wider field, and one in which there were much greater gaps in the evidence. It would therefore be worse than useless to try to trace here the whole course of their investigations. Instead, we shall present merely a partial picture of what they and their successors eventually found, in a form that can be useful even to a student who knows no language but English. Below are listed a set of Latin and English pairs of words that we can derive from the same Indo-European roots. It should be emphasized, shouted, and reinforced by a flourish of trumpets that *in no case did the English word come from the Latin one.* Biologists do not say that man was descended from monkey, but that man and monkey apparently had a common ancestor. English *has* borrowed a great many words from Latin — among others, *paternal* and *piscatorial.* But these words preserve much of their Latin form. *Father* and *fish* are cousins rather than children of *pater* and *piscis.*

pater	father	tu	thou	caput	head
piscis	fish	tres	three	cornu	horn
frater	brother	[1]thugater	daughter	[2]hortus	garden
fero	bear (carry)	[1]thura	door	hostis	guest
[2]bursa	purse	duo	two	genus	kin
[2]bucca	pouch	duco	tug	gelidus	cold

You will notice that in each subgroup the relation between the initial consonants is regular, but that the degree of resemblance between the rest of the words varies considerably. This is because the shift of the initial consonants is independent, while any of the other sounds may have been affected by one or more additional influences. All of these could be systematically explained, but it would take a good many pages.

If you examine the whole set you will find that the initial consonants of the Latin words in the first column are labials, those in the second are dentals, and those in the third are palatals. Dividing them horizontally, those at the top are voiceless stops, those in the middle are fricatives, and those at the bottom are voiced stops. In other words, the same sort of changes have hap-

[1] These examples are from Greek rather than Latin, since the phoneme /θ/ disappeared from Latin by another sound shift which had nothing to do with this one.

[2] Some linguists are not sure that these pairs are cognate, but their sounds are in the proper relationship, and no other explanation has been found.

pened to consonants with something in common. These changes can be summarized by such statements as the following:

Indo-European voiceless stops, preserved as such in Latin (and most other Indo-European languages), *shifted to become fricatives in Germanic. At the same time, fricatives shifted to voiced stops, and voiced stops shifted to voiceless stops.*

This explanation is deliberately oversimplified. If you want to go into comparative linguistics seriously you will have to learn it in a somewhat more accurate and very much more complicated form. For instance, we have reason to believe that some of the Latin consonants, though nearer to the (hypothetical) original Indo-European sounds than the English ones are, had already changed somewhat in a manner that will not even be mentioned here. But most students of English will probably find this explanation adequate; and they may even find it useful. Even if you do not know any Latin as such you know thousands of English words borrowed from Latin, and you are likely to encounter others at any time. It is quite often possible to recognize one by noticing that the appropriate consonant shift would make it close to an English word of Germanic origin. And if you are studying any Germanic language you can often recognize a strange word by applying the sound shift in the opposite way.

The shift (still in its oversimplified form) can be shown schematically as in the following diagram.

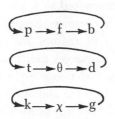

There are several points that need explanation.

1. It is convenient to think of these shifts as simultaneous, since otherwise the logical result would be to leave only one sound in each series. In a fuller explanation a chronological order of shifting could be shown.

2. /x/ stands for a sound like that in German *doch*. It appears in our spelling as *h*, but this letter formerly represented a sound much more strongly aspirated than it is now — a palatal fricative which bears the same relation to /k/ as /f/ does to /p/ or/θ/ to /t/.

3. If you try simply to memorize this diagram, you may easily get mixed up. But if you understand the phonetic relations you can reconstruct it completely from any pair of Latin and English words to which it applies. If you remember *pater* and *father*, for instance, you have $p \rightarrow f$. The only other labial sound to which *f* can go is *b*, and *b* must go back to *p*. It doesn't matter whether you put the palatals or the dentals next, but you must be sure to put the voiceless stops under *p*, the fricatives under *f*, and the voiced stops under *b*.

The list of cognate words given above is sufficient to prove that there is a systematic relation between the sound systems of English and Latin. This list could be extended greatly, and a more extensive analysis would show clearly what need only be stated here — that the shift occurred in Germanic before that language broke up into various branches. Unfortunately, the list could not be extended to such an extent that we could simply apply the principles discovered to a passage of Latin and come up with anything like a complete English translation.

There are a number of reasons for this. I have mentioned several times that all languages are always changing, and one of the kinds of change that occurs is in the makeup of the vocabulary. Some words drop out and are replaced by others. Some linguists are convinced that this process occurs in all languages at a constant rate. The evidence for this theory is both complicated and fragmentary, and I do not know enough about the subject to evaluate it; but there is certainly an arguable case. Just why all languages drop some perfectly good words and replace them by others that seem no better cannot be explained by any general theory, though there are clear enough reasons in some individual cases. At any rate, we do not find exactly the same pairs of cognates if we compare English and Latin, English and Greek, or Latin and Greek. Each language has dropped some items from the common heritage that both the others have retained.

Another difficulty is that while the initial consonants in our cognates show a dependable relationship, there is a good deal of apparent irregularity in the later ones. For one thing, a consonant that occurred after an unstressed syllable sometimes shifted differently from one that occurred initially or after a stressed one. For another, some consonants have been affected by later sound changes that have nothing to do with Grimm's Law. Almost all the apparent irregularities can be confidently explained as really regular when we take into account all the forces at work; and the few that cannot now be explained may yield to later investigation. But it takes more than an elementary knowledge to handle such complications, and we shall not go into them here.

34. THE HEAVY GERMANIC STRESS. In some languages all the syllables are pronounced with nearly equal force, and the primary stress — such as it is — may shift from one syllable to another in different inflected forms of the same word. For instance, in the present indicative active of the Latin verb *vocō*, the forms *vocō*, *vocās, vocat,* and *vocant* all have the stress on the first syllable, but the forms *vocātis* and *vocāmus* have it on the second. In the Germanic languages the stress was both heavier and less variable. It regularly fell on the first syllable of a word unless that syllable was a mere prefix. The other syllables were pronounced so lightly that it was easy for them to weaken or drop off entirely, and a great many of them did. Most of our old Germanic words have

been reduced to monosyllables in this way. We do have a good many polysyllables of Germanic origin, but they are mostly the result of combining several different roots. Thus *hlafweard* (guardian of the loaf) went through such stages as *hlaford* and *lavord* on its way to becoming *lord;* but we combine the short form with other elements to make such newer words as *warlord, lordship,* and *lordliness.*

English words borrowed from non-Germanic languages very early are likely to be shortened in exactly the same way. Thus we get *priest* from *presbyteros.* More recent borrowings may keep all their syllables, but some of them will be pronounced much more lightly than their cognates in other languages. Thus the Spanish *extraordinario* has seven full syllables. In the English *extraordinary* only two have a full pronunciation with clear vowel sounds. The others are either somewhat slurred or omitted entirely. In extreme cases the pronunciation becomes /strɔnri/.

35. THE THREE BRANCHES OF GERMANIC. Sometime after Germanic broke off from Indo-European it divided into three main branches, known as North, East, and West Germanic. From the first of these we get the Scandinavian languages, with the exception of Finnish, which is not of the Indo-European family. There is now no active survivor of the second, but Gothic lasted long enough to leave a written record which is of great linguistic importance because it preserves specimens of the language in a considerably earlier form than has come down for any of the other branches. Aside from its importance to linguists, Gothic is recommended to anyone who would like to attain a complete mastery of a literature, since all that remains is part of a translation of the Bible by Bishop Ulfilas or Wulfila, for which ponies are readily available.

The West Germanic branch in turn split into two main divisions known, from the comparative altitudes of the regions in which they developed, as High and Low German. The official language of modern Germany is a High German dialect, though

many of the spoken dialects in the northern part of the country
are Low German (Plattdeutsch). Yiddish is also basically High
German, though it contains a considerable number of Hebrew
words, and it is usually written and printed in Hebrew characters — perhaps the most striking example we have of the fact
that spoken language is affected comparatively little by the way
it happens to be written. High German is distinguished from
the Low principally by the second or High German sound shift,
which occurred much later than the one covered by Grimm's
Law. It will not be discussed in detail here, but it is the explanation of such correspondences as those mentioned earlier in this
chapter between English *two* and German *zwei,* English *three*
and German *drei,* and so forth. A working knowledge of it is
extremely useful to any English speaker learning German.

36. THE GENEALOGY OF ENGLISH. Low German split still further
into a number of dialects, from which are descended the Plattdeutsch mentioned above, Dutch-Flemish, Frisian, and — in at
least three strands — Old English. Two of these are Anglian and
Saxon. The third may or may not be Jutish, but it is the dialect
of the Germanic settlers in Kent, parts of Hampshire, and the
Isle of Wight, which definitely differed in a number of ways from
both of the others. Of the three, Anglian has had the strongest
influence on the development of standard Modern English, but
neither of the others is negligible. It is healthy to realize that
even at its very beginning as a national language English did
not have one correct form, but several overlapping and competing forms, each "best" in its own area. The interworkings of these
three during the past fifteen centuries are enormously complex,
and our evidence is so fragmentary that we shall never know all
the details; but we can, and in this book I shall, attempt to trace
the main lines.

It should be clear by now that fitting Modern English into our
language chart is no simple matter. Its basic grammatical patterns and most of its commonest words have developed from

three interweaving strands of Old English, but it has also borrowed a good deal from Scandinavian, Latin, French, and Greek, and odds and ends from many other languages. If we considered the whole vocabulary, giving the same value to rare words as to common ones, we would have to classify English with the Romance languages, since the words we have borrowed from Latin and French considerably outnumber the ones we have inherited from Old English. But since both the basic structure and the core of the vocabulary have developed from Germanic origins, the classification used here seems on the whole most reasonable.

CHAPTER FOUR

Old English

37. THE BEGINNINGS OF ENGLISH. Until the middle of the fifth century the part of Britain which is now called England was inhabited by the Britons, who spoke a variety of the Celtic rather than the Germanic branch of Indo-European. Some four hundred years earlier this territory had been conquered by the Romans, organized as part of the Roman Empire, and supplied with several legions of Roman troops. At first the legions were used principally to keep the native Britons in order. When they had achieved this purpose their mission was changed to protecting the inhabitants from raids and invasions from various directions, but especially from the northern part of the island, which is now Scotland. The Scots had not yet come over from Ireland, and this territory was then occupied by the Picts, a probably non-Indo-European people who had inhabited the whole island before the Britons came in and pushed them north. Since the Romans never conquered Pictland, they built a protective wall across the island and manned it with their legions, meanwhile discouraging the Britons from any military activities of their own.

But about 409 the whole Roman Empire was in such serious trouble that the legions were withdrawn for service nearer home. This left the Britons, whose military traditions had lapsed for some centuries, at a disadvantage against the northern raiders. They struggled without much success for some forty years; then they had to face a new, and eventually calamitous, series of invasions. Some Germanic tribesmen from the west coast of the European continent had been raiding Britain even during the Roman occupation, and archaeologists have found evidence of a few small permanent settlements. The withdrawal of the legions and the disorganization that followed opened the way to much more extensive settlement, and three tribes soon conquered much of England. The two larger ones were the Angles and the Saxons, but the identity of the third group has never been settled. Bede called them Jutes, and this name will be used here, since no more satisfactory one has been found; but we simply do not know who they were or exactly where they came from. The Angles took possession of about the northern two-thirds of what is now called England (from Anglaland) after them. The Saxons took over most of the southern third, leaving only Kent, part of Hampshire, and the Isle of Wight to the Jutes. All three tribes spoke Low West Germanic dialects so much alike that they could understand each other, and Old English might be described as the result of a gradual fusion of the three. The fusion was by no means complete. Considerable regional differences remained for centuries, and at times increased. Even today many of them persist in popular speech. But the language of the whole country soon came to be known as English, and developed increasing differences from the dialects of the continent.

The history (or rather the collection of conflicting theories) of the relations between the Germanic invaders and the earlier Celtic inhabitants of Britain is an interesting subject in itself, but it does not have much connection with the development of the language, and there is enough confusion within our own subject to make it inadvisable to borrow trouble from elsewhere. Whether the Angles, Saxons, and Jutes slaughtered, enslaved, or simply drove out the Britons, they borrowed only some place-names and a very small handful of ordinary words from their victims.

The very tiny Celtic influence on English is really an amazing fact, especially when we consider how enormously English has borrowed from other languages. Not only the Britons were Celts; so were the Scots (though probably not the Picts) who had been harassing them. For many centuries varieties of Celtic were the normal languages of Wales, Ireland, and most of Scotland, not to mention Cornwall in southern England and Brittany just across the channel in France. Even now it is only the Cornish variety which has completely died out, though the other languages are now decidedly secondary — even in Eire, which is making a strenuous effort to be as un-English as possible. Yet in all this time English has borrowed scarcely more from Celtic than it has from Chinese.

There is, of course, an explanation of sorts. The English were converted to Christianity by missionaries steeped in the Graeco-Roman tradition, which was reinforced by their education for centuries. They were invaded, oppressed and sometimes ruled by the Danes, conquered and administered by the French. Their borrowings from these sources can be attributed to both pressure and need. Some words were literally forced into their language, and others were needed to fill out gaps in English. Still others were internationally current, and thus often seemed preferable to purely local words. Probably some were adopted out of simple snobbery. Neither necessity, international currency, nor snobbery gave the English any reason to borrow much from their Celtic neighbors, so they didn't. But it still seems curious.

38. PRE-CHRISTIAN ENGLAND. We know amazingly little about fifth- and sixth-century England, and that little is pieced together from various kinds of indirect evidence. No histories have survived, and there is not the slightest reason to suppose that any were written during this period. Archaeology gives us a little evidence of how the early English lived, but our strongest impressions come from the Germanic traditions, mostly continental, that were handed down (with continual modifications) for generations before they were put in writing. These contain all sorts

of exaggerations and distortions, but we can take a brief look, for whatever it is worth, at the picture they present.

On this evidence the early English, like the continental tribes-men, were an able and vigorous group of people, but they seem to have gone on for some time within a fairly narrow range of ideas and ambitions. They lived by hunting, fishing, and farm-ing, relaxed by eating, drinking, and listening to songs, and de-voted most of their more serious energy to fighting. Sometimes they fought for gain, and sometimes for one emotional reason or another; but always in the background was a firm, even re-ligious, belief that fighting was the proper business of man, and that the only respectable way to die was in battle.

Their religion, like their language, was obviously a part of their Indo-European heritage. If we compare their gods to those of the Greeks and Romans we of course find many differences, but the resemblances are far too great to be attributed to mere coincidence. Woden and Frigga were not exactly like the Greek Zeus and Hera, but then neither were the Roman Jupiter and Juno; and if you read enough Greek mythology you soon find that Zeus and Hera were not always like themselves. When stories are handed down for centuries they inevitably change as the interests and beliefs of the tellers and the audience change; and the Indo-European peoples, spreading over millions of square miles through thousands of years, developed some really remark-able changes. But behind them all are the signs of a common origin that cannot be hidden. There are the gods, neither all-good nor all-powerful, but worthy (on the whole) of worship, and certainly worth propitiating. And behind them are the three fates, whom the Romans called Parcae and the Germanic tribes Norns — old women beyond passion or personal interest, somehow laying out the lines of the future with which even the gods cannot tamper.

There is, in general, nothing comparable to the Christian idea of heaven. In the Germanic accounts, especially, not even the gods can look forward to an eternity of peace (which would certainly bore them) or happiness. They are temporarily ahead of their equally powerful enemies, the Giants, but the final battle — Ragnarok or Götterdämmerung — is still to come. For this battle Woden will need all the human heroes that he can get, though he knows that even with their help he cannot win. Accordingly he keeps a corps of beautiful (but rather hefty) young female recruiting officers. These are the Valkyrie — a word that means "choosers of the slain." It is their duty to watch over battles; and whenever they see a worthy champion at the very peak of his valor and performance, they arrange for an enemy weapon to kill him. Then they take his spirit to Valhalla — the Hall of the Slain — where he goes into training for Ragnarok. Each day he fights gloriously with his peers. Each night, his wounds healed, he feasts with his companions, with plenty of ale and appropriate song. And in the end the great fight against the Giants will come, and it will really be the end, for neither side can win. They will destroy each other and the very earth on which they have lived, and nothing will remain but utter chaos.

Neither such a life nor such a vision of the future would appeal to everybody, but the Germanic tribesmen seem to have found them adequate for some centuries. At least those who settled in Britain apparently found nothing in either the life or the ideas of the Romanized Britons (by most standards a considerably more advanced people) that they cared enough about to adopt. Whether they slaughtered, enslaved, or drove away the Britons, they went on living their own habitual lives in the new space they had acquired. They did not even bother to take over the towns and villas they found, but destroyed them or left them to rot while they built their own farm houses as they had on the continent.

39. HISTORICAL BACKGROUND OF THE OLD ENGLISH PERIOD. It is usual to divide the development of the English language into three great periods: Old English, from the middle of the fifth century to about 1100; Middle English for the next four hundred years; and Modern English from about 1500 on. These divisions are of course arbitrary. There was no sudden change in the

language at either 1100 or 1500, and even the gradual developments took place at very different rates in different parts of the country. However, there are real differences between the three stages, and these dividing dates will do as well as any others.

Before considering the Old English language it will be well to take a brief glance at the historical framework of the period. The very large Anglian territory was soon divided into two major areas — Northumbria from about the Scottish border to the River Humber, and Mercia from the Humber south to the Thames. There were dialectal as well as political differences between the two, so that during the Middle English period Northumbrian developed into Northern English, and Mercian split into East and West Midland. Just south of the Thames, on the eastern side, the originally Jutish territory came to be called Kent, and retained dialectal characteristics of its own even after it came to be controlled by the West Saxon kings who ruled (when they could manage it) the whole southern fifth of the country.

It took the English (as we may now call the Angles, Saxons, and Jutes) about a hundred and fifty years to gain control of most of England. This process was not a unified national effort but a tangle of local enterprises, frequently interrupted by fights among the English themselves; and we know very little about the details. Not a single contemporary piece of writing either in English or by an Englishman has survived, and we don't even know of any that have been lost. Our ignorance is highlighted by the attention historians have to pay to the one surviving Latin account, by a Welshman named Gildas. It is a Jeremiad rather than a history, and so obviously unreliable that it would be completely neglected if there were any other source. As it is, we can only hope that a few of the things he reports may be more or less true.

In an age so committed to the keeping of records as our own this situation may seem incredible, but it is quite typical of the pre-Christian Germanic peoples. They had an alphabet — the Runic one — which they used for magic spells and for inscriptions on wood, stone, or metal, but not for extended compositions of any kind. Their literature was transmitted orally, and they had no interest in history as we conceive it — a systematic account of exactly what happened, and when, and where. They were vitally interested in the exploits of their heroes, but cheerfully unconcerned with either geography or chronology. Everything beyond living memory had simply happened "way back then," in a location that was either unspecified or subject to change according to taste.

Toward the end of this period of expansion, in 597, Roman missionaries landed in Kent and began the systematic conversion of England to Christianity. The Welsh had been Christians since Roman times, but had showed no interest in converting their heathen oppressors, who in any case would probably not have been very receptive to anything they had to offer. Also, Irish missionaries had converted most of Scotland, and there were certainly some individual Christians farther south. But the movement that changed the country from a pagan to a Christian one began when St. Augustine of Canterbury, sent by Gregory the Great, landed at Thanet with thirty-nine companions and received official permission to spread the new religion. There was of course some opposition, but progress was surprisingly fast.

Among other things that the Christian missionaries introduced was the habit of extended writing. Most of the people were still illiterate, but within the church an amazing tradition of scholarship developed, so that in little more than a century England had become one of the centers of learning for the entire western world. Bede (673–735) was probably the ablest and most learned scholar of his time, and has been called "the teacher of the Middle Ages." To us the most interesting of his encyclopedic writings is his *Ecclesiastical History of the English People.* He shows only occasional interest in purely secular affairs, and when he does deal with them he has to depend almost entirely on oral tradition; but he sifted this so carefully and intelligently that he is by far our best authority for the early Old English period.

Probably most of the writing that was done, and certainly most of what has survived, was (like Bede's) in Latin. We have, however, a fair amount of English poetry from about 650 on. Most of this was written in the north of England, and consequently in the Anglian dialect, but it has come down to us only in much later West Saxon manuscripts. Since the idea of copying with letter-by-letter accuracy almost never occurred to a medieval scribe, it is only occasionally that a typical Anglian form has been preserved.

The explanation for this indirect preservation is that from about 787 on Scandinavian raiders, especially Danes, began to harry the north of England, and from about 850 they began to make permanent settlements there, until they controlled the whole Anglian territory. The procedure of the early raiders was simple: whatever they wanted, they took; whatever they could not use, they killed or destroyed. They were particularly thorough in the destruction of books, which were not only useless to them, but suspected of containing magic spells which might be dangerous in the hands of their enemies. In the latter half of the ninth century it seemed probable that the Danes would take over the whole country; but Alfred the Great, king of Wessex, managed to stop their expansion and keep the southern part of England free. Thereafter the Danes, even in the territory they continued to control, were gradually absorbed into the more numerous English people.

40. ALFRED AND ENGLISH PROSE. The place of Alfred is as important in a history of the English language as it is in a political history of England. He was distressed by the decay of learning in England since the great days of the eighth century, and did his best to remedy it by having the books he considered most essential translated into English. He himself translated Pope Gregory's *Pastoral Care,* though he tells us that he had to have two priests, a bishop, and an Archbishop help him to understand the Latin; and he took at least some part in translating the general history of Orosius and Boethius' *Consolation of Philosophy.* It is generally believed that he also at least inspired the English version of Bede's *Ecclesiastical History* and the

compilation of the group of annals collectively known as *The Anglo-Saxon Chronicle*, which was begun during his reign.

Obviously English prose would have had to start some time, with or without King Alfred, and we need not here go into the argument about exactly how much of the work associated with his name should actually be attributed to him, or how much influence it had in encouraging the use of prose during succeeding generations. But we can be perfectly sure that without these works we would know much less about Old English than we do. Our knowledge of what may be called Alfredian prose is particularly important because in Old English manuscripts the vocabulary of prose differs from that of poetry much more than it does in most languages, or in most later periods of English. Considered as literature, the poetry is much more impressive; but it is in the prose that we find the roots of later English.

Alfred's successful resistance to the Danes was not the end of the trouble with them. Throughout the tenth century there was a great deal of raiding of England by Danes from the continent, and in the early years of the eleventh century Danish kings actually reigned in England. But during this time the descendants of the earlier Danish invaders had become so mixed with the English, that they usually joined them in the struggles with the newer raiders.

In 1066 England was conquered by the Normans under William, and the effect on the language was as great as on other sides of life. Perhaps the simplest way to explain what happened is to say that with Frenchmen in control of almost everything, nothing written in English could be very important or effective. Apparently very little was written in English, and certainly very little has survived, between the conquest and the beginning of the twelfth century. When we begin to find again a considerable body of native material, the language has changed so much that we call it Middle rather than Old English.

41. THE SOUNDS OF OLD ENGLISH. Old English differed from Modern English in the phonemes of which it was composed, in

the distribution of those phonemes which are common to both stages, and in the representation of the phonemes in writing. Briefly, it contained two phonemes which have since been lost: /x/, which had the value of *ch* in such German words as *nicht* and *doch*, and was spelled as *h;* and /y/, which was a rounded front vowel with approximately the value of French *u* or German *ü*. It did not contain the /ʒ/, which came in during the Middle English period. The voiced and voiceless members of the three pairs /v/ and /f/, /ð/ and /þ/, and /z/ and /s/ were not distinct phonemes, but allophones — voiced between vowels, voiceless elsewhere.

These features will be discussed in more detail when we examine some specimens of Old English text, but it is necessary to get a few facts about the vowel system straight before we go into the intervening discussion of the parts of speech. There were nine vowel sounds, each of which could be either long or short; and the long vowels were, to the best of our knowledge, simply prolongations of the short ones, and not the diphthongs which are called long vowels in Modern English. However, there was no distinction in spelling between the open and close *e* and the open and close *o*. We can therefore distinguish between the members of these two pairs of sounds only because of what we know about the later development of the words in which they occur. Since there is not enough text in this book to give students a chance to become familiar with differences that are not indicated by the spelling, the differences between the open and close sounds will therefore be disregarded in the very broad phonemic transcriptions.

Long vowels were occasionally, but not usually, marked in the manuscripts. Here they are marked in the discussion of the parts of speech because it is important to emphasize such differences as that between *bite* which developed into modern *bit,* and *bīte* which developed into modern *bite.* They are not marked in the specimens of text because there more students seem to find them confusing than useful.

The short vowels give little trouble, but the following table of
the long vowels should be studied:

Name	Spelling	Phonetic value	Compromise phonemic representation
long a	a	[ɑː]	/ɑː/
long digraph	æ	[æː]	/æː/
long open e	e	[ɛː]	/eː/
long close e	e	[eː]	/eː/
long i	i	[iː]	/iː/
long open o	o	[ɔː]	/oː/
long close o	o	[oː]	/oː/
long u	u	[uː]	/uː/
long y	y	[yː]	/yː/

42. THE STRUCTURE OF OLD ENGLISH. Old English differs from
Modern English not only in its sounds and its vocabulary (which
will be discussed later), but in the way in which the words are
put together to form sentences. The difference is often summarized by the statement that English has developed from a
synthetic to an analytical language. A synthetic language is one
in which the relations of words are shown primarily by their
inflectional forms. An analytical language is one in which differences in form have largely disappeared, and relations are shown
primarily by word-order, supplemented by such "function words"
as prepositions and auxiliary verbs.

The English shift from one type to the other has been a matter
of changing emphasis rather than of absolute conversion. Word-
order had some importance in Old English, and inflections have
some importance now. Often the two supplement each other.
But when they conflict we have to decide which one to believe.
Consider such a sentence as "Him saw I." From the synthetic
point of view it obviously means "I saw him," since *I* is in the
normal form for a subject, *him* in the normal form for an object,

and the order of the words is a secondary matter. An ancient Saxon would interpret it (with the words in a slightly different form) in this way without the slightest hesitation. But the natural reaction of almost any contemporary American would be that the sentence meant "He saw me," and that the speaker was either very ignorant or indulging in baby-talk. An unusually fanatical grammarian might insist that the sentence "really" means "I saw him," but even he probably would not carry his theories very far. If he saw a sentence like "Sally and him invited my wife and I to breakfast," he would accept the obvious meaning and simply say that the sentence contained a couple of errors.

The drift toward analytical structure had begun even before the Germanic tribes left the continent, and was continuing all during the Old English period. That is, more and more inflectional forms which had once been different were coming to be identical, and therefore losing much of their signalling power. The heavy stress on the root syllables made it easy to slur the endings. More or less simultaneously a reliable word-order was developing. We could argue indefinitely about whether the new word-order had to develop when the inflections dropped out, or whether the inflections were lost because the new word-order made them unnecessary. It seems simpler to say that both tendencies were at work, and we don't know which was more important. But the dropping of inflections was happening a little faster than the development of a word-order to replace them. That is, people sometimes depended on inflectional differences that were no longer there to depend on, and ambiguous sentences often resulted.

A student cannot be expected to master Old English grammar without a far greater experience with the language than this book provides; but even a very sketchy outline of it can be useful in showing how some of the features of Modern English originated. Many points of usage which seem utterly unreasonable when considered in isolation can be readily understood when recognized as survivals from an earlier system. Moreover, it is obviously impossible to study the development of a language intelligently without having a firm, if not particularly detailed, idea of what it was like at the beginning.

The kind of Old English discussed is late West Saxon, since that is the only dialect in which enough manuscripts have been preserved to give us adequate evidence. Even in this one dialect there is a good deal of variation in the forms, which is not surprising. We have no evidence at all that English grammar was ever studied during either the Old or Middle English periods. So far as we know, people learned English by simple absorption, and there were no accepted standards to keep their practices uniform. In this chapter the paradigms (sets of inflectional forms) have been simplified by leaving out most of the variants.

Students who are not thoroughly familiar with the terminology of traditional grammar may find it useful to read the first part of Chapter 9 before continuing with this one. In that chapter grammatical theory is considered in much more detail than is included here.

43. NOUNS. Old English nouns, like Latin ones, occurred in a number of different declensions with different sets of endings. We do not know why this was so. Possibly the "original Indo-European" was already a mixture of languages with different characteristic declensions. At any rate, some of the Old English declensions can be shown to be related to those in such languages as Greek and Latin, while others are either of purely Germanic origin or were borrowed by the Germanic peoples from some other language they encountered after separating from the other Indo-Europeans.

In Old English nouns the separate ablative case had already disappeared, and the running together of other originally distinct forms had gone further than in Latin. The paradigms for five nouns are given below. They should all be examined carefully, but only the *stān* declension is worth memorizing, since this is the one from which the modern pattern developed.

	stone (m.)	*word* (n.)	*gift* (f.)	*ape* (m.)	*foot* (m.)
Singular					
Nominative	stān	word	giefu	apa	fōt
Genitive	stānes	wordes	giefe	apan	fōtes
Dative	stāne	worde	giefe	apan	fēt
Accusative	stān	word	giefe	apan	fōt
Plural					
Nominative	stānas	word	giefa	apan	fēt
Genitive	stāna	worda	giefa	apena	fōta
Dative	stānum	wordum	giefum	apum	fōtum
Accusative	stānas	word	giefa	apan	fēt

Notice that two of the declensions do not have the -*s* ending in the genitive singular, and that only the *stān* declension has it in two cases of the plural. What has happened since is that the *stān* declension has been simplified in form and extended in use, so that it now takes in most of the nouns that originally belonged to others. But both the -*en* plural of *ox* and the unchanged plural of such words as *sheep* and *deer* go back to other declensions. Notice also that in the *fōt* declension the variation between the two vowels is not simply between singular and plural. In such expressions as "He was six foot tall" *foot* does not come from the singular, but from the dative plural *fōtum*, which could mean (all by itself) "to the extent of — feet."

There are several declensions besides the ones illustrated above, and all the declensions had subclasses with certain phonetic peculiarities. As we might reasonably expect, a number of irregular forms (not indicated above) are found, since the competing analogies put a considerable strain on the memory. When irregular forms occur very rarely, they are considered to be mistakes. When they occur frequently, they are considered legitimate variants.

The nominative case is used primarily for a word that is, or refers to, the subject of a sentence. The genitive is primarily the case of possession, but (as in Modern English) may also indicate various other relations, such as kinship, authorship, and member-ship in a group. The accusative is primarily the case of the direct object. The dative, which was originally used primarily as the indirect object, has taken over most of the functions of several lost cases. It is used after most prepositions, and is also often used alone where a prepositional phrase would now be required (for example, *fōtum*, two paragraphs above).

In *stān* and *word* the nominative and accusative forms are alike in both the singular and the plural. If they were alike in all declensions Old English would have only three cases. But in *giefu* and *apa* differences between the nominative and the accusative have been preserved, though some other original differences have been lost. We therefore have to recognize four cases as existing in Old English nouns, and it is on the whole convenient to show each one in every paradigm, though there is no one noun that keeps the forms for all four distinct.

Even at the risk of monotony it is worth repeating that all the forms were originally distinct; in fact there were twice as many to be distinct as are shown above. The Indo-European nouns had eight cases — the vocative, locative, ablative, and instrumental as well as the four shown above. This obviously made a good many forms to remember and keep separate, so that it was easy to make mistakes, either by using wrong forms or by slurring pronunciation so that originally different forms came to be pronounced alike. When the same mistakes were made often enough and long enough they stopped being mistakes — after all you can't blame a baby for not making a distinction that his great-grandfather forgot to pass along to his grandfather.

We can still find all eight cases in Sanskrit. Russian has six; but Latin nouns usually have only five, and Greek and German nouns, like Old English ones, only four. Modern English has only two, and French and Spanish only one. Nobody knows why the rate of change has been so different, but then nobody really knows how the cases started in the first place. One guess is that the various endings were originally separate words used to show special relations — something like prepositions except that they

came after the words to which they pointed, so that they might
be called "postpositions."

44. PRONOUNS. The personal pronouns have retained more of
their original inflections than any other class of words in the language simply because people hear and use the various forms so
often that they are less likely to forget them or get them mixed up.
Even in this group, however, there have been some losses and
some changes, as you can see by examining the paradigms below.

45. THE PERSONAL PRONOUNS.

		FIRST PERSON	SECOND PERSON	THIRD PERSON		
				Masc.	*Fem.*	*Neut.*
Sing.	*Nom.*	ic	ðū	hē	hēo	hit
	Gen.	mīn	ðīn	his	hiere	his
	Dat.	mē	ðē	him	hiere	him
	Acc.	mē	ðē	hine	hīe	hit
		(earlier mec)	(ðec)			
Dual	*Nom.*	wit (*we two*)	git (*ye two*)			
	Gen.	uncer	incer			
	Dat.	unc	inc			
	Acc.	unc	inc			
		(earlier uncit)	(incit)			
Plur.	*Nom.*	wē	gē	hīe		
	Gen.	ūre	ēower	hiera		
	Dat.	ūs	ēow	him		
	Acc.	ūs	ēow	hīe		
		(earlier ūsic)	(ēowic)			

The dual number disappeared so long ago that most people are
amazed to learn that it ever existed, yet it had a very reasonable
origin and has left a few traces in other parts of the language.
As a matter of logic it is rather curious that we consider the
difference between singular and plural — one and more than
one — so important that it has to be indicated every time we use

a noun or pronoun, while the difference between two and millions can be neglected. The series one, two, and more than two (which is still found in many languages) at least has an anatomical basis, since it goes back to a stage when people counted on their hands rather than their fingers. Children still seem to go through this stage quite regularly. When they are very young *one* and *two* are distinct numbers, but *three, seven,* and *twenty* are synonyms — interchangeable terms for that confusing number that is too large to be grasped by either hands or mind. Our habit of saying "the *younger*" of two but "the *youngest*" of three or more is clearly a leftover from the same classification. Another occurs in the phrase "every *other* one" for "every *second* one." *Other* originally meant either "second" or "different" — these are identical if you can't count higher than two. To avoid confusion we eventually had to borrow *second* from French.

The old distinction between dative and accusative cases has now been completely lost; generally the dative form has survived. The old accusative forms *mec, ðec, ūsic,* and *ēowic* were dropping out in favor of the corresponding dative forms even in Old English times. Since then *him* and *hiere* (her) have driven out *hine* and *hīe.* The only old accusative form that has remained is *hit,* in the form *it.*

In the third person there has actually been an increase in the total number of forms. In Old English all the forms began with *h,* and some of them were ambiguous. This ambiguity was increased in late Old and early Middle English when some of the originally distinct forms came to be pronounced (and therefore spelled) alike. Even the masculine and feminine singular forms became identical in some dialects — obviously an intolerable situation. Accordingly *she* was developed, probably by borrowing from the demonstrative pronoun (see below), and the plural forms which developed into *they, their,* and *them* were taken over from the Scandinavians who had settled in England.

If you will pronounce the Old English forms carefully you will see that those which remain in the language have changed less than the spelling would seem to indicate. Even *gē* and *ēow* are

less strange than they look if you remember that *g* before a front
vowel regularly came to be pronounced as *y*; and *ēow*, when
pronounced with the stress on the *o*, sounds a good deal like *you*.

46. DEMONSTRATIVE AND INTERROGATIVE PRONOUNS. The only
other Old English pronouns which need be mentioned in a brief
survey are the demonstrative and interrogative ones. Not all the
forms that occur in manuscripts are given here, and even the
ones listed need not be memorized, but they are worth careful
examination because of later developments; for though the inflection has since been much simplified, some of the forms which
have been lost as cases of pronouns have been retained in the
function of adverbs — *then, there, when,* and *why.* The modern
that-those had (with additional variants) the following forms:

	Masculine	Feminine	Neuter
Singular			
Nominative	sē	sēo	ðæt
Genitive	ðæs	ðǣre	ðæs
Dative	ðǣm	ðǣre	ðǣm
Accusative	ðone	ðā	ðæt
Instrumental	ðȳ		ðȳ

Plural (all genders)	
Nominative	ðā
Genitive	ðāra
Dative	ðǣm
Accusative	ðā

This word had a number of uses. As an adjective it was sometimes equivalent to modern *the,* sometimes to the stronger *that.*
As a pronoun it was originally demonstrative: "Ðæt was god
cyning" — "That was a good king." But it soon came to be used
also as a relative: ". . .ðā sceolde cuman ðǣre helle hund ongēan
hine, *ðæs* nama wæs Ceruerus, *sē* sceolde habban þrīo hēafdu"
— "then (they say) came the hound of that hell to meet him

whose name was Cerberus, *who* (they say) had three heads."
The habit of using *that* for all genders now seems convenient,
but the disappearance of a genitive form for *that* is a real loss.
The use of the interrogative *who* and *which* as relatives did not
develop until much later.

You will notice that in the masculine and neuter singular there
is a fifth case, the *instrumental*. This case, which was originally
used to designate the thing by means of which something was
done, had extended its uses until it was generally equivalent to
the Latin ablative; then it disappeared as a separate form in all
nouns, in some pronouns, in the weak declension of adjectives,
and in the feminine gender and plural number everywhere.
Some grammarians list every dative form in the language as
"dative and instrumental"; but it seems simpler to limit its mention to the places where it demonstrably occurs — in a few
pronouns and in strong adjectives. (Weak and strong declensions
of adjectives will be discussed in the next section.)

The other demonstrative pronoun, ðēs, ðēos, ðis (modern *this*)
was inflected just as completely, and with even more variations
in its forms, but has left fewer traces in Modern English.

The interrogative pronoun had lost its separate feminine forms,
and has no plural. It is declined as follows:

	Masculine	*Neuter*
Nominative	hwā	hwæt
Genitive	hwæs	hwæs
Dative	hwǣm	hwǣm
Accusative	hwone	hwæt
Instrumental	hwī	hwī

The modern forms *who, whose, whom,* and *what,* plus the now
separate words *when* and *why* can be traced to this pronoun.
In Old English times hwǣr (*where*), hwȳ (*why*), and hū (*how*)
had already broken off. The first of these was apparently an
otherwise lost feminine form, and the others may have been.

47. ADJECTIVES. In Old English the adjective was the most highly inflected of all the parts of speech. It had the same cases as the noun, plus the instrumental. It had forms for all three genders, singular and plural, since it had to agree with the noun it modified. Like Modern German, it had a "weak" declension for use whenever it was preceded by a limiting word, such as the definite article or a possessive or demonstrative pronoun; and a "strong" declension whenever it was not preceded by such a word. (You are hereby advised to accept this as a fact and not worry about why. *I* don't know — though I could say so in a more long-winded way.) And of course there are the three degrees — positive, comparative, and superlative — to multiply all the possible endings by three, to a total of a hundred and eighty.

	STRONG DECLENSION			WEAK DECLENSION		
	Masc.	*Fem.*	*Neut.*	*Masc.*	*Fem.*	*Neut.*
Sing.						
N.	gōd	gōd	gōd	gōd-a	gōd-e	gōd-e
G.	gōd-es	gōd-re	gōd-es	gōd-an	gōd-an	gōd-an
D.	gōd-um	gōd-re	gōd-um	gōd-an	gōd-an	gōd-an
A.	gōd-ne	gōd-e	gōd	gōd-an	gōd-an	gōd-e
I.	gōd-e		gōd-e			
Plur.						
N.	gōd-e	gōd-a	gōd		gōd-an	
G.	gōd-ra	gōd-ra	gōd-ra		gōd-ena	
D.	gōd-um	gōd-um	gōd-um		gōd-um	
A.	gōd-e	gōd-a	gōd		gōd-an	

Naturally enough our ancestors had begun to find these too many to keep straight even before the time of the earliest manuscripts that have come down. Many of the other endings had become identical, especially in the weak declension. But we may be devoutly thankful that in Middle English times speakers developed the habit of showing the relation of an adjective to its noun by position rather than agreement in form, so that the only trace of all these complications that remains is *-er, -est* endings for comparative and superlative degrees of short adjectives.

48. VERBS. None of the parts of speech has changed as much between Indo-European and Modern English as the verb. The Latin verb *vocō,* which preserves the original system fairly well, has over a hundred physically different forms, not counting duplications. Eighty-five of these are "finite" — each with a special, limited function which cannot be explained by less than five terms specifying *person, number, tense, mood,* and *voice.* By contrast, the English equivalent *call* has only the four forms *call, calls, called,* and *calling,* and of these only *calls* is finite, and thus the equivalent of a particular Latin form. The other three have various uses.

We have made up for the lost inflections by various devices. To indicate subjects we use a combination of more pronouns and a consistent word-order instead of personal endings; and in place of inflections for tense, mood, and voice we have developed an extensive system of auxiliary verbs, supplemented by adverbial expressions of time and such conjunctions as *if* and *though.* Thus *vocārētur* may be translated as *if he were to be called.*

The changes, which will be discussed in more detail in Chapter 9, began even before Germanic split into its various groups. The number of inflected tenses was reduced to two, compared to the Latin six. By the time of the earliest English records the inflected passive voice had disappeared, and so had differences of person in the plural of both moods and in the singular of the subjunctive. As the conjugation of *bītan* on page 82 below shows, there were only twenty-four theoretically different finite forms left; and when we eliminate duplications, there were only nine. But the development of verb combinations had not kept pace with the disappearance of inflections.

49. STRONG AND WEAK VERBS. But although the conjugation of each individual verb had greatly simplified, the variations be-

tween different verbs remained extremely complex. There were
two types of verbs, known as *strong* and *weak*, each divided into
several classes. In the strong verbs the past tense was formed by
a change in the root vowel, as in the modern *sing, sang*. This is
the normal development of a general Indo-European characteristic. The weak verbs were a special Germanic invention. They
indicated the past tense by what is called a "dental suffix" (see
page 85 below). Eventually this became the general or "regular" way of forming past tenses, and many verbs which had
originally had vowel changes were remade on the new model.
Those that did not were credited by certain philologists with a
sturdy independence of character — hence the name "strong
verbs." But it doesn't seem fair that the class which did on the
whole win out should be called weak.

50. THE STRONG VERBS. The strong verb *bītan* (*bite*) is conju-
gated as follows:

	Indicative		Subjunctive
	Present		*Present*
ic	bīt-e	ic	bīt-e
ðū	bīt-st (-est)	ðū	bīt-e
hē	bīt-ð (-eð)	hē	bīt-e
wē	bīt-að	wē	bīt-en
gē	bīt-að	gē	bīt-en
hīe	bīt-að	hīe	bīt-en
	Past		*Past*
ic	bāt	ic	bit-e
ðū	bit-e	ðū	bit-e
hē	bāt	hē	bit-e
wē	bit-on	wē	bit-en
gē	bit-on	gē	bit-en
hīe	bit-on	hīe	bit-en

Several things are worth noticing about this paradigm.

1. Short vowels are not followed by doubled consonants — this spelling convention developed much later. Instead, long vowels are here indicated by a line over them. Unmarked vowels are short. Also, long vowels are simply prolongations of the short ones, not the quite different diphthongs sometimes called long vowels in Modern English.

In addition to its finite forms, the Old English verb had a present participle (*bītende*), a past participle (*biten*), and an infinitive (*bītan*). Both participles were used like adjectives much more often than in such constructions as *was biting* and *had bitten,* and both could be declined like adjectives. The infinitive was a separate form, as in other inflected languages.

2. The difference between the long and short *i* is important. From the long *i* we get such modern forms as *bite;* from the short *i, bit.*

3. The past indicative shows two different vowel stems, one for the first and third persons singular, the other for all other persons. This distinction is not preserved in any Modern English verb, but it has resulted in much confusion. In some verbs the vowel of the plural has been generalized, so that we now say not only *they bit* but *he bit.* In other verbs it is the singular form that has been generalized, so that we now say either *he* or *they wrote* (which is the regular phonetic development of the old singular *hē wrāt*). It is simply a matter of chance that we haven't preserved the other forms, *writ* and *bote.* Actually, *writ* competed with *wrote* in Standard English for several centuries, and is still used in some dialects. *Bote* can be found in place of *bit* in earlier literature, but seems to have died out completely. In a few verbs, like *sink* and *shrink,* the two possible forms are still competing.

4. In both tenses and in both moods one form had already been generalized to serve for all three persons in the plural, and in both tenses of the subjunctive one form had come to serve for all three persons in the singular. Some forms (ic bīte, ðū bite) had already become identical in the indicative and subjunctive,

and others (wē biton, wē biten) needed only a little slurring to become so.

51. CLASSES OF STRONG VERBS. Old English had something over three hundred strong verbs, divided into seven classes, as shown by the following examples:

	Infinitive	Preterite singular	Preterite plural	Past participle
Class I	bītan	bāt	biton	biten
Class II	crēopan	crēap	crupon	cropen
Class III	drincan	dranc	druncon	druncen
Class IV	stelan	stæl	stǣlon	stolen
Class V	tredan	træd	trǣdon	treden
Class VI	bacan	bōc	bōcon	bacen
Class VII	crāwan	crēow	crēowon	crāwen

The first six of these classes show a vowel variation based on *ablaut,* which may be defined briefly (if not clearly) as an independent vowel change. In Indo-European differences in pitch were more important than they are today, and different inflected forms of a given word might have different pitches on the root syllable. The most important result of this is that we often find related forms containing an /e/ when the pitch was high, and an /o/ when the pitch was low. As far as we can tell, neither of these vowels developed from the other. The "original" vowel has been lost, and we can trace the words back only to the stage where /e/ and /o/ appear.

These six classes all had an /e/ as the root vowel in the infinitive and an /o/ in the past singular; but these sounds had a different phonetic environment in each of the six classes, and therefore developed differently. For instance, in Class I the /e/ or /o/ was followed by an /i/, and the resulting diphthongs developed in one way. In Class II the second element in the diphthongs was /u/, and in Class III there were no diphthongs, but the development of the vowels was influenced by the fol-

lowing /n/. The details of all the steps of change are too complicated to go into here; but, wild as the changes may look, they
are both regular and predictable if you know all the phonetic
forces at work. Our sounds inevitably influence each other, as
you can see if you will try to pronounce the phoneme /e/ in
exactly the same way in the five words *bet, bell, bent, berry,* and
bay.

The changes in Class VII have a different origin. The verbs
in this group were originally reduplicating. That is, they formed
their preterites by doubling the root syllable. The repeated syllables were first somewhat differentiated, as in the Latin verbs
fallō-fefellī and *parcō-pepercī*. Later, in Germanic, the extra
syllable was dropped, but the vowel change remained.

At this point it would be a rather silly exercise to memorize
the vowel changes in the seven classes of strong verbs — especially since these classes all have subclasses not here indicated.
But there are some useful things that can best be understood by
considering some of the differences here displayed. As we noticed
in *bītan,* the vowel of the preterite singular is usually different
from that of the preterite plural, either in quality or length. Another thing to notice is that the /on/ ending of the preterite
plural has now been completely lost, but that the /en/ ending
of the past participle has been treated very irregularly. In some
verbs, such as *rise, rose, risen,* it has been completely preserved
in Standard English. In some, such as *find, found,* it has been
completely lost — nobody now says *founden*. And in many it is
preserved only in certain uses, principally adjectival, as in
a drunken man and *his bounden duty,* compared to *he had drunk*
and *he had bound*.

We should also notice that such verbs as *bake* and *crow* have
completely lost their older inflections, and are now regular weak
verbs.

52. THE WEAK VERBS. The weak verbs originally formed their
preterites by the addition of /ode/, /ede/, or /de/, endings which

have come down to us (though not respectively) as /d/ (*earn-earned*), /t/ (*look-looked*), and /id/ (*wound-wounded*). Usually the root vowel did not change, but sometimes it did, as in the verbs from which we get *buy-bought* and *tell-told*. Thus all the regular verbs in Modern English are weak, but not all the weak verbs are regular. Any verb that adds /d/, /id/, or /t/, or changes /d/ to /t/ (*send-sent*) is called weak, whether or not there is also a vowel change.

When vowel changes do occur in weak verbs, they are not the independent or ablaut changes of the strong verbs, but are caused by the influence of neighboring sounds. There are a number of possible influences, and when several of them happen to be at work on the same word the development can be very complicated and the results may seem most peculiar; but the working of each influence is amazingly regular, and if we know enough about the earlier forms we can see that the evolution of such apparently erratic pairs as *think-thought* is exactly predictable.

Weak verbs had the same vowel in the singular and plural of the preterite, and almost always had this same vowel in the past participle. The past participle ended in /ed/ rather than /en/, so that when personal endings disappeared in the preterite the two past forms became identical.

53. CHANGES IN CLASSIFICATION. Of the 312 strong verbs recorded in Old English, slightly over a third have completely disappeared from the language. Of those that remain, two-thirds have become weak. Thus we now say *crowed* instead of *crew*, *helped* instead of *holp*, and *washed* instead of *wesh* or *woosh*. This shift toward a regular pattern is comparable to the shift of most nouns to the *stān* declension. But as so often happens in the development of a language, a strong current in one direction is accompanied by a much smaller eddy in the other. A few originally weak verbs, such as *dig* and *fling*, have developed strong forms which have driven out the weak ones; others, like *chide* and *thrive*, now have

strong forms competing with the weak ones; and still others, though weak in Standard English, have such forms as *brang* and *squoze* in some dialects. Each of these developments is simply a matter of incorrect analogy, and it would be impossible to prove that forms now scorned are essentially any worse than those which have become correct simply because everybody has made the same mistakes.

54. ADVERBS. In Old English, adverbs are not discoverably a separate part of speech. But certain prepositions and conjunctions and some case-forms of certain nouns, pronouns, and adjectives came to be used in one or more of the ways covered by the familiar definition — "a word that modifies a verb, adjective, or other adverb." Grammarians committed to this definition later called these words and forms adverbs when they were so used.

The *-ly* ending which is now so characteristic of adverbs was originally a noun, *līc,* meaning *body* or *shape.* From it we get the word *like* — "of the same shape." It then came to be used to make adjectives from nouns, usually in the weakened form of *-ly.* Thus *manlike* and *manly* are of identical origin. When the original meaning had been more or less forgotten, the ending was also used to make secondary adjectives from existing adjectives. Thus we find *glædlic* along with *glæd* (glad), and even *fæstlic* along with *fæst.* The Anglo-Saxons often used the instrumental cases of these words — either the simple or the compound ones — to modify verbs and adjectives as well as nouns. They could thus say either "Hē sang *glæde*" or "Hē sang *glædlice.*" Grammarians often say that this case-form "developed into an adverb," but there was no perceptible development; our ancestors were simply broadminded about their modifiers.

During the Middle English period the feeling somehow arose that the *-ly* ending was the natural way to form adverbs, and the general pattern for such pairs as *beautiful-beautifully* was firmly set. Some old adjectives in *-ly* remained, and still do — *manly, friendly, goodly,* and so forth; and the adverbial use of some of the short forms, such as *fast* and *hard* continues to be recognized. But other "flat adverbs" such as *quick* and *slow* are often condemned as incorrect, though they have been in continuous respectable use ever since Old English times.

55. PREPOSITIONS, CONJUNCTIONS, AND INTERJECTIONS. These three classes of words were uninflected in Old English, as they are now. The first two have considerably increased in number, so that we can show connections more precisely than used to be possible. I can think of no other useful generalizations to make about them.

56. SUMMARY OF OLD ENGLISH INFLECTIONS. Old English nouns, pronouns, and adjectives were inflected to indicate gender, number, and case. The adjectives were also inflected for comparison (*big, bigger, biggest*). Verbs were inflected for person, number, tense, and mood, and there were a few traces (too slight to be worth discussing in this chapter) of inflection for voice. These are the only kinds of form changes that are recognized as inflections. Such endings as *-ish, -ly, -ment,* and the *-er* in *baker* (as distinguished from the *-er* in *bigger*) are called *derivational suffixes* rather than inflections. There is positively nothing to gain by wondering whether such endings are "really" inflections or not. The classification is arbitrary.

We have now lost the inflections for gender, person, mood, and voice so thoroughly that the few remaining traces can be (and sometimes are) treated as isolated idioms, without ever mentioning these grammatical concepts. The other four kinds of inflection are still active, though not nearly so necessary for communication as they used to be.

57. SPECIMEN OF OLD ENGLISH. We may now examine a simple specimen of Old English. If we carefully copied a bit from an old manuscript (and modernized the punctuation) we might get something like this:

Fæder ure þu þe eart on heofonum, si þin nama gehalgod; to-becume þin rice; geƿurþe þin ƿilla on eorðan sƿa sƿa on heofonum; urne gedæghƿamlican hlaf syle us to dæg and forgyf us ure gyltas sƿa sƿa ƿe forgyfað urum gyltendum; and ne gelæd þu us on costnunge, ac alys us of yfele, soþlice.[1]

Maybe you recognize it at sight, and if it were read aloud by somebody who understood it you would almost certainly recognize it; but it surely looks strange. However, much of the strangeness is caused simply by the forms of a few of the letters. English printed in Gothic type or in the Greek alphabet would also look peculiar, though it would not really be a different language. If we substitute modern characters for the unfamiliar ones, but make no other change, we get the following, with a very rough phonemic transcription that includes some guesses about when unstressed vowels lost their distinctive characteristics.

Fæder ure thu the eart on heofonum, si thin nama
fæːder uːre θuː θe eart ɔn heɔvɔnum siː θiːn nɑmɑ

gehalgod; to-becume thin rice; gewurthe thin willa on
jehɑlgɔd to bəkume θiːn riːtʃe jəwurðe θiːn wilɑ ɔn

eorthan swa swa on heofonum; urne gedæghwamlican
eɔrðɑn swɑ swɑ ɔn heɔvɔnum urne jədæjxwɑmliːkɑn

hlaf syle us to dæg; and forgyf us ure gyltas swa swa
xlɑf syle uːs to dæj ɑnd fɔrjyf uːs uːre jyltɑs swɑ swɑ

we forgyfath urum gyltendum; and ne gelæd thu us on
weː fɔrjyvɑθ uːrum jyltendum ɑnd ne jəlæd θuː uːs ɔn

costnunge, ac alys us of yfele, sothlice.
kɔstnuŋe ɑk ɑlys uːs ɔf yvele soːθlitʃe

Here the text is a transliteration — that is, a transcription into a different (in this case only partly different) alphabet. The Old English ƿ (*wyn*) has been replaced by its modern equivalent, *w;*

[1] Kaiser, p. 6.

and both ð (*eth*) and þ (*thorn*) have been replaced by *th*. You
can probably now recognize the Lord's Prayer.

You will notice that the phonemic transcription contains two
characters that do not appear in transcriptions of Modern English.
The /x/, with the value of *ch* in German *doch*, has already been
explained in the discussion of the sound shift in Chapter 2.
Old English *h* is believed to have retained this value when it
occurred finally or before a consonant. When it occurred before
a vowel it had apparently changed into the sound we use today,
though perhaps a little stronger. The /y/ originally represented
a rounded front vowel like the French *u* or the German *ü*. If
you round your lips as if you were going to say /u:/, and then
try (but without straining) to say /i:/, you will find that you
automatically make this sound. In later English this sound disappeared, and *y* was used interchangeably with *i*. A number of
minor points are debatable, but if you read the passage aloud
with reasonable expression, and pronounced the words as indicated, you would probably be understood by any carefully preserved West Saxon you happened to meet — which is perhaps
as much as you could hope for this early in the study.

To know that this passage is an Old English version of the
Lord's Prayer is interesting, but not in itself very enlightening.
To learn anything really useful from it we must examine it very
carefully; and we must make a special effort to see whether any
of the changes that have taken place in the language since it was
written are *systematic*. The importance of looking for systematic
developments cannot be overemphasized, since it makes the difference between having to learn every detail as a separate item
and learning a much smaller number of principles that can be
applied again and again. No system works perfectly, and we
have to make many adjustments, but the gain is still enormous.
If we look at the passage in this way, here are some of the things
we shall find:

1. A number of endings and other unstressed syllables which
have since weakened or dropped off entirely.

a. *Endings.*

Old English	Modern English
ure	our
heofonum	heaven
nama	name
thin	thy
willa	will
eorthan	earth
urne	our
gyltas	guilts
forgyfath	forgive
urum	our

Notice particularly the different forms of the possessive adjective — *ure, urne,* and *urum* — as it agrees with different nouns. Because some weakening had already taken place, the same form is used in the nominative singular (*fæder ure*) and accusative plural (*ure gyltas*), but *urne* is used in the accusative singular and *urum* in the dative plural.

b. *Other unstressed syllables.*

Old English	Modern English
gehalgod	hallowed
to-becume	come
gedæghwamlican	daily
gelæd	lead
alys	loose

2. *Certain changes in word order.*

Old English	Modern English
Fæder ure	our Father
to-becume thin rice	Thy kingdom come
urne gedæghwamlican hlaf syle us	give us our daily bread

We need not worry about whether these changes were the causes
or the result of the dropping of endings, or a little of both. But
when endings no longer give a reliable indication of the way
words are related, we need a dependable word-order to take
their place.

3. *Evidence that at least one vowel has shifted regularly.*

Old English	Modern English
ure	our
thu	thou

In a longer passage, and with the long vowels marked, we should
find evidence of a very general change of this sort.

4. *Some changes in the values of consonants.*

Old English	Modern English
gehalgod	hallowed
dæg	day
gedæghwamlican	daily

The old English *g* (originally /g/ in all positions) had already
changed to /j/ in West Saxon when next to a front vowel, and
was later spelled as *y*. The *g* in Modern *give* etc. shows an Anglian
influence. After a back vowel *g* later came to be pronounced and
spelled as *w*. Thus we get *day* from *dæg*, but *dawn* from *dagian*.

5. *The ambiguous function of some Old English symbols for
   fricatives.*

Old English	Modern English
heofonum	heaven
yfele	evil

In these words the substitution of modern *v* for old *f* does not
represent a sound change. In Old English the pairs /f/ and /v/,
/s/ and /z/, and /θ/ and /ð/ were not separate phonemes, but

pairs of allophones. There were no contrasting pairs of words like modern *feel* and *veal, rice* and *rise, ether* and *either* (/fi:l-vi:l; rais-raiz; i:θər-i:ðər/). These fricatives were usually voiceless when initial or final, but voiced between vowels. That is why we still have so many pairs like *calf-calves, cloth-clothes,* and *house-houses* (the *e* in *house* is a late spelling convention, and does not represent an Old English sound).

Thus Old English *f* can represent either /f/ or /v/, and *s* can represent either /s/ or /z/. The two letters *þ* and *ð* were used interchangeably, according to the taste of the writer. A good many people have thought that one *must* represent the voiced and the other the voiceless sound, but their most strenuous efforts have not dug up any evidence.

The sort of analysis we have just indicated may at first seem impossibly slow and cumbersome. You may think it would be much simpler just to get a translation to show you what the original means. Certainly a translation can be helpful, but it will seldom do the whole job. If it is in normal Modern English it often fails completely to show how the original was put together. If it tries to reflect the original exactly it is always clumsy, and sometimes almost meaningless. Whichever it is, it must be supplemented by some analysis to be of any value.

Let's take another look at the clause "urne gedæghwamlican hlaf syle us to dæg." If you saw it alone without knowing where it came from it would probably convey absolutely nothing to you. When a translation tells you that all together it means "Give us this day our daily bread" you collect an odd bit of information, but you haven't really learned anything of value — certainly nothing that is likely to help you with other passages. The important question is, how and why does it mean what it does? To get at the answer to this question you must examine, compare, use your reason, guess, check your guesses, and — but only when nothing else works — memorize.

Once you know the gross meaning it is obvious that *us to dæg* means *us today.* With this clue you should be able to disentangle *daily* from *gedæghwamlican.* Notice that in both these words a *g* has changed to a *y*. Maybe it happens often, so concentrate on the fact for a moment. If you don't remember it after these first occurrences, you will after a few more, if you keep your mind alert for such things. And do other long Old English words tend to lose some of their less important syllables? (We have just seen that some of them do.) Next, there must be some word for *our*, and *urne* seems to be the obvious one. It does look a little like *our*, and it looks even more like *ourn*. Could it be that that "ignorant" form is really the survival of a perfectly good Old English form that has somehow been lost in the Standard language? This seems likely — and now you'll never forget *urne*.

That leaves *syle* and *hlaf* to mean *give* and *bread*. Doesn't seem probable. "Give us our bread — syle us our hlaf." Can't be the same words, but they do sound a little like something. Could it be "sell us our loaf?" *Loaf* looks all right, especially with *daily*. A little change in meaning, but it must be the same word. Could *sell* ever have meant *give?* It means "give for something" instead of "give for nothing." But does *give* always mean "give for nothing?" You have certainly heard a clerk say "I can give you some nice apples today," and he didn't mean that they were free. Maybe *sell* was used that way so often that it changed its meaning permanently. And there you have it.

If you study the passage thoroughly you will find that only four of the words have completely disappeared from the language: *ac, costnunge, gewurthe,* and *si. Rice*, cognate with German *Reich*, has almost gone, but we do have the compound form *bishopric*. All the others are still in the language in some form or other. They may look utterly strange at first, but it is possible to get at them when you know how to go about it.

In short, there are a number of steps to take in the early stages of reading any unfamiliar language.

1. Examine a passage carefully to see what you can get from it directly.

2. Figure out, look up, ask, or otherwise discover what each of the "hard" parts means, and as nearly as possible, why it

means that. Anything that you can connect with something you already know is much more likely to stay with you.

This step — a really thorough translation — is as far as even most thoroughly conscientious students ever get. It is a very silly place to stop, because you have done most of the work and got very little of the reward. Therefore:

3. While your information is fresh in your mind, *read* the passage — that is, look at it and react to it directly. Do not allow yourself to say, or even to think, that *syle* means *give*. You have found out what *syle* meant to the Saxons. Let it mean the same thing to you. Then and only then will you actually be reading the passage.

This last step is not hard; but a great many people never think of it as even possible, so they never attempt it. Translating should be merely an intermediate step.

This is not mere theory. I am speaking from the kind of personal experience that it makes a man feel very silly to recall. At school and college I studied French for several years, got good grades in it, and began to read — I thought — French books for pleasure. I got to the point where I could translate very accurately and quite fast — perhaps thirty pages an hour. It did not occur to me that I was not reading French, but I wasn't. Every time I saw a French word I thought of the English equivalent, and reacted to that. I was not reacting directly to the French words — one part of thinking in French — simply because it had never occurred to me that I could. It took months of actual living in France to get me on the right track.

You may think "Of course — that's what it always takes," but that is not true. When the time came for me to learn German I had realized that a direct reaction was possible, so I started to use one at once. When I first encountered *auf wiedersehen* I analyzed it; *to* (or maybe *upon*) *again see*. Reasonable enough — or at least as reasonable as *good-bye* or *so long*. Anyhow, the Germans used it, and so could I. Thereafter when I encountered it I would not think (however rapidly) "ah, yes — that means *good-bye"* or even *"To again see."* I had realized that what *auf wiedersehen* really means is simply — *auf wiedersehen*. It required no translation, so I read it or heard it or spoke it in German. I didn't know much German, but I knew that much. And pretty soon I knew some other bits, and then they began to fit together and come pretty fast. I learned to use German in a small fraction of the time it had taken me to use French, because I was going right after it.

I do not offer this as a brilliant discovery of my own. A great many people knew it long before I did, and I should have learned it much earlier. But since many people have obviously not learned it yet, I pass it on here for what it is worth.

58. "THE CREATION." Here is a somewhat longer passage to investigate, taken from a sermon by Aelfric, Abbot of Eynsham, usually considered the greatest writer of Old English prose. It is followed by a quite literal translation, and a recommended way of studying it is indicated below.

Ealle gesceafta, heofonas and englas, sunnan and monan, steorran and eorðan, ealle nytenu and fugelas, sæ and ealle fiscas God gesceop and geworhte on six dagum; and on ðam seofoðan dæge he geendode his weorc, and geswac ða and gehalgode ðone seofoðan dæg, forðan ðe he on ðam dæge his weorc geendode. And he beheold ða ealle his weorc ðe he geweorhte; and hie wæron ealle swiðe gode. Ealle ðing he geworhte buton ælcum antimbre. He cwæd: "Geweorðe leoht!" And ðærrihte wæs leoht geworden. He cwæð eft: "Geweorðe heofon!" And ðærrihte wæs heofon geworht, swa swa he mid his wisdome and his willan hit gedihte. He cwæð eft, and het ða eorðan ðæt heo sceolde forðlædan cwicu nytenu. And he ða gesceop of ðære eorðan eall nytencynn and deorcynn, ealle ða ðe on feower fotum gað: ealswa eft of wætere he gesceop fiscas and fugelas, and sealde ðam fiscum sund and ðam fugelum fliht; ac he ne sealde nanum nytene ne nanum fisce nane sawle, ac heora blod is heora lif, and swa hraðe swa hie beoð deade, swa beoð hie mid ealle geendode. Forðy is se man betera, gif he gode gedihð, ðonne ealle ða nytenu sindon; forðan ðe hie ealle gewurðað to nahte, and se man is ece on anum dæle, ðæt is on ðære sawle; heo no geendeð næfre.[2]

The text is here slightly normalized, to avoid a few unrewarding complications; the punctuation is modernized; and so is the alphabet except for the character ð. It has been translated as follows:

> All creatures, heavens and angels, sun and moon, stars and earth, all beasts and birds, the sea and all fishes God created and wrought in six days; and on the seventh day he ended his work and ceased, and hallowed the seventh day, because on that day he ended his work. And he beheld then all his works that he had wrought, and they were all exceedingly good. All things he wrought without any matter. He said, "Let there be light," and instantly there was light. He said again, "Let there be heaven," and instantly heaven was made, as he with his wisdom and his will had appointed it. He said again, and bade the earth bring forth living cattle, and he then created of earth all the race of cattle, and the brute race, all those which go on four feet; in like manner of water he created fishes and birds, and gave the power of swimming to the fishes, and flight to the birds; but he gave no soul to any beast, nor to any fish; but their blood is their life, and as soon as they are dead they are totally ended. Therefore is man better, if he grow up in good, than all the beasts are; because they will all come to naught, and man is in one part eternal, that is in the soul; that will never end.

59. ANALYZING "THE CREATION." No one method of studying language works best for everybody, but many students have found it profitable to follow the steps indicated here:

1. Go over the original twice, rather slowly but without strain, to see how much you can get from it with no outside help and no great effort. Probably it won't be very much — a number of words, a few phrases that are clear, and perhaps a few more that you feel you almost understand. It will of course help a good deal if you are familiar with the Bible.

[2] Kaiser, p. 1.

2. Read the translation twice, rather carefully.

3. Go over the original again, without referring to the translation, and see how much more you can now understand. Certainly some words which meant nothing at the first approach will now be clear. You will get much better results if you try to *read* it this time, pronouncing the words, at least mentally, and grouping them for rhythm as the punctuation suggests. Most important of all, don't let yourself translate anything you don't have to. By now, for instance, you will certainly know what "heofonas and englas, sunnan and monan" are — so let them be that, and don't blight your progress by calling them something else.

4. Now — and only now — go back and forth between the original and the translation. At this stage a pencil can be very useful. (But *not* a pen — by no means a pen.) Under each word that still seems either meaningless or arbitrary draw a line. In the first two lines you might have to mark *gesceafta, nytenu, fugelas,* and *gesceop.* Look at the words for each of these in the translation, and see if you can find any clue as to how the Old English words can mean what they do. *Fugelas* is not too hard. Try *ou* instead of *u* as in *ure-our,* and a *w* instead of *g* as in *gehalgod-hallowed.* That gives you *fowelas,* and it is not hard to believe that our word for barnyard birds could have once meant birds of all kinds.

Then there is *nytenu* for *beasts.* If you have never heard of neat's foot oil you may have to give up on this one. But if you have, and know that *neat* once meant *cattle,* you will realize that still earlier it could have had a broader meaning. *Gesceafta* and *gesceop* are definitely harder, but they do offer some clues. First, they look as if they might be related, and the fact that they are translated as *creatures* and *created* confirms this. You should remember from the Lord's Prayer that an initial *ge-* regularly disappeared later, so you can disregard that element. You then have *sceafta* and *sceop.* You will soon find out that you have to be a little broadminded about Old English vowels; but if the words are related the consonants must be either identical or related. Now *p* and *f* are both labials, so a relation is at least possible. You can't be sure, but it looks promising. And *fiscas* for *fish* shows that *sc* can change to *sh,* so the words must be pronounced something like *shaft* and *shop.* You can't make anything directly from *shaft,* so try *shop.* "God created everything, God shop everything." No. Let's be broadminded about vowels. "God created everything, God *shap* everything, God *shape* everything" — that's it. God *shaped* everything. So the *sceafta* must be the *shapings* — "the things he created or shaped."

At this point you may think I am making it sound much easier than it really is, and perhaps you are right. Certainly, unless you are very much brighter than I am, you will miss some relations that seem obvious after they are pointed out, and you will sometimes go off on a false track. This sort of examination involves a good deal of effort, and some of the effort is wasted, but on the whole it is much more effective than simply trying to memorize equivalents.

At this point you may want to see how many other words you can figure out for yourself before examining the clues given below; but here are some more things you should, sooner or later, consider. The words are given in the order of their appearance rather than alphabetically.

englas This word, originally Greek, but borrowed into English from Latin, became so thoroughly a part of the language that it is treated exactly like a native word, both in the change of *a* to *e* and in the form of its inflectional ending. It is the only word in the passage of foreign origin.

geworhte Our two words *worked* and *wrought* go back to this source. If you remember that *h* was pronounced /x/, you can see that the form *work* is an easy development. *Wrought* is an example of what is called *metathesis,* which means the shift of a vowel sound to the other side of a consonant sound. This is particularly likely to happen when the consonant is a "rolled r." There is a tendency for an extra vowel to develop on the other side. Then the new vowel may get the stress that was originally on the old one. Finally, the old vowel drops out. A clear example of this is the Old English ðurh, which developed first into *thorough* (preserved in a special meaning), then into *through*. In *third*, from older *thrid*, the movement was the other way.

seofoðan   The n of *seventh*, which is missing here, was probably preserved in Anglian, though it may have been restored by analogy.

weorc   Notice that *weorc* has the same form in the accusative singular and plural. Sometimes the form of the modifying adjective will tell which it is. Sometimes you have to guess from the context.

forðan   This word, and *forðy*, which occurs a few lines further along, are both compounded of the word *for* and a case-form of the word ðæt. It may seem curious that one is translated *because* and the other *therefore*, but consider the following sentences: He sat down because he was tired.
                      He was tired; therefore he sat down.

ðe   The word *the* originated as an unstressed form of *that*. The unstressed ðe is often used after a stressed form (here ðan), apparently to give a little extra flexibility. It need not be translated.

hie   We have now differentiated the initial sounds of *he, she, it,* and *they,* but in Old English all forms of the third-person pronoun began with *h*. Compare *heora* for *their,* and the feminine form *heo,* used to refer to the feminine noun *sawle*.

antimbre   The prefix *an-* can be disregarded.

cwæð   The spelling with *qu* was introduced during the Middle English period by French scribes, who had no *w* in their alphabet.

forðlædan   Notice that this compound is exactly equivalent to *produce,* which literally means "lead forward."

nytencynn   The kin (race) of domestic animals.

deorcynn *Deor* meant any wild animal before it was specialized to mean a certain kind.

sealde The past tense of *syle,* which occurs in the Lord's Prayer.

ne This was the original word for *not.* It could be made more emphatic by expanding to the phrase *ne a wiht — not a bit (whit).* This later contracted, first to *naught,* later to *not. Ne* also can mean *nor.*

hraðe *H* later dropped out of the initial combinations *hl, hn,* and *hr.* Nothing is *rathe* nowadays except a poetic primrose, but we still have *rather,* which is exactly equivalent to *sooner,* though used in a more limited way.

beoð Our modern verb "to be" is a mixture of four verbs, *aren, beon, sindan,* and *wesan,* each of which was once complete.

dæle The meaning *part* is preserved in the phrase "a good deal of," and in the term for giving each card player his share of the cards.

There remain, of course, a certain number of words that have left no traces in the language, such as *geswac* and *gedihte;* and there are a few others, such as *ælce* (modern *each*) that have changed so much in meaning that recognizing the relation is of no particular help. But a very large part of the Old English prose vocabulary will yield to this sort of examination. You will not, of course, remember permanently everything that has been said about every word discussed above; but you won't forget it all, either. If you make a serious attempt to learn Old English (or any other language) it is very economical to spend a good deal of extra time at first in a close examination of this sort. If you do, your knowledge will soon snowball, and you'll save a great deal more time than you have used up.

Once you have made the examination, go back to Aelfric's original, and see how many of the underlinings you can now afford to erase, because the words now mean something to you. And if you have written in the meanings of any of the words, erase them, too. You can't really read the original if your eye is attracted by a translation. If you have no interest in learning a language, and desire only to avoid embarrassment in case your instructor asks you to translate something in class, you can afford to gloss freely and indelibly with a pen. Otherwise not.

You will notice also that some words appear in different forms, for instance *fiscas* as a direct object, but *fiscum* as an indirect object; but these inflectional endings are not as much needed as they would be in Latin, since there has already been a good deal of development toward a standard word-order — which is, of course, one reason why they soon disappeared. There are, however, many sentences in Old English which are misleading unless you pay close attention to the significance of the endings.

60. VOCABULARY REPLACEMENTS. A closer look at the translation will also show some interesting things about the difference in vocabulary between Old and Modern English. (The translation is not mine, since I did not want to take any chance of either exaggerating or minimizing the difference.) Here it is again, this time with every word which is not of Old English origin in italics:

> All *creatures,* heavens and *angels,* sun and moon, stars and earth, all *beasts* and birds, the sea and all fishes God *created* and wrought in six days; and on the seventh day he ended his work and *ceased,* and hallowed the seventh day, *because* on that day he ended his work. And he beheld then all his works that he had wrought, and *they* were all *exceedingly* good. All things he wrought without any *matter.* He said, "Let there be light," and *instantly* there was light. He said again, "Let there be heaven," and *instantly* heaven was made, as he *with* his wisdom and his will had *appointed* it. He said again, and bade the earth bring forth living *cattle,* and he then *created* of earth all the *race* of *cattle,* and the *brute race,* all those which go on four feet; in like *manner* of water he *created* fishes and birds, and gave the *power* of swimming to the fishes, and flight to the birds; but he gave no soul to any *beast,* nor to any fish; but *their* blood is

their life, and as soon as *they* are dead *they* are *totally* ended.
Therefore is man better, if he grow up in good, than all the
beasts are; *because they* will all come to naught, and man is in
one *part eternal,* that is in the soul; that will never end.

In the original the only borrowed word is *angels,* which ex-
presses a concept that simply did not exist in English until it was
introduced by Christianity; but in the translation a seventh of
the words are from Danish, French, or Latin sources. There is
nothing fancy about these borrowings. Aelfric's sermon was
clearly addressed to rather simple people, and the translator has
apparently tried to reflect the directness and naturalness of the
style. He has to say *beasts* or *animals* (also from French) instead
of *nytenu,* because no Old English synonym has survived. He
could of course have translated ðærrihte as *right then* instead of
instantly, but some readers would find that almost humorously
chummy. In short, all of the borrowed words are familiar, and
most of them are so much a part of our everyday thinking that
it is rather hard to believe we could ever have managed without
them. Our language has been greatly enriched by such borrowings, but we have lost something, too. *Swiðe,* once you are used
to it, is more direct and forceful than the rather artificial *exceedingly;* and though we can still say *flight* for *fliht,* we now
have to say *the power of swimming* where Aelfric could say
simply *sund.*

61. THE ROMANS IN BRITAIN. It naturally requires the reading
of a good deal more material than can be included in this book
to develop anything like a mastery of Old English; but the prose,
at least, is not as hard as it is sometimes made to seem, if it is
approached by analysis rather than as a mechanical exercise in
memory. One more selection is offered, with no clues other than
a few glosses, as a sort of aptitude test.

Æfter þæm þe Romeburg getimbred wæs syx hunde wintra
and seofon and syxtig, Romane gesealdon Gaiuse Juliuse seofon
legian, to þon þæt he sceolde fif winter winnan on Gallie. Æfter
þæm þe he hie oferwunnen hæfde, he for on Britannie þæt

iglond, and wiþ þa Bryttas gefeaht, and gefliemed wearþ on
þæm londe þe mon hæt Centlond. Raþe þæs he gefeaht eft wiþ
þa Bryttas on Centlonde, and hie wurdon gefliemede. Heora
þridde gefeoht wæs neah þære ie þe mon hæt Temes, neah
þæm forda þe mon hæt Welengaford. Æfter þæm gefeohte him
eode on hond se cyning and þa burgware þe wæron on Ciren-
ceastre, and siþþan ealle þe on þæm iglonde wæron.[3]

winnan, to make war   *raþe,* soon after
geflieman, to put to flight   *eode on hond,* surrendered
                      burgware, citizens

62. THE LATIN ELEMENT IN OLD ENGLISH. It is easy to find examples of Old English that show more foreign influence than
the passage from Aelfric. A few dozen words had been borrowed
from Latin even before the tribesmen left the continent. These
were mostly terms that reflected Roman activities in war, road-
building, and trade, along with their considerably more advanced
cuisine. Thus we find *camp* (*battle*), *pil* (*javelin*), *weall* (*wall*),
stræt (*road*), *mil* (*mile*), *pund* (*pound*), *mynet* (*coin*), *win*
(*wine*), *cytel* (*kettle*), *cycene* (*kitchen*), *cuppa* (*cup*), *disc*
(*dish*), *ciese* (*cheese*), and *pise* (*pea*). One reason that we know
that many of these words are borrowings from Latin rather than
Germanic cognates is that they have not undergone the consonant shift covered by Grimm's Law. If they had come straight
down from Indo-European, *camp, ciese, cuppa,* and *cytel* would
begin with *h* rather than *c, pise* and *pund* with *f* rather than *p,*
and so forth. And even if they did not occur in surviving manuscripts we could tell that some of them were early borrowings
because their vowels have changed in exactly the same way as
the vowels of native words in the same relative positions, while
words borrowed much later have been preserved in a form much
closer to their Latin originals. When related forms appear in a
number of other Germanic dialects as well as English, we assume
a continental origin.

[3] From King Alfred's translation of Orosius, Kaiser, p. 56.

Between their coming to England and their conversion to Christianity the English borrowed no more from the Latin than from the Celtic vocabulary of the Romanized Britons. The word *castra*, which meant first a military camp, later any walled and inhabited place, is about the only one we can be sure of. This occurs in a great many place names, usually as *-caster* in the north (*Lancaster*) and as *-cester* or *-chester* in the south (*Worcester, Winchester*).

After the conversion to Christianity began, borrowings from Latin were naturally increased. We cannot always be sure whether a particular word was borrowed before the move from the continent or in the early part of the seventh century, and a few of the words included in the list on p. 104 may belong to this period. Others include many words connected with the new religion and with the living habits of the missionaries and their successors, who obviously imported a few characteristic garments and household furnishings and a great many vegetables, herbs, shrubs, and even trees.

How much the form of a Latin word changed after getting into English depends on three things. First, the sounds of which it was composed, since some sounds are, during any given period, more stable than others. An extreme example of this is the fact that the Indo-European word for *mouse* came down in Latin and in English in the identical form *mūs*, since none of the three phonemes of which it is composed underwent any change in either the Italic or the Germanic branch during this period. More generally, during the development of English short vowels have been far more stable than long ones, and both the dental and the labial consonants have been more stable than the palatal ones.

Second in importance is the date of entry. For instance, during the seventh century the kind of change known as *umlaut* was active in English. This is a kind of vowel-attraction. In its most important form, a front vowel in the second syllable of a word has the effect of changing the vowel in the first syllable from a back to a front position. Since the vowel in the second syllable later disappeared in English, and other changes also occurred to complicate the picture, umlaut is rather too complicated to discuss intelligibly here, but we can mention three things about it: it is the cause of such irregular plurals as *men, mice,* and *feet,* and the irregular past tenses of some weak verbs; it explains why the vowels in all forms of some words are further forward than those in cognate words in other languages (for instance *bench,* compared to *bank* borrowed from French); and it affected only those Latin words which came in before the end of the seventh century.

The third factor is the kind of usage into which words come. Those that are used by everybody tend to change much more than those known only to the educated minority. The effect of this difference is particularly obvious in pairs of words from the same root, one with a tangible reference known to everybody, the other a more abstract term which most people had no occasion to use. Such pairs as *deacon* and *diaconate, bishop* and *episcopal, pope* and *papacy* are examples.

It is often impossible to tell whether a conservative form is the result of late borrowing or learned use, because the question of just when a foreign word becomes a part of English is by no means simple. Lexicographers can often date the earliest appearance of a word in a surviving manuscript; but a word may have been used for centuries before it happens to appear in writing which has been preserved. On the other hand, a writer may at any time use a foreign word which does not really become a part of the language until much later, if ever.

At any rate, between four and five hundred words of Latin origin appear in Old English manuscripts. About a hundred of them do not seem to have been completely naturalized, and a good many others — like many native words — later went out of use; but most of them have been part of the language ever since. Since we have continued to borrow from Latin, some of them have been reintroduced in a form nearer the original. Thus we have *monastery,* whose unchanged vowel shows that it is a later borrowing than *minster* — both from *monasterium.* Such pairs as these are called *doublets*. *Mint* from *moneta* has the doublet *money*, originally from the same source, but coming into English through French, where the sound changes were quite different. Still later we based *monetary* directly on the Latin word.

63. THE SCANDINAVIAN ELEMENT. Another language which had an important influence on Old English was Scandinavian, although most of the evidence of that influence does not appear in writing until the Middle English period. The Danes and Norwegians who first raided and then settled in England during the latter half of the Old English period spoke North Germanic dialects which had much the same basic vocabulary as the West Germanic dialects of the Angles and Saxons, though they differed considerably in their inflectional endings and in the development of a few of the phonemes. Moreover, the Scandinavians had much in common with the English in ancestry, traditions, and way of life. Once they adopted Christianity — which they agreed and began to do after their defeat by Alfred in the battle of Ethandum in 878 — there was no major obstacle to prevent their blending with the English in a far more complete way than the English had ever mingled with the British.

The amalgamation of the two groups was far from peaceable. There were periods of bitter fighting between the English and the Danes almost until the time of the Norman conquest; but then there had always been bitter fighting among the English themselves, and no doubt would have been if the Danes had never come. We should not forget that loyalties during this period were primarily personal rather than national. In the later battles between the Danes and the English the "Danish" armies from the northeast undoubtedly included a good many Englishmen; and if the English armies from the southwest did not include Danes, it was only because there were not many Danes in that part of England.

Under these circumstances it was inevitable that the two languages should modify each other. Before they died out completely (which was not until well into the Modern English period) the Scandinavian dialects were undoubtedly influenced by English, though they left no written records to prove this; and English — at first locally and then nationally — was greatly influenced by Scandinavian.

It is hard to measure this influence with anything like precision, for several reasons. For one thing, such classifications as North and West Germanic are arbitrary, and the language of the Angles was in some ways more like that of the Scandinavians than that of the Saxons. Moreover, it was Anglian territory that the Danes settled in, and manuscripts preserved from any part of this territory are extremely scarce. It is therefore often impossible to tell whether a word or form which does not appear in writing until much later was originally Scandinavian, Anglian, or a combination of both, and there is naturally some disagreement among scholars about the probabilities. The complete accuracy of the word lists and statistics given below cannot, therefore, be guaranteed, and it would not be useful to attempt here a minute examination of all the evidence; but the picture presented seems to be approximately correct.

First, there are over 1,400 Scandinavian place-names in England, of which the most easily recognizable contain such endings as *-by, -thorpe,* and *-thwaite.* Then in the general standard vocabulary there are about nine hundred words almost certainly of Scandinavian origin, and about as many more which are probably Scandinavian or which clearly show some Scandinavian influence. And finally, in the non-standard dialects there are some thousands of Scandinavian words which are certainly English to the speakers of these dialects. In general, the Scandinavian coloring is stronger the farther north we go. It is particularly strong in Lowland Scottish, as we can see from the poetry of Robert Burns. And of course it is always possible for a word in any dialect to move into the standard language, so that we have probably not seen the last of importations yet. Moreover, the mere number of borrowed words, even if we count everything possible, does not indicate the full strength of the Danish influence. The nature of these borrowings must also be considered.

In general the English borrowed from Latin only words that they needed to indicate new things or new ideas introduced by the Romans. They are all from what are called the "open" parts of speech — nouns, verbs, adjectives, and adverbs. We are still borrowing words of these kinds from many languages, and inventing new ones, largely from Greek and Latin roots. They are important additions to our language; but they do not greatly affect its structure, and they do not very often drive native words out of the language.

The Danish influence was quite different and much more intimate. There were comparatively few new words for new things and ideas, such as technical war, shipping, and legal terms, and most of these have not survived, though *law* and *outlaw* are interesting exceptions. Most of the borrowings were of everyday terms, and many of them drove out established English words. The nouns *egg, fellow, freckle, garden, guess, leg, root, skin,* and *sky;* the verbs *call, get, give,* and *take;* the adjectives *flat, loose, low, odd,* and *weak* — these are only a few of the more surprising importations.

Even more remarkable are the words *they, their,* and *them, both* and *same, till,* and *with.* These are not mere items in the vocabulary, but parts of the basic structure of the language. It is true that there are not many of them, but it is almost incredible that there should be any at all, because such words are just not borrowed from one language to another. Even the form *are* is often attributed to Danish influence, though it can also be traced to Anglian.

As far as form is concerned, we may divide the Danish borrowings into three classes: those identical, except for their inflectional endings, with their English equivalents; those recognizably related to their equivalents, but with some difference of sound; and completely unrelated synonyms. Of the third class there is not very much to say. It is certainly surprising that the English gave up *niman* for *take* and *welkin* for *sky,* but they did. With words of the first class we can only prove a borrowing when we know (from later Old Norse literature) that the Scandinavian meaning was different from the English one. Thus *with* is common to both languages, but in Old English it meant *against*, a meaning preserved in the combinations *withstand* and *notwithstanding*. In Scandinavian it had the sense of accompaniment, a meaning expressed in Old English by *mid*. If we say, about the two World Wars, that we fought *with* the British, we are using the word in its Scandinavian sense; but if we say that we and the British fought *with* the Germans we are using it in its original English sense. Probably the most important effect of words which were identical in the two languages except for their endings is that they increased the tendency to drop these endings almost entirely.

The most interesting Scandinavian borrowings are those of the second class, consisting of obviously related words with some difference in their sounds. The principal correspondences are these:

1. Germanic /g/ remained /g/ in all positions in Scandinavian, but changed to /j/ (usually spelled *y*) before a front vowel and to /i/ (usually spelled *i* or *y*) after one in English. Thus Chaucer's normal form of *give* is *yive* or *yeve*, while the modern form is of Scandinavian origin. So is the form *egg*, of which the normal English development was *ei*, which is found in Chaucer, and was still competing with *egg* in Caxton's time.

2. The other palatal stop, /k/, also remained in Scandinavian, but changed to /tʃ/ in English. Thus *cyrice*, borrowed from Greek through Latin, has given us the two words *kirk* and *church*.

3. The combination /sk/ remained in Scandinavian but changed to /ʃ/ in English. If you drop a porcelain cup on a hard floor, the cup will probably *shatter* while the pieces of it *scatter*.

4. The Germanic diphthong /ai/ developed differently in the two languages, eventually resulting in /ei/ (spelled in various ways) in our words from Scandinavian, and /ou/ (usually spelled

o) in our words from Old English. Examples are *nay* along with *no* and *hale* along with *whole* (the *w* in this word is a late spelling convention). There were some other differences in vowel development, but they are too complicated to be discussed here.

When both the Scandinavian and the Old English form survived we may get either a regional difference like that between *kirk* and *church,* or a semantic difference like that between *scatter* and *shatter* or between *hale,* with its more limited meaning, and *whole.* Thus the Old English *scyrte* and its Scandinavian equivalent both meant a long, smocklike garment. The time came when this might be called either a skirt or a shirt — a rather wasteful pair of synonyms. Somehow both terms became specialized, *skirt* for the lower half and *shirt* for the upper. The same sort of thing happened with *dike* and *ditch,* both of which used to mean both the trench and the long mound formed alongside it by the earth removed. Here the Scandinavian form has been specialized to mean the upper part, and the Old English one the lower. Other comparable pairs, now specialized, are *yard* (which comes from *geard,* so that the change to /y/ is normal) and *garden, shrub* and *scrub* (in its botanical sense), and probably *shell* and *scale* (of a fish).

With the scarcity of written evidence that has come down to us it is impossible to know just when each of these words came to be habitually used in English; and it is sometimes impossible to be sure whether a word with such a typically Scandinavian beginning as /sk/ was actually borrowed from Scandinavian, or was merely a Scandinavian mispronunciation (which eventually became established as correct) of an Old English word beginning with /ʃ/. When two sounds compete there is bound to be some confusion. For instance, we have the two words *screech* and *shriek.* Obviously they ought to be *shreech* and *scriek,* each a respectable descendant of its own tradition. Instead we have two hybrid forms.

Even before the Norman Conquest some French words began to appear in Old English, but they were so few in comparison with those that came in during the Middle English period that it is not worth while discussing them here. And since the greater number of Latin borrowings occur rather seldom, most of the writing that has come down to us is so thoroughly Germanic that a German or Scandinavian student can learn to read it with rather less effort than an English or American one, since many of the words that have completely disappeared in Modern English have cognates still in use in the other Germanic languages. This seems rather unfair; but the tables are turned with Middle English, in which a native speaker can recognize innumerable words that have no meaning in Scandinavian or German.

CHAPTER FIVE

The Middle English Period

64. THE NORMAN CONQUEST. The pivotal event in English history, linguistically as well as otherwise, was the conquest by the Normans in 1066. The Anglo-Saxon invasion had been simply a movement of Germanic tribes to a new territory. These tribes pretty well cleared out all traces of what had preceded them, and went on living very much as they had on the continent. Their conversion to Christianity of course modified many of their values and attitudes, and for a while they added a considerable development of learning to their ordinary pursuits of fighting and farming. When the Danes conquered much of England the result was a setback rather than a forward step, since these invaders wiped out most of the progress that had been made, and had very little new to contribute. In the six centuries before the Conquest England had been a unified kingdom for only two brief periods — for about forty years in the middle of the tenth century, and for about twenty years under the Dane, Cnut, in the early part of the eleventh. It had never really been an organized country. The Normans not only unified it quickly and more or less permanently, but brought in a very different language and culture. By the time they were finally absorbed by the English both the country and the language were unlike anything else in the world.

The kingdom of Cnut collapsed under his successor in 1042. Edward the Confessor, a legitimate English claimant who had grown up in exile in Normandy, was called to the throne, and was the nominal king for the next twenty-four years. Actually the country was ruled by a number of independent and highly competitive earls, the most important of whom was Harold of Wessex. Edward was much admired (by interested people) for his piety and generosity to the church. There was not much else to admire him for, and he was a very ineffectual king. His sympathies and interests remained French rather than English, and he brought a number of French favorites to take important positions at his court. Being childless, he also seems to have promised to make his second cousin, William, Duke of Normandy, his heir. He had no right whatever to do this, but it gave William a claim of sorts. The natural heir was Harold; but he had once been a prisoner of William's and (according to William) had promised, for the sake of his freedom, not to contest the latter's claim.

When Edward died in 1066 Harold was elected king and immediately faced trouble on two sides. The Norwegians had raised an army to invade England from the north, and William was preparing to cross the channel. Harold defeated the Norwegians, but in the same year William defeated him at the Battle of Hastings. The fight was close, but when it was over the English had no organization with which to continue an effective resistance. In a remarkably short time William not only gained control of all England but organized it so thoroughly that it has been essentially one country ever since.

A little must be said about his background. Shortly after Alfred's victory in 878 had stopped the Danish expansion in England (and possibly for this reason) Scandinavian bands began taking over a part of northern France. They were called *Northmen* (*North-manni* or *Nortmanni* in contemporary manuscripts), and in a later contraction, *Normans*. Their history in Normandy was quite different from that of the Germanic conquerors of England. They took over the political and military control of their new territory both more rapidly and more efficiently than the English did; but they adopted the language as well as many of the customs of the people they had conquered. We can only guess why. Maybe they married more of the native women, and paid more attention to them. Maybe they, unlike the English, were impressed by the higher civilization they found. None of the explanations offered really seems adequate, but the fact remains that within a surprisingly short time they were speaking a sort of French and had apparently dropped their old language entirely.

65. THE FEUDAL SYSTEM. They also adopted the system of feudal tenure that had been developing in the continental remains of the Roman Empire — a system that, with all its disadvantages, had the seeds of a stronger and more effective central government than was likely to come out of the loose and almost tribal organization that was in use among the other Germanic peoples. In theory feudalism was a neat pyramidal structure rising from the broad base of the peasantry through the various levels of the nobility to the monarch at the top. The underlying principle was that nobody owned any land outright, but that each of the various levels had certain rights in it, and certain duties connected with those rights. A king was lord of his whole realm, but since he obviously couldn't be everywhere at once, either to farm or protect it, he divided it into fiefs, each controlled by a vassal in chief. These owed the king a share of their crops, financial contributions on certain specified occasions, and above all a specified amount of military service. As long as they faithfully fulfilled these obligations they were lords within their own territories. The king could not legally take the land from them, and he had very little to say about how they managed it or how they ruled their subjects. Moreover, their rights passed to their heirs, and the king could not revise the original distribution even though he might see that it was not working out at all well.

In a similar way the large holdings of a vassal in chief would be divided among lesser noblemen, down to the simple knights, who were the lowest members of the ruling class. A knight's holding was parceled out to peasants, who did the actual farming and other physical work. They were bound to the land; that is, they could not leave to find a better place, nor could the knight take their holdings from them. They had to work and fight for him, but he had to protect them, just as his lord owed him protection in return for service. Except for the king at the top and the peasant at the bottom, everybody had duties extending both up and down, and could count on help from both above and below. It was a beautifully symmetrical and strongly interlaced structure.

But when we turn from theory to recorded practice we find that the symmetry has pretty well disappeared, and that its solidity and efficiency are delusive. To consider only a few of the more obvious distortions, fiefs changed hands by marriage, inheritance, and conquest. A nobleman who had collected a few might owe allegiance to several different overlords, who might well be at war with one another, leaving an interesting question of where his true allegiance lay. A duke, or even a count, who had collected enough might become more powerful than his royal master. And it was perfectly possible for two nobles to owe feudal allegiance to each other for different parts of their holdings. Altogether, the possibilities of chaotic disturbances were plentiful, and the history of medieval Europe indicates that they were abundantly realized.

From humanitarian and democratic viewpoints there are all sorts of objections to the feudal system, but from the viewpoint of a reigning monarch the chief one was that a vassal might become sufficiently powerful to rise against the king. William had had enough experience on the continent to be well aware of this danger, and when he set up his own system in England he took appropriate precautions. Inevitably, he parceled out the kingdom among his followers, in proportion to their rank and value to him; but as far as possible he avoided giving them large, unified holdings. Instead, he gave them scattered fiefs which would be less likely to provide centers of power. He also took the unusual, though not original, precaution of insisting that each minor vassal should take an oath of allegiance directly to him, which took precedence over his duties to any intervening lord. And he reinforced his authority by instituting a system of royal courts throughout the kingdom, which further limited the powers of the nobles, and laid the foundations for the traditional English belief that a strong king was the people's best protection against an oppressive nobility. At the same time he let it be known that the old laws were still in effect except when they were specifically changed. The great importance of this was that the most effective laws in England were local customs rather than national edicts. The English in each district, even on each manor, already had a very strong determination to proceed according to tradition, and the royal attitude gave them some support. There were certainly times and places where they were horribly oppressed by their overlords, but they never sank to the position of the continental peasantry. The continuance of their old traditions had its effect in aiding the preservation of their language.

There is no evidence that William's restraint was caused by any kindly feelings. He was cold, selfish, avaricious, and utterly ruthless. He could, and on occasion did, slaughter thousands to make the point that rebellion was not profitable. But he took no pleasure in cruelty, and he was too intelligent to take any action that seemed likely to stir up more trouble than it was worth. Moreover, he wanted to encourage the theory that he was a legitimate successor to the throne rather than a simple invader. Above all, now that the kingdom was his he wanted it run as efficiently and as profitably as possible.

66. The Organization of the Country. Naturally most of the important positions in the country went to Normans and other Frenchmen. William did not want anybody in power who was not on his side. He apparently had no prejudice against Englishmen as such, and was quite willing to leave in authority anyone who would work with him, unless he needed the position for one of his own men — which he usually did. Feudal followers had to be rewarded if they were to remain faithful. Ecclesiastical posi-

tions of importance were treated in exactly the same fashion as secular ones. This was necessary on two counts. Not only was the church a more pervasive spiritual and social influence than it is today, but it was in control of much land, and of the laymen who worked, and on occasion defended, that land. A bishop or abbot therefore had to be considered in his feudal as well as his spiritual functions. Also, the church had a monopoly of education, so that a country simply could not be administered without what amounted to a clerical civil service.

We don't know how many Normans and other Frenchmen William brought to England, nor what proportion of them later returned to France. One estimate, which seems as reasonable as any other, is that about 20,000 of the foreigners stayed — enough to form an adequate cadre for the organization of the country. There was not, as far as we know, any concerted effort to drive out English. It was simply that the new ruling class naturally spoke French, and saw no reason to change. A few of them, usually not on the highest levels, had to learn enough English to give orders. Aside from that, if the English wanted to learn French, let them. Some did — it was one way to get ahead. A great many more of them had to learn some French words, and these words gradually became a part of English.

For some two hundred years French remained the normal language of the nobility. During this period the kings and many nobles had possessions on both sides of the Channel, and divided their time between the two. On the whole they seem to have considered themselves Frenchmen who held estates in England, rather than Englishmen. But early in the thirteenth century this condition came to an end. In 1204 Normandy was permanently lost to the English crown, and during the next half-century the nobles either had to choose between keeping their English and French holdings, or had that choice made for them. Those who kept their English holdings soon became English because there was no longer anything else for them to be.

This development of a national feeling among the nobility was probably assisted rather than delayed by a new wave of French influence. Henry III, King of England from 1216 to 1272, was completely French in his sympathies, and imported thousands of Frenchmen to fill most of the important positions in his administration. These were not from Normandy, but from various other provinces, and their speech was closer to the Central French from which the modern standard language has developed than to Norman French — especially as that was now spoken in England. Their influence probably did something to prolong the official use of French in England. On the other hand the Norman English, especially but not exclusively those they had displaced, naturally hated them, and began to feel much more English by contrast. By the end of the century French was dying out as the primary language even of the nobility, and during the fourteenth century it lost most of its official status. About 1350 English began to be used in the schools, and by 1386 it had pretty well superseded French there. In 1362 a parliamentary statute ordered the use of English in all lawsuits. The records of guilds, of towns, and of parliament itself were kept in French until well into the fifteenth century, but it is clear that this was a matter of traditional conservatism, and no longer reflected the language in which business was actually transacted.

67. THE SUBMERGENCE OF ENGLISH. Thus during several centuries English disappeared as an official language, and for the first few generations of this period it very nearly disappeared as a written one. From the Conquest to about 1200 the only English document of much importance that has come down is the Peterborough version of the Anglo-Saxon Chronicle, which contains annual entries running down to 1154. The language of the last few years shows some differences from that of the earlier ones, but it is still essentially Old English. It seems reasonable to suppose that the chronicle was kept up by a monk who was both old and oldfashioned, and that it breaks off when he died simply because there was no one left to continue it.

There is no reason to suppose that much other writing in English during this period has been lost. With the French in

control of practically everything there can have been little reason
to write English. At least above the primary level (about which
we know very little) the language taught in the schools was
Latin, which was still regarded as the one important language of
Christendom, and used for the most important documents of all
kinds. The language in which Latin was taught was French,
which was used, when Latin was inappropriate or impracticable,
for all important affairs, as well as the everyday affairs of practically all people of either education or position. Who was to
write in English, and why?

Accordingly, if we consider only the written language for this
early period, we are likely to feel that English was almost
swamped out of existence, and that it made a most remarkable
comeback in the thirteenth and fourteenth centuries. But the fact
is that English was always the only language of the great majority
of the people; and in an age when so few of them were directly
affected by education there was never any real chance that it
would be supplanted.

68. THE DIVERSITY OF MIDDLE ENGLISH. It is of course possible
that in the years immediately after the Conquest many of the
French really expected their language to become general throughout the country, but by 1200 it seems to have been obvious to
everybody that this was not going to happen. If the ordinary
people were to be reached at all, they had to be reached in their
own language; and a large number of works, mostly for the
good of their souls, were either composed in or translated into
English of various sorts.

Since Old English has come down to us almost entirely in
rather late West Saxon manuscripts, it is easy to think of it as a
fairly uniform language; and our whole training encourages us to
think of Modern English as basically a standard language with
well-codified rules, fringed with a number of dialects, inferior in
kind, which for most purposes do not have to be seriously considered. In the Middle English period, on the other hand, we are
confronted with such a mass of conflicting material that it is

very hard to keep in mind any consistent idea of what "the language" was. We can, if we like, talk of the development of the four major dialects — Northern, East Midland, West Midland, and Southern. Or we can add Kentish and talk of the five major dialects, or split some of the others and make it nine. Whatever number we use, we should realize that until the very end of the period none of them approached the status of a standard language for the whole country; and the differences between them were so great that we find scribes translating from one to another for the benefit of their neighbors. The following excerpts from Trevisa's translation of Higden's Latin *Polychronicon* (1385) give some idea of the situation late in the fourteenth century. (The forms of the words have been modernized, but the syntax has not been altered.)

> Also English men, though they had from the beginning three manner speech, southern, northern, and middle speech in the middle of the land, as they came of three manner people of Germania, nonetheless by mixing and mingling, first with Danes and afterward with Normans, in many the country language is impaired; and some use strange wlaffing, chytering, harring, and garring grisbitting. . . .
>
> . . . for men of the east with men of the west, as it were under the same part of heaven, accord more in sounding of speech than men of the north with men of the south. Therefore is it that Mercians, that be men of middle England, as it were partners of the ends, understand better the side languages, northern and southern, than northern and southern understand either other.
>
> All the language of the Northumbrians, and specially of York, is so sharp, slitting, and rasping, and unshaped, that we southern men may that language hardly understand.[1]

This passage obviously contains some sectional bias. Those speakers who used the "strange wlaffing, chytering, harring, and garring grisbitting" might conceivably have had equally unpleasant things to say about other dialects; and the Yorkshiremen (unless they differed remarkably from their descendants) would

---

[1] Kaiser, pps. 516, 517.

have been very hard to convince of the superiority of Southern English. Moreover, the explanation of the origin of the differences is not quite accurate. We now trace the Northern dialect to Northumbrian, and the "middle speech" — East and West Midland — to Mercian, both of which were basically Anglian dialects in Old English times. The Southern dialect developed from the speech of the other two "manner people," though some scholars prefer to treat Kentish, which was of Jutish origin, separately. But at least the separate origins, the chief foreign influences, and the current diversity are all brought out.

Our knowledge of these dialects is far from complete, and there are differences of opinions on some points. What we think we know is based only in part on the surviving manuscripts. We also depend on forms and constructions that have persisted in the spoken dialects of Modern English. To take a very simple example, we believe that the Southern English voiced the /f/ and /s/ sounds at the beginnings of such words as *for* and *see,* as their descendants still do in certain rural areas. Southern manuscripts support the voicing of the /f/ very thoroughly, since they usually spell *for* as *vor.* But they neither support nor contradict the voicing of the /s/, since most scribes did not use the letter *z* at all, but used *s* for the voiced as well as voiceless sounds, as we still do in many words today. However, it seems likely that two such similar sound changes occurred about the same time; and since the /z/ pronunciation in Southern dialects is recorded in very early Modern English (for instance, when Edgar poses as a peasant in *King Lear*), we have good reason to believe that it was current in Middle English.

69. SOME PECULIARITIES OF MIDDLE ENGLISH MANUSCRIPTS. We are so used to relying on careful editing and printing that it takes either a good deal of exposure or a strenuous effort of the imagination to realize what books were like before the new practices gradually developed. Some of the difficulties of copying long manuscripts, day after day, on very expensive material, are im-

mediately obvious. Physical conditions did not make them easier
— always a quill or reed pen, often a bad light, and little or no
heat in an English winter. But we must add to these a complete
lack of certain reference works, techniques, and above all established conventions which we now take for granted, but which
actually took many generations after the introduction of printing
to develop. During the whole of the Old and Middle English
periods there was not a grammar, a dictionary, or even a spelling
book of English in existence. There was not even complete agreement about the alphabet — either the letters of which it was composed or the sounds that some of these represented. And there
was certainly nothing like the modern procedure of proofreading
in any general use, for the apparently simple idea of reproducing
anything with literal accuracy — that is, getting it right letter by
letter — does not seem to have occurred to many people. After
all, if the man you were copying spelled the same word in a number of different ways, why should you be fussy? And even if he
didn't, others did. An unusually careful scribe might copy word
for word — or try to. A less particular one would copy sentence
by sentence (if he could tell where all the sentence divisions
were), thus introducing a good deal of variation, some of it inten-
tional, some not. And a really broadminded one would add,
delete, or modify wherever he felt inclined to. The freedom with
which even able and honorable scholars often altered their texts
may seem utterly horrifying to a modern student who has been
taught that it is sinful to make a silent correction of even a letter
or a comma; but neither the conditions nor the traditions of
modern accuracy had yet developed.

Even in Latin manuscripts of works whose text was particularly
respected, and on which scholars had been busy for centuries,
the variations that occur are amazing and sometimes completely
bewildering. In English manuscripts all the difficulties are compounded. Consider, for example, the problems of a monk born
in the north, belonging to a monastery in the midlands, and
assigned to copy a manuscript composed in the south — to take

a fairly simple case. Letter-by-letter copying would not only be painfully slow (have you ever tried to copy exactly an extensive passage in an unfamiliar dialect?), but worse than useless, because who wanted those silly southern perversions? He might try to do it word by word, but that brought up again and again and again the question of which form for each word — the one he had grown up with, the one his colleagues used, or the one he saw at the moment? Almost inevitably he would do a little of each. We may find it incredible, but there was simply no *right* way to spell anything, unless the scribe was a dogmatic reformer like Orrm (see pages 135–136), who invented his own rules — which nobody else ever followed. Otherwise each man's spelling had to be some sort of compromise between an attempt to represent the sounds he heard and a recollection of the way or ways he had most often seen a word spelled before.

And what should he do about completely unfamiliar words or forms in the strange dialect? Guess at them and substitute what seemed reasonable in his own dialect, or just copy them, rightly or wrongly (and some handwritings were hard to read even then) and leave the guessing to somebody else? Or compromise by trying to copy the word and adding a synonym or an explanation, right or wrong? We could go on with his problems, but we are trying to keep the case simple. It is easy to understand that our manuscripts seldom show any dialect in as pure a form as we should like to see it. Except for the very few autograph originals that have come down to us, any manuscript must be some kind of compromise between at least two idiolects, often separated by many miles and many years. And even an autograph manuscript is likely to reflect to some extent the author's reading in various dialects rather than simply the sounds of his own speech.

With the documentary evidence in such a confusing state it is not possible, in an introductory text, to give a detailed account of the various dialects through the centuries. To do so without reference to the texts would be to offer an exercise in memorizing which would be almost meaningless, especially to students who do not already have a thorough knowledge of Old English; and to do so with illustrative examples would require more texts than could reasonably be handled, not to mention innumerable explanations that many of the forms that actually occur really ought to be quite different. The obvious alternative — and the one we shall take — is to discuss Middle English as if it were much more uniform than we know it was, with only occasional references to time and place. We can then come back to earth by examining rather casually a few assorted examples, and then quite closely a specimen from Chaucer, whose dialect has three advantages: it is not far from the main line of development; it is comparatively easy to approach; and it is much the most rewarding. Finally there will be a selection from Malory, whose language, aside from the spelling and a few peculiarities of syntax, is almost modern.

70. SOUND-CHANGES IN MIDDLE ENGLISH. The most important sound-changes that occurred in Middle English may be summarized as follows:

Vowels: Old English long *a* (/ɑ:/) changed to long open *o* (/ɔ:/) except in the Northern dialect. This open *o* changed again to long close *o* (/o:/) early in the modern period. Thus *bān* became *bone,* *hām* became *home,* and *stān* became *stone.* In each case the silent final *e* is simply a modern spelling convention. Such forms as *bane, hame,* and *stane,* which can be found in the Border ballads and the poetry of Burns, are of course Northern. On the other hand, Old English short *a* lengthened in open syllables (that is, when followed by a single consonant followed by a vowel). This accounts for such words as *name* (/nɑ:mə/), in which the *a* was originally short.

Old English *æ* (/æ/) changed to *a* (/ɑ/). It later changed back to its original value in most words, but by this time we had lost the useful symbol *æ,* which would have prevented much ambiguity if we had retained it.

Old English *y* (/y/), both long and short, unrounded to become /i:/ or /i/ except in the south, though the *y* spelling remained common.

71. DIPHTHONGS. The original Old English diphthongs all simplified to become single vowels, and a new set of diphthongs developed. This set of changes is too complicated to be discussed here, but split development of *eo* is worth mentioning. In most of the country the second element dropped out, so that *bēo* gives us *bee* (Middle English /be:/, Modern English /bi:/), *trēo* gives us *tree*, and so forth. But in the south the second element rounded the first one, so that we get such forms as *bo* and *tro*, pronounced like the German ö.

72. CONSONANTS. Old English double consonants were actually pronounced as such. In Modern English the double pronunciation is used only when identical consonants are accidentally brought together in the formation of compounds, such as *bookkeeper* and *part-time*. Otherwise the double letter is used only as a spelling convention. The change occurred during the Middle English period, but cannot be precisely dated.

In the earliest English the letters *c* and *g* consistently had the "hard" values /k/ and /g/ wherever they occurred; but in West Saxon these sounds were fronted before the front vowels *e, i,* and *y*. In such positions /k/ became /tʃ/, /sk/ became /ʃ/, and /g/ became /j/. You will notice that each of these changes involves moving the tip of the tongue farther forward in the mouth to pronounce the consonant. It is thus a natural, though not inevitable, change to make in the neighborhood of a front vowel. There is a conflict of opinion (with evidence on both sides) about whether the same changes took place in Anglian territory and were later reversed under Scandinavian influence, or whether Anglian was always more like Scandinavian in this respect. But there is no doubt that during the Middle English period the original sounds were current in the Northern dialect, while the fronted sounds were general in the rest of the country. This accounts for those contrasting pairs of words mentioned on pages 110–111, as well as for many other Northern variants found in Middle English texts.

In Old English the letter *h* was originally pronounced as /x/ in all positions. In Middle English, if not earlier, this weakened in the initial position to something like the modern /h/. Then it dropped out completely in the initial combinations *hl, hn,* and *hr.* In the south it also dropped out in the combination *hw,* but in the north it actually strengthened to a /k/ in this position.

The initial combinations *gn, kn,* and *wr* continued to be fully pronounced until the modern period.

Possibly as a result of French influence the two fricative sounds /f/ and /v/ became contrasting phonemes instead of allophones of the same phoneme; and so did the /s/ and /z/ sounds. It seems reasonable to suppose that /θ/ and /ð/ became differentiated at the same time, though the evidence is less conclusive. This development did not spread to the south, where these fricatives were always voiced.

73. Loss of Inflections. The most important structural change in Middle English was the weakening and eventual loss of most of the inflectional endings, compensated by the development of a standard word-order. The changes that affected Chaucer's dialect will be described later in some detail. In general, the *m* of the dative changed to *n,* and the vowels in all endings except the present participle weakened to /ə/, generally written as *e,* but sometimes as *i, y,* or *u.* Later the *-en,* from whatever source, weakened to *-e,* and still later the *-e* dropped. In early Middle English the present participle ended in *-and* in the north, in *-end* in the Midland territory, and in *-ind* in the south. Later the modern form in *-ing* became general throughout the country, presumably by confusion with the verbal noun (gerund) in *-ing,* though the exact process followed is not clear. On the whole these changes took place most rapidly in the north and most slowly in the south.

Two explanations for these changes are often given. The first is that contact or "rubbing" with French had the effect of wearing off many of the inflectional endings. This sounds reasonable, but it does not seem to have happened in similar situations elsewhere in the world. The second is that during the long period when English was spoken largely by uneducated people the complications of the old inflections were too much of a strain, and they were therefore forgotten. This also sounds superficially reasonable, but it does not allow for the fact that these complications had developed during ages when all men were illiterate; and they were certainly no greater than those that can be found today in some languages which have not yet developed a written tradition. Moreover, very similar changes have taken place in the Scandinavian languages, with no foreign occupation to explain them. We might as well admit that we don't know why the structure changed, but it did.

74. BORROWINGS FROM THE FRENCH VOCABULARY. There can, however, be no question about the influence of the French vocabulary. During the time when the invaders were in control of so many sides of life, their words for a great many things became *the* words, and were used in English as well as French. Many other borrowings, though less necessary, seem natural enough. Snobbery on the part of part of the English probably accounted for some, and laziness on the part of the French for others. It is a very general rule that when two languages are in contact because of a conquest, the language of the conquered people is affected much more than that of the conquerors. We cannot tell how fast the French influence worked in speech. There have been studies of the rate of appearance of French words in English writing, but the picture they present must be considered very conservative. Aside from the fact that many words must have been current for generations before they happened to be used in a document which happened to be preserved, a good many Middle English authors say specifically that they are writing for people who know no French. It is reasonable to suppose that they would avoid any French words that were not

thoroughly established, and perhaps many that were. For what the evidence is worth, when writings in English begin to reappear about 1200 they show no more than a sprinkling of French words. The number of new ones appearing grows steadily until about 1400, when it begins to taper off.

A good many of the words borrowed might be called technical terms in those areas where the French influence was particularly strong, such as government, law, religion, and military affairs. To take just a few examples of each, we find under *government* not only that word itself but *assembly, authority, council, court, crown, empire, majesty, mayor, parliament, reign, royal, state, statute, tax,* and *treaty.* Under *religion* we have *baptism, clergy, communion, confession, creator, damnation, devotion, faith, friar, immortality, miracle, parson, pastor, reverence, saint, trinity,* and *vicar.* Under *law* (which rather curiously is not from French), we have *assault, attorney, bail, bar, bill, crime, decree, felon, fine, judge, justice, plaintiff, prison, sentence,* and *trespass.* And among our *military* terms are *arms, army, battle, captain, combat, defense, enemy, guard, lieutenant, navy, sergeant, siege, skirmish, soldier,* and *spy.* All these lists could be made very much longer, and we could add lists from other fields, such as social life and organization, food and clothing, learning and the arts. But perhaps these are enough to indicate some of the areas in which we would now be helpless without our French words. We should also notice that a large part of these are not gap-fillers, like so many of the earlier borrowings from Latin, but importations which drove out established native synonyms.

Moreover, it was not only in such special areas as those mentioned above that large-scale borrowing occurred. Here are a few of the general-purpose words that came in: *able, age, aim, air, blank, brief, bucket, bushel, carry, change, clear, cover, damage, debt, double, dozen, eager, easy, envy, error, face, fault, feeble, folly, gay, gentle, grain, grief, hardy, hasty, honor, horrible,* and so on down the alphabet. It would be hard for the most fanatical believer in "good old Anglo-Saxon" to avoid these words or a great many others just as much a part of our everyday language.

But French did not, like Danish, supply any function words. Such few apparent exceptions as *because* and *during* developed their present uses after having been borrowed as "full" words.

75. CHARACTERISTICS OF NORMAN-FRENCH WORDS. It is obvious that some of the borrowings listed above are almost or exactly like Modern French words, while others are quite different. One reason is that the earliest borrowings are from Norman French, while many of the later ones are from the Central French which eventually became the standard form of the language. Early French, like English, existed in a number of dialects, and the Norman one had a number of characteristic features, of which three are especially noticeable. (1) The initial Latin *ca* combination was preserved in Norman, while in Central French it changed to *ch* plus a vowel which varied according to the other sounds in the word. Thus *catch, cattle,* and *cavalry* are all from Norman, while *chase, chattel,* and *chivalry* are somewhat later borrowings from Central French. (2) Many Norman words begin with *w,* while their Central equivalents begin with *gu.* The pairs *warden* and *guardian, warranty* and *guarantee* are examples. (3) The combinations *sc, sp,* and *st* are frequent in Latin words, and usually remained in their Norman derivatives; but in Central French the *s* usually disappeared before the twelfth century. (Most modern French words in which the *s* remains are late borrowings from Latin.) Thus such words as *coast, cost, establish, feast,* and *forest* show a Norman origin.

76. LEARNED AND POPULAR WORDS. Not all the peculiarities of our borrowings from French can be explained by Norman origin. Words introduced from any other language by scholars writing or translating are often called "learned words," and those introduced in common speech are called "popular words" — the reference being to the populace, not to popularity. There is no firm line between the two kinds, but there is a general difference worth considering. Learned borrowings are more likely to retain their original form and meaning, since they are — as long as they

remain "learned" — used mostly by people with more than an average interest in precision. Popular borrowings are more likely to be modified to resemble native words and to change with the general drift of the language. They are also likely to combine with native elements to make new compounds, and to extend their original meanings very freely.

77. INDIRECT INFLUENCE OF FRENCH. Whether or not French influenced the changes in English structure, it certainly did more than add to the vocabulary. For one thing, its long use as the language of all important affairs delayed the development of a standard dialect of English. In every European country various regional dialects were in use on a more or less equal basis during the early part of the Middle Ages; and in every country one or another of these eventually attained the prestige of a national language. In France, for instance, the dialect of the Île de France — the country around Paris — won out quite early simply because that area became the center of power and influence, political, economic, and intellectual. It was not only the official language but the one generally adopted by influential people throughout the country. The assorted provincials brought into England by Henry III during the thirteenth century seem to have used it quite generally. But it was not until much later that the dialect of London developed a comparable prestige, simply because for some centuries French rather than any kind of English was the language of opportunity.

Moreover, the French borrowings were so extensive that they changed the whole balance of the language and prepared the way for the incomparable hospitality to words from other languages that English has shown ever since. The English vocabulary is now much the largest in the world, and well over half of it comes from French and Latin sources. It is often impossible to tell from which source an originally Latin word was actually borrowed; but even the direct Latin borrowings were certainly made easier by the fact that many French words were already in the language.

78. OTHER FOREIGN INFLUENCES ON MIDDLE ENGLISH. Direct borrowings from Latin not only continued but increased during the Middle English period. A list of examples would not be very informative, but it is worth mentioning that they were almost entirely learned words, and the greater part came in by way of translations of Latin books. As a result, they have since undergone no such changes as affected the Old English popular borrowings. They were usually somewhat modified to make them seem legitimately English, as by changing the endings *-abilis* and *-atus* to *-able* and *-ate;* but the fact that they could always be checked against their established Latin forms tended to prevent any further changes.

Most of the Scandinavian borrowings first appear in English documents during this period, though (as pointed out on page 111) they may have been in the spoken language for centuries. Moreover, their use was still spreading, so that many words which are found only in northern documents in the thirteenth century spread even to the London area by the fifteenth. There was also a sprinkling of words from many other languages, but not enough from any one to constitute a sizable influence.

79. LOSS OF NATIVE WORDS AND WORD-ELEMENTS. With so many French and Latin words coming in, a considerable number of native words dropped out of use. In some instances this seems to be a matter of simple cause and effect. It is easy to understand why *ætheling* gave way to *noble* at a time when almost all the nobility were French, and why the same sort of thing happened with technical terms for military affairs, the law, and so forth. It is not nearly so easy to understand why *earm* gave way to *poor* and *lyft* to *air*. In these and many other cases there seems to be no national principle involved. Moreover, not all the lost words were replaced by French or Latin ones. *Eek,* for instance, gave way to the equally English *also*, and *niman,* after some centuries of competition, to the Scandinavian *take*. Many of the changes can only be explained by reference to the well-known (but itself unexplained) fact that gradual replacement

of words is always occurring in every speech group, whether or not there is an outside source of supply. But the rate of turnover in England was certainly increased during this period. It is well known that more than half of our words come from French and Latin sources, but it is not generally realized that we have preserved a very much higher proportion of the Roman than of the Old English vocabulary. Something like five-sixths of the words recorded in Old English have disappeared. This figure is somewhat deceptive, since many of the lost words are recorded only in poetry and may never have had much currency in ordinary speech, but it is still impressive.

More significant than the loss of individual words is the great reduction in use of those prefixes and suffixes with which new words used to be freely made. In early Middle English such prefixes as *be-, for-, to-,* and *with-,* and such suffixes as *-hood, -lock, -red,* and *-ship* were added to roots whenever it seemed useful and appropriate. By the end of the period these elements seem to have lost any specific, independent meaning; they were therefore seldom used in new combinations, and retained only in well-established words which were understood as wholes and not by analysis of their parts. A few clearcut prefixes, such as *over-, under-,* and the negative *un-* remained; and so did such suffixes as *-ful, -ish, -less, -ly,* and *-ness.* But on the whole the tendency was to use Latin rather than native elements in the formation of new words.

80. MIDDLE ENGLISH SPELLING. Anything like a complete treatment of Middle English spelling would be impossibly complicated, but a few general statements can be made to ease the approach to the selections in the following sections.

1. Those words that now begin with *wh-* were spelled in Old English with *hw-,* which obviously better reflects their pronunciation. But the Old English *h,* as we have already seen, was used for a stronger sound than the modern one — the fricative /x/. Apparently this sound (in this position) was weakening in

the south, but remained strong in the north. In both areas French scribes (who were not used to a strong *h*) seem to have found *hw*- an incredible way to indicate it. In the north they generally spelled the word *hwat*, for instance, as *quat* or *quhat*. In the midlands they were likely to reverse the initial letters, as we still do; and in the south we find such spellings as *wat, ouat,* and *uat*.

2. Scribes knew that a good many words of French or Latin origin began with a silent *h*, but they didn't always know which ones. Thus we may find *onor* for *honor* and *habundant* for *abundant*. Moreover, some scribes might pronounce an initial *h* where we do not, or vice versa. *Heten* occurs for *eten* (*to eat*), and *ost* for *host*. The following procedure is therefore extremely useful: if you don't recognize a word that begins with *h*, try it without and see what you get; and if you don't recognize a word that begins with a vowel, try it with an initial *h*.

3. The letters *u* and *v* are interchangeable. Thus we may find *uanite* for *vanity* and *vp* for *up*. Printers later tended to use *v* initially, whether for the vowel or the consonant sound, and *u* in other positions; scribes were less consistent.

4. The letter *y* had ceased to be used for the rounded front vowel (which was now generally spelled *u* in those areas where it was retained), and had become simply a variant form of *i*, with which it could be interchanged in all positions. Thus *lady* may be spelled *ladi*, and *yes* may be spelled *ies*.

5. The letters *i* and *j* are also interchangeable in certain positions, but not in all. Either may appear initially before a vowel, as in *iustice* for *justice* or *Iohn* for *John*; and *j* may appear as the second half of a doubled *i* (see 6, below), or in Roman numerals. Roman seven, for instance, may be indicated as *vii, vij,* or *vjj*.

6. Long vowels may be indicated in any of three ways:

   a. Not only *e* and *o* but *a* and *i* were often doubled. Thus we may find *caas* for *case* and *tiim* or *tijm* for *time*.

   b. In early Middle English a final *e* indicated a pronounced syllable. In later Middle English it often indicated merely that the preceding vowel was long.

c. In the Northern dialect vowel length was often indicated by an *i* immediately after the vowel. Thus we may find *rois* for *rose* or *maid* for *made*.

7. In diphthongs *u* and *w* were interchangeable. Thus *foul* and *fowl* are merely variant spellings, not distinct words.

8. The letter ȝ (*yogh*) was used in at least four different ways:

a. For /x/, in which value it alternates with *h* and *gh*, and *ugh*.

b. For /dȝ/, in which value it alternates with *g*.

c. For /j/, in which value it alternates with *y* or *i*.

d. For /z/, especially in inflectional endings.

There are times when it seems to have still other values, but these are enough to indicate that it should always be considered with care, to say nothing of suspicion.

9. The alternation of *g* and *y* (or ȝ) in such words as *give* or *yive* and *again* or *aȝayn* is not strictly a matter of spelling, since different dialectal pronunciations are indicated; but it is worth mentioning at this point.

81. THE ORRMULUM. In the paraphrase of the Gospels called the *Orrmulum* the modern convention of doubling consonants to indicate short vowels is used hundreds of years before it was generally adopted, and even in positions where we do not now regard it as necessary — for instance finally, and before another, different consonant. *Orrm* or *Orrmin* (he gives his name both ways) is the only Englishman before the modern period who has left us a plan for a definite system of spelling reform. Unfortunately, there is no evidence that anybody ever showed the slightest interest in following it. Possibly the reason is that none of his contemporaries or early successors ever succeeded in reading as far in his book as the explanatory passage quoted below, since his version is almost inconceivably dull. He is never contented with saying the same thing twice if he can find a way to say it three times, and he usually can. But his attempt at consistent spelling gives us some valuable information about pro-

nunciation, and he does have the advantage of being easier to read (for a few lines) than most of his contemporaries.

Annd whase wilenn shall þiss boc   efft oþerrsiþe writenn,
Himm bidde icc, þatt hēt wrīte rihht,   swasumm þiss boc himm tæcheþþ
50   All þwerrtūt, affterr þatt itt iss   uppo þiss firrste bisne,
Wiþþ all swillc rīme, alls her iss sett,   wiþþ allse fele wordess,
Annd tatt he loke wel, þatt he   an bocstaff wrīte twiʒʒess,
Eʒʒwhær þær itt uppo þiss boc   iss writenn o þatt wise.
Loke he wel þatt hēt write swa,   forr he ne maʒʒ nohht elless
55   Onn Ennglissh wrītenn rihht te word;   þatt wite he wel to soþe.

Annd ʒiff mann wile witenn whi   icc hafe don þiss dede,
Whi icc till Ennglissh hafe wennd   goddspelless hallʒhe lare:
Icc hafe itt don forrþi þatt all   crisstene follkess berrhless
Iss lang uppo þatt an þatt teʒʒ   goddspelless hallʒhe lare
60   Wiþþ fulle mahhte follʒhe rihht   þurrh þohht, þurrh word, þurrh dede.
Annd tærfore hafe icc turrnedd itt   inntill Ennglisshe spæche,
Forr þatt I wollde bliþeliʒ   þatt all Ennglisshe lede
Wiþþ ære shollde lisstenn itt,   wiþþ herrte shollde itt trowwenn.
Wiþþ tunge shollde spellenn itt,   wiþþ dede shollde itt follʒhenn.
65   To winnenn unnderr crisstenndom   att Crist soþ sawle berrhless.
Annd godd allmahhtiʒ ʒife uss mahht   annd lusst annd witt annd wille,
To follʒhenn þiss Ennglisshe boc,   þatt all iss haliʒ lare,
Swa þatt we motenn wurrþi ben   to brukenn heffness blisse.

Am[æn]. Am[æn]. Am[æn].[2]

Translation:

And whoever shall want to write this book over again
I pray him that he write it right, so as this book teaches him
50   All throughout, the way that it is in this first example
With all such measure as here is set down, with all so many words,
And that he look well, that he one letter write twice,
Always where it upon this book is written in that way.
Let him look well that he write it so, for he can not else
55   In English write the words right; let him know that well in truth.

[2] Kaiser, p. 212, ll. 48–68.

And if anybody wants to know why I have done this deed,
Why I have turned into English the gospel's holy lore:
I have done it because all Christian folk's salvation
Depends upon that one thing, that they gospel's holy lore
60 With full might follow right, through thought, through word, through deed.
And therefore have I turned it into English speech,
Because I would gladly that all English people
With ear should listen to it, with heart should believe,
With tongue should pronounce it, with deed should follow it,
65 And win under Christianity through Christ true salvation of soul.
And that God Almighty give us power and desire and wit and will,
To follow this English book, that is all holy lore,
So that we may be worthy to enjoy heaven's bliss.

Amen. Amen. Amen.

Since neither this text nor this sub-dialect is a particularly re-warding subject of study except for specialists, no notes are given.

As proof that the statements on pages 122–124 about varia-tions in manuscripts are not exaggerated, here is a selection from the *Cursor Mundi* as it appears in two manuscripts. It would be easy to find versions that differ much more; actually this is simply the first passage reproduced from two different manu-scripts that came to hand when an illustration was needed. A detailed analysis of the contrasting features would be out of place here; but MS *C* is closer to the Northern original, both in time and place, than MS *T*. Even a casual line-by-line inspection will show some of the things — by no means all — that could happen in copying.[3] Line 156 is particularly interesting. *Heven* (*u* and *v* were interchangeable at this time) is an old Northern verb meaning "to avenge"; but since it suggested nothing but *heaven* to the Midland scribe, he changed the whole line to fit in with this word.

---

[3] To facilitate this, a translation of the *C* version is given. Most of the changes made in the *T* version are reasonably obvious.

	MS C	*MS T*
	Þis Herods had regned thritte[4] yere;	Heroude had regned þritty ȝere,
	Quen Iesus Crist vr lauedi bere;	Whenne þat Marie Iesu bere;
155	Siþen he regned yeres seuen.	Siþen he regned þries seuen.
	His wranges godd on him sal heuen,	Fer he brouȝte him self from heuen
	Þat fals, þat fell, þat goddes fa,	Þat false feloun goddes fo
	Þat soght his lauerd for to sla!	Souȝte his lord for to slo.
	Hu had he hert to sced þair blod	How had he hert to shede her bloc
160	Þat neuer did til him bot god!	Þat neuer dud but good?
	Þat wili wolf, þat fox sa fals	Þat wilful wolf þat ferde so fals
	Bath gain fremd and freindes als,	Aȝeynes fremde and frendes als
	O carles costes al til vnknauin,	His delful dedes most be knowen;
	And was manqueller til his auen.	Monqueller was he to his owen.
165	Þat gredi gerard als a gripe,	Þat gredy gerarde as a gripe
	His vnrightes biginnes to ripe,	Now his wrongis bigonne to ripe;
	And of his seruis mani dai	And for his seruyse mony a day
	Nu neghes tim to tak his lai.	Þenne coom tyme to take his pay.[5]

Translation (C version):

	This Herod had reigned thirty years,
	When Our Lady bore Jesus Christ;
155	Afterward he reigned seven years.
	God shall avenge his wrongs on him,
	That false, that wicked, that God's foe,
	That sought to slay his Lord!
	How had he heart to shed their blood
160	That never did to him (anything) but good!
	That wily wolf, that fox so false
	Both against strangers and friends also,
	Oh churl's actions all to (those) unknown,
	And (he) was mankiller to his own.
165	That villain greedy as a vulture,
	His misdeeds begin to ripen,
	And for his service of many a day
	Now the time is near for him to receive his (punishment of the) law.

---

[4] The spelling *thritte* is not a misprint. The scribe of MS C is exceptional in regularly distinguishing between the voiced and voiceless dental fricatives, using Þ for the former and *th* for the latter.

[5] Kaiser, p. 223, 11.153–168.

82. ALYSOUN. The Southern lyric "Alysoun" is here given with
only a few clues rather than either a translation or an analysis
on the theory that a student is more likely to feel some of its
charm if he misses a bit here and there than if he has to dissect
it too laboriously. It is worth several readings and some discussion.

Bytuene Mersh ant Aueril	*springtime*
When spray biginneþ to springe,	
Þe lutel foul haþ hire wyl	*little bird*
4 On hyre lud to synge.	*in her language*
Ich libbe in loue-longinge	*I live*
For semlokest of alle þynge,	*seemliest, most attractive*
He may me blisse bringe,	*"He" can mean "she" in this dialect*
8 Icham in hire baundoun.	*captivity*
An hendy hap ichabbe yhent,	*hendy : pleasant yhent : caught*
Ichot from heuene it is me sent,	*I wot (know)*
From alle wymmen mi loue is lent,	*averted*
12 Ant lyht on Alysoun.	

On heu hire her is fayr ynoh	*she has blond hair*
Hire browe broune, hire ege blake,	
Wiþ lossum chere he on me loh;	*lovesome expression laughed*
16 Wiþ middel smal ant wel ymake.	*made*
Bote he me wolle to hire take	*unless*
Forte buen hire owen make,	*for to be mate*
Longe to lyuen ichulle forsake	
20 Ant feye fallen adoun.	*fey : ready to die*
An hendy hap, *etc.*	

Nihtes when y wende ant wake,	*wind, turn*
Forþi myn wonges waxeþ won,	*my cheeks grow pale*
Leuedi, al for þine sake,	*lady*
24 Longinge is ylent me on.	*come to me*
In world nis non so wyter mon	*wise*
Þat al hire bounte telle con;	
Hire swyre is whittore þen þe swon	*neck*
28 Ant feyrest may in toune.	*maid*
An hendi, *etc.*	

Icham for wowyng al forwake,	*worn out by waking*
Wery so water in wore;	*behind a dam (weir)*
Lest eny reue me my make	*steal mate*
32 Ychabbe yȝyrned ȝore.	*yearned a long time*
Betere is þolien whyle sore	*endure*
Þen mournen euermore;	
Geynest vnder gore,	*fairest under apparel (gear)*
36 Herkne to my roun.	*secret*
An hendi, *etc.*[6]	

83. THE LONDON DIALECT. The dialect from which standard Modern English is derived is basically East Midland, with a fairly strong southern influence, and weaker influences from other parts of the country. This is the dialect of the upper classes of London and its neighborhood, and therefore of the court, the capital, the economic center, the ancient universities, the most influential of the public schools, and the center of the publishing business. The kind of language spoken in any of these places would have had a certain prestige, and the fact that they were all combined in one neighborhood allowed them to reinforce each other. We have already seen that the inevitable emergence of this dialect as the standard language happened late because of the importance of French for several centuries. If it had happened earlier the development would certainly have been somewhat different. London itself was on the border between the southern and the East Midland territories. This location, combined with its political and economic importance, naturally resulted in some shifts in the proportions of its population, and consequently in the nature of its dialect. In the early part of the Middle English period this was distinctly Southern. By Chaucer's time it was basically East Midland, though it still preserved a number of southern features which have since been lost.

It must be emphasized that while this dialect was the ancestor of standard Modern English, it was not yet standardized in the way to which we have since grown accustomed. Its prestige was

[6] Kaiser, p. 466.

sufficient to make many people throughout the country attempt to comply with it, at least in writing. But nobody had yet written its rules; and while some snobs who used it undoubtedly looked down on all outsiders, many of these outsiders were happy and satisfied with their own varieties.

84. THE TEXT OF CHAUCER. It may be well to say a few words about the nature of a modern text of Chaucer before examining a specimen. We have no manuscripts of his work from his own hand, or even from his lifetime; and those manuscripts which we do have, being unusually numerous and from all over the country, show a wild variety of readings. All of them contain some obvious mistakes — a fact which would not have surprised Chaucer in the least. Among his minor poems is one addressed to Adam, his own scribe, calling down a mild curse on him if he doesn't learn to copy more carefully, because Chaucer has to spend so much time correcting his mistakes. And at the end of *Troilus and Criseyde* he sends the book off with a prayer including the lines:

> And for ther is so gret diversite
> In Englissh and in writyng of oure tonge,
> So prey I god that non myswrite the
> Ne the mys-metre for defaute of tonge.

We do not know whether Adam reformed, but other scribes mis-wrote and mismetered the poems so thoroughly that not until the present century was a reasonably satisfactory restoration of the text accomplished.

Not to be too technical, the general procedure has been to study the relations of all the manuscripts. Then the Ellsmere MS, which is generally accepted as the best, is taken as the base, and corrected from other good manuscripts only when there is a very definite reason to believe that their readings are more faithful to the original. (An editor cannot simply take whatever reading he prefers, no matter where he finds it.) The spelling is not corrected simply to achieve consistency (as in the use of *i*'s and *y*'s), but only when it is obviously wrong and interferes with either the sense or the meter. This is particularly important in the matter of final *e*'s, since many which were pronounced as separate syllables in Chaucer's time became silent soon after his death. We do not know just how Chaucer spelled, but he was obviously careful. We can therefore be reasonably sure that he wrote a final *e* only when it was "organic" — that is, when it was still pronounced as a weakened form of an old inflectional ending, or when it had a syllabic value in a French borrowing. But after these organic *e*'s had all become silent, scribes who saw them in old manuscripts had no way of knowing that they had ever been pronounced, and therefore looked on them as mere spelling variants, about which there was no reason for them to be careful. A modern editor must therefore be particularly careful to remove inorganic *e*'s and to restore organic ones whenever possible.

85. SPECIMEN OF CHAUCER. Here are the first eighteen lines of the *Canterbury Tales,* with a phonemic transcription, followed by a rather thorough analysis and some suggestions for profitable study. Lines 19 to 100 are then given with slighter notes.

Whan	that	Aprill	with	his	shoures	soote
hwɑn	ðat	ɑ:pril	wiθ	hiz	ʃu:rəz	so:tə

The	droghte	of	March	hath	perced	to	the	roote,
ðə	dru:xt	ɔf	mɑrtʃ	hɑθ	persəd	to	ðə	ro:tə

And	bathed	every	veyne	in	swich	licour
ɑnd	bɑ:ðəd	evəri	vein	in	switʃ	liku:r

Of	which	vertu	engendred	is	the	flour;
ɔf	hwitʃ	vertju	endʒendrəd	is	ðə	flu:r

Whan	Zephirus	eek	with	his	sweete	breeth
hwɑn	zefirus	e:k	wiθ	hiz	swe:tə	bre:θ

Inspired	hath	in	every	holt	and	heeth
inspi:rəd	hɑθ	in	evəri	holt	ɑnd	he:θ

The	tendre	croppes,	and	the	yonge	sonne
ðə	tendrə	krɔpəz	ɑnd	ðə	juŋgə	sunə

Hath in the Ram his halve cours yronne
haθ in ðə ram hiz halvə kurs irunə

And smale foweles maken melodye,
and smalə fu:ləz ma:kən melodiə

That slepen al the nyght with open ye
ðat sle:pən al ðə ni:xt wiθ opən iə

(So priketh hem nature in hir corages);
so prikəθ hem natju:r in hir koradʒəz

Thanne longen folk to goon on pilgrimages,
ðan lɔŋgən folk to gɔ:n ɔn pilgrimadʒəz

And palmeres for to seken straunge strondes,
and palmerəz fɔr to se:kən straundʒə strɔndəz

To ferne halwes kowthe in sondry londes;
to fernə halwəz ku:θ in sundri lɔndəz

And specially from every shires ende
and spesiali frɔm evəri ʃi:rəz endə

Of Engelond to Caunterbury they wende,
ɔf eŋgəlɔnd to kauntərburi ðei wendə

The hooly blisful martir for to seke
ðə hɔ:li blisful martir fɔr to se:kə

That hem hath holpen whan that they were seeke.
ðat hem haθ holpən hwan ðat ðei wer se:kə

86. CHAUCER'S PHONEMES: CONSONANTS. Chaucer had one consonant which has since been lost, the palatal fricative /x/, spelled *gh*, which is made by raising the tongue so close to the roof of the mouth as almost to make the stop /k/. The sound resulting from the friction in this narrow gap is like that represented by *ch* in German or in Scottish dialect.

His /l/ and /r/ were pronounced rather more clearly than in Modern English, and had less tendency to modify or be modified by neighboring sounds. Thus *talke* is pronounced almost like *talc* plus the schwa sound, rather than as /tɔ:kə/. In such words

as *ferme, first,* and *word* the /r/ is definite and the vowels remain
respectively /e/, /i/, and /o/ instead of all changing to /ə/ as
in the modern derivatives.

Chaucer's other consonants were apparently identical with
ours, except that he probably had no /ʒ/. The distribution of
some sounds was, however, rather different. See below under
Pronunciation.

87. SHORT VOWELS. Chaucer's short vowels were approximately
the same as ours, except that it is generally believed that he had
no /æ/ sound, but pronounced *that,* for instance, as /ðat/ rather
than /ðæt/.

88. LONG VOWELS. Chaucer's long vowels are pronounced more
like those in Spanish or Italian than like the so-called long vowels
of Modern English. As the transcription indicates, it is generally
believed that they really were long vowels rather than diphthongs
— that *me,* for instance, was pronounced /me:/ rather than /mei/.
The /ɑ:/, /i:/, and /u:/ sounds give little trouble. In Middle
English generally there was a distinction between the long open
and close *o* sounds, /ɔ:/ and /o:/, and between the long open
and close *e* sounds, /ɛ:/ (a symbol we have not previously used,
which stands for the vowel sound in *breath*) and /e:/.

89. PRONUNCIATION. To read Chaucer as if his language were
misspelled Modern English is about as satisfying as it would be to
play a Beethoven sonata off-key on a tin whistle. In the first six
lines of the "Prologue," for instance, none of the couplets would
rhyme and no line would have a satisfactory rhythm, to say
nothing of the subtler relations between sound and sense. We
cannot, of course, tell precisely how Chaucer pronounced every
word. He lived in a time and place where pronunciation varied
a good deal, and he certainly did not always pronounce the same
words in the same ways. His poetry is not so fragile that it won't
stand a reasonable degree of variation, but it cannot be successfully distorted into an entirely different system.

The aim of this section is simply to show a beginning student how to make an approximation of a fourteenth-century pronunciation so that he can read Chaucer in a workable way. The differences between the open and close long *e* and *o* sounds are disregarded both here and in the transcription, not because they are not real, but because they are distracting to beginners. If you concentrate on them you are likely to lose too much of the rhythm. Moreover, they are not indicated in most texts, and Chaucer himself often disregarded them. The simplest thing is to pronounce them whichever way seems more natural in a given word — remembering that in a word like *reed* the choice is between /re:d/ and /rɛ:d/ — it can't possibly be /ri:d/, and *rood* can be /ro:d/ or /rɔ:d/, but not /ru:d/.

1. Final *e*'s in native words represent weakened inflectional endings. In words borrowed from French they are syllabic, as they still are in French poetry, though not in prose. Both kinds of *e*'s are normally pronounced, though with the value of /ə/ rather than /e/. Failing to pronounce them when required will do more than anything else to destroy the rhythm. They are, however, light syllables, and should never be exaggerated. Moreover, they are normally elided when immediately followed by a word beginning with a vowel or an *h,* and often when followed by a word beginning with a *w.* If they occur at the end of a line they should be pronounced regardless of the sound with which the next line begins. This may sound rather complicated, but if you remember that Chaucer's verse, though not rigidly regular, is pretty dependably rhythmical, you won't make many mistakes if you pronounce them lightly wherever they seem to fit naturally into the metrical pattern.

2. In familiar words vowels usually have the same length as in their modern form. The one important exception is that words from French are stressed on the last full syllable, as in *couráge* and *melodíe,* and the vowels in these syllables preserve a length that has been lost with the shift of the stress forward. In unfamiliar words a vowel is usually short when it is followed by two

different consonants, a double consonant, or a final single consonant. It is always short when it is unstressed. Otherwise it is usually long.

3. The short *u* should be pronounced as in *put* rather than as in *but*. Moreover, an *o* was often written instead of a *u* when it came next to *m, n,* or *v,* to avoid confusion growing out of the peculiarities of medieval handwriting. Thus such words as *love, some,* and *sun* are pronounced with a *u* rather than an *o* sound, regardless of how they are spelled. Otherwise all the short vowels may be pronounced as in Modern English.

4. The long vowels are pronounced as follows:

lady	rhymes approximately with modern *body*			
me	"	"	"	"	*hay*
I	"	"	"	"	*see*
good	"	"	"	"	*toad*
muse	"	"	"	"	*refuse a*

Since the Old English long *u* was already represented by the vowel-digraph *ou,* the *u* with a long sound occurs only in words from French.

5. The letters *i* and *y* are interchangeable, and so are the letters *u* and *w* when they occur as the second element of a diphthong. *Ai* and *ei* regularly rhyme, but scholars disagree as to whether they should be pronounced as in modern *day* or *die,* or somewhere in between. Without argument, but because some choice is necessary, the *day* pronunciation is used in this book.

au normally had the value of *ow* in modern *how.* It may have had a slightly different value when followed by *n.*

ou represents several different sounds, and the best clue to its value in any word is the modern pronunciation of that word. When the modern sound is /ɑu/, as in *now* and *ground,* the Middle English sound was /u:/. When the modern sound is /ou/ as in *soul* or *grow,* or /ɔ:/ as in *thought,* the Middle English word may be pronounced with the same value: *soule*-/soulə/, *growen*-/grouən/, *thoughte*-/θɔ:xtə/.

eu has the value of the now unfamiliar combination /eu:/ thus *few* is pronounced /feu/ rather than /fju/.

6. Final *s* is voiceless in stressed syllables. *Was* rhymes with *glas*(s).

7. The initial combinations *gn,* *kn,* and *wr* are fully pronounced.

8. Students who know French should resist the temptation to pronounce Chaucer's borrowings from that language as in modern French. The letter *j* and the combinations *ch, ge,* and *vowel plus nasal* indicate the same sounds in borrowed as in native words. French, too, has changed in the past six hundred years.

90. VOCABULARY. Many of Chaucer's words have come down to us with no noticeable change, others with changes so slight that they are easy to recognize. Ability to see through changes and identify words varies greatly, but practice and technique will help anybody. Consider line 3:

> And bathed every veyne in swich licour

Four of the words are identical in spelling with their modern forms, and thus easy to recognize however you pronounce them:

> And bathed every _____ in _____ _____

Some students will immediately recognize two others, *veyne* and *licour*. Others will not be able to identify these words by their eyes alone; but if they take the trouble to pronounce them they will see that *veyne* might be either *vein* or *vain*, or perhaps even *vane*, while *licour* must be either *liquor* or *liqueur*..

The best way to decide between these possibilities is to pronounce the words in context rather than in isolation. It then seems obvious that *veyne* must be *vein* and *licour* must refer to the sap running through it. If you know that *liquor* was formerly used where we now use *liquid*, the problem is solved. If you don't know that, but can figure out that *liquor* is even now a more general term than *liqueur* and used to be more general still, you have learned something. Sometimes it is worth confirming these shifts in meaning by using a glossary or dictionary, but often you can be confident that a meaning you had never connected with a word *must* be intended in a given passage because:

First, it seems like a reasonable variation of a familiar meaning; and *second*, it is the only such variation that makes sense in the context.

Unless both these things are true, you had better look up the word. But if both *are* true, you had better *not* look it up. You are learning to react directly to the author's language, and it is better to develop confidence in your ability to do this, even if you make an occasional mistake, than to be overcautious.

The still unidentified word in line 3, *swich*, is a little harder. If you pronounce it alone you get nothing but *switch*, which makes no sense here. If you pronounce the whole line you may guess that the nearest reasonable word is *such*, which is right. If you haven't managed this guess there is no reason for shame.

There are a number of other words in the passage which you should have a fair chance of recognizing through the unfamiliar spellings, particularly if you read and pronounce them in context rather than in isolation. Thus *Aprill* guarantees the meaning of *shoures*, and if it is with these that the *droghte* of March has been *perced*, March must have been dry. The two words *flour* and *sonne* are worth special consideration, because our first impression is likely to be misleading, and our second may well be that Chaucer is mistakenly using the wrong homonyms. But the habit of distinguishing in spelling between such pairs as *son-sun* and *flour-flower* is not only later than Chaucer's time but a completely artificial device which we now use erratically and sparingly, though we are accustomed to think of it as very important when we do use it. *Flour* began simply as "the *flower* of the grain," just as we can still speak of "the *cream* of the crop" — and we do not use a special spelling for that metaphor. *Son* and *sun* are of different origins but have become exact homonyms, just like hundreds of other pairs which we do not distinguish in spelling. Of course we'd better follow the established conventions in Modern English, but it saves confusion if we remember that they did not exist in the fourteenth century.

With such words as *al* (*all*), *nyght* (*night*), *slepen* (*sleep*), and *smale* (*small*) simple recognition is enough, but with others some adjustment in meaning is needed. *Vertu*, for instance, is not used in its most usual modern sense, but as in the phrase "by *virtue* of." *Foweles* is not limited to barnyard birds, nor *corages* to heart-felt feelings of bravery. *Palmeres* were not card-sharps, but travelers who proved they had been to the Holy Land by bringing back palm-leaf souvenirs. An Irishman would recognize *strondes* (*strands*) as meaning *shores* more readily than an American; and not everybody who celebrates *halloween* knows that this means the night before All *Hallows* (*Saints*) Day. The clue to *kowthe* is the negative form *uncouth* — by etymology simply "unknown," but with its original meaning now transformed by natural snobbery.

Some of the words may cause even more trouble. It is not easy to recognize *soote* as *sweet*, especially when *sweete* occurs four lines below. But if you ask the natural question, "Why did Chaucer use the two different forms?" try to ask it without indignation. Indignation interferes enormously with language learning. He probably used the two forms because he heard them both every day, and he selected whichever seemed to him to sound better in a particular line. *Soote* of course rhymes with *roote;* and the repetition of vowel sounds in *sweete breeth,* while not necessary, is at least to some ears more attractive than *soote breeth.* It is really quite unlikely that Chaucer was deliberately playing a nasty trick on a later generation.

You may well find that you cannot connect *holt* (*grove*) and *eek* (*also*) with anything you know, or recognize the *Ram* as one of the signs of the zodiac, to which you have perhaps been giving little thought lately. It will be natural for you to identify *croppes* with modern *crops,* though if it occurs to you that holts and heaths are curious places for them to be growing you may look the word up and discover that it meant *shoots*. At first *yronne* may look like about the way you'd expect Chaucer to spell *iron*, but you'll soon learn that *y-*, like Old English and German *ge-*, is often a prefix indicating a past participle.

At any rate, the best way to think of Middle English is as a foreign language to which you are lucky enough to have a great many clues, rather than as English which an evil conspiracy has messed up beyond convenient recognition. You may well think that in the last few paragraphs we have been overdoing the clue business, and that it would be much easier simply to look up all the troublesome words in a glossary. This is true; but in the long run it wouldn't be nearly so profitable. To memorize the translation of a few lines is a basically childish procedure. To learn to read those same lines is a considerable step toward a worthy accomplishment. For the first few pages it is a job of considerable difficulty for almost anybody. But if you do it intelligently, so that you are learning something about the language as you go along, and not merely trying to find modern equivalents for the unfamiliar words, your speed and ease of reading will increase at a quite surprising rate. A good memory is of course most useful in language learning, but deliberate memorizing should be reserved for rather important occasions when nothing else will serve. Take the two words *eek* (*also*) and *holt* (*grove*). If you know German you can connect *eek* with *auch* and *holt* with *holtz*, and you will probably never forget them. If you don't, you might pause to think that if you *eke out* something you do it by using something else *also*. And if this is too forced, spend a few moments trying to get it fixed in your memory, because it is obviously a useful word that is likely to appear often. If you forget *holt*, you can afford to, because it may be quite a while before you see it again. In short,

First, try to connect every new word with something you already know.

Second, make a special effort with words that seem likely to occur frequently.

91. GRAMMATICAL STRUCTURE. By the fourteenth century a good many inflectional endings had either disappeared completely or had been worn down to a few blurred and often ambiguous forms. The fact that this weakening of inflections went so far before the standard word-order that was to replace them had fully developed causes some trouble, but not very often. There are, however, a few points that it is distinctly helpful to bear in mind.

92. NOUNS. The stān declension of Old English became simplified and almost completely generalized during the Middle English period. Originally, as we have seen (page 74), it was declined as follows:

	Singular	*Plural*
Nominative and Accusative	stān	stānas
Genitive	stānes	stāna
Dative	stāne	stānum

By Chaucer's time it had reached its modern state except for some differences in the convention of writing. Thus:

	Singular	*Plural*
Common case	ston	
Genitive case	stones	all cases stones

1. The long *a*, here as elsewhere, changed to a long open *o*, and somewhat later to a long close *o*. The length might or might not be indicated in the spelling.

2. The dative case dropped out of general use, and was preserved only in a few set phrases known as *petrified datives*. Thus Chaucer says *to bedde* instead of *to bed*. Perhaps the most interesting example of this construction is *on live* (meaning *in life*), from which we get the modern form *alive*. The vowel of the dative is preserved, and the /f/ had been voiced to a /v/ because of its intervocalic position.

3. Because of the general weakening of the vowels in endings, *stonas* came to be pronounced, and therefore spelled, like *stones*.

4. Since both the genitive singular and the common plural form now ended in *-es*, it was natural to extend this form to the genitive plural which had originally lacked the *s*. The convention of using apostrophes to make a visual distinction between the audially identical forms *stones, stone's,* and *stones'* did not develop until much later.

Although most of the words which had originally belonged to other declensions had been attracted to the *stone* pattern, with the *s* in both the genitive and the plural, a number still resisted. Thus Chaucer says "his lady grace" (line 88) where we should now use *lady's,* and "his hors were goode" (line 74) where we should use *horses.* He also uses many more plurals in *-en* than have survived. In some other Middle English texts these *-en* plurals are even more widespread. In fact, in early Southern texts so many nouns have this form that it, rather than the *-s* plural, might have been expected to become general.

93. PRONOUNS. Among the personal pronouns Chaucer uses *ich* and occasionally *ik* as well as *I* in the first person; *his* for *its* (which had not yet been invented); and *hem* and *hire* or *here* for *them* and *their.* He also uses a few contractions not immediately obvious. Thus *art thou* and *hast thou* may appear as *artow* and *hastow,* and *so thee ich* as *so theech* (for "so may I thrive" — *thee* here is a verb, not a pronoun). In other texts so many forms of the pronouns appear that it would not be profitable to discuss them here.

94. ADJECTIVES. The very highly inflected Old English adjectives had been simplified to a maximum of two forms in each degree — one with and one without a final *-e.* The final *-e* could be used when the adjective was in weak position or when it agreed with a noun in the plural; but this form disappeared in the fifteenth century.

95. VERBS. Old English had ten major classes of verbs, seven strong and three weak, with variations in each class that occurred when neighboring sounds influenced each other in various ways. A natural result was that speakers often made mistakes in their use. Our grammatical habits are pretty largely based on analogy, and when too many conflicting analogies are possible, some confusion is bound to result. During the Middle English period a very considerable modification of the old inflections took place in a very irregular fashion. Since the weak verbs were much more numerous than the strong ones, and also more nearly regular, it was easier for them to survive, and this is on the whole what happened.

About half of the 312 strong verbs in Old English have completely disappeared. This does not prove anything, because a great many words of all sorts have given way to synonyms. But half of the remaining ones have shifted to the weak conjugation, which does show the force of the more general analogy. And many of those which are still strong do not have the forms which would normally have developed, but different ones caused by mistaken analogy with other verbs. All these tendencies began during the Old English period and continued during the Modern period; but the confusion of forms was particularly acute in Middle English.

There was also a considerable confusion of the inflectional endings. In Chaucer's usage the *að* ending of the present indicative plural has disappeared, and the *-en* ending, which was originally used only in the subjunctive, has taken its place. Moreover, the infinitive ending in *-an* and the past indicative plural ending in *-on* have been weakened to *-en*. And finally, this new all-purpose ending is in the process of further weakening, so that in any of its uses it can appear as either *-en* or simply *-e*. Thus we have the infinitive *to seken* in line 13, but *to seke* in line 17, and the past indicative plural as *they weren* in line 40, but *they were* in line 41. As past participles we have *holpen* (line 18), *spoken* (line 31), and *riden* (line 48) in contrast with *come* (line 23), *yronne* (line 8), and *yfalle* (line 25). And the prefix *y-* (from Old English *ge-*) which appears in the last two of these, is as optional as the final *-n*. Thus, though the form is *come* in line 23, it is *ycome* in line 77. It is perhaps worth special mention that *been* appears as an infinitive (*to been*) and indicative (*they been*) as well as a participle.

This may sound like a very confusing state of affairs, but it needn't be. After all, in Modern English we say *to put, they put* (present or past), and *they have put,* and ambiguity very seldom results. Once we realize that Chaucer's *-e* and *-en* endings are versatile, they give very little trouble.

Chaucer does, however, preserve the *-(e)st* ending in the second person and the *-(e)th* ending in the third person of the present indicative, in contrast with the *-e* ending of the present subjunctive.

In some of the other Middle English dialects the verb endings were quite different. They will be discussed later in order to avoid confusion here.

96. NEGATIVES. The Middle English use of negatives is quite different from ours. In the first place, the theory that "two negatives make an affirmative" (which is reasonably true of classical Latin) had not yet been misapplied to English. As long as they were used with different words, negatives reinforced rather than canceled each other (as most of us still feel that they do, even though we have been trained not to use them that way ourselves). Thus in lines 70–71 we find:

> He *nevere* yet *no* vileynye *ne* sayde
> In al his lyf unto *no* maner wight.

Notice also that here the simple negative is *ne*, as it usually is at this time, though the stronger *nat* is also found. *Ne* may also mean *nor*, and *ne . . . ne* regularly means *neither . . . nor*.

Chaucer also uses such forms as *nis*, *nadde*, and *nolde* where we use *isn't, hadn't,* and *wouldn't.* In other words, with the common auxiliary verbs beginning with a vowel or the weak consonants *h* and *w*, the contraction was formed from *ne* plus the verb rather than from the verb plus a weakened form of *not*. Thus *nis* is equivalent to *is not, nas* to either *has not* or *was not*, and *nere to were not*. The only remnant of this construction that has survived is the phrase *willy-nilly*, from *will he, nill he — whether he wants to or not*.

A change in such a fundamental construction as this is most unusual. It may be explained by the fact that *not* began as a weakened form of *naught*, which in turn is a condensed form of the phrase *ne a wiht*, meaning *not a bit*. We usually put a modifying phrase after a verb rather than before it; and even when the phrase was condensed beyond recognition, the inherited order apparently seemed more natural, just as even today *he cares not* seems more normal than *he not cares*, though neither is the usual expression.

97. IMPERSONAL CONSTRUCTIONS are much more common in Middle than in Modern English. Compare the following expressions:

> He will do it   if he pleases.
> if he likes.
> if it pleases him.
> if it suits him.

The four *if* clauses have roughly the same meaning, but two of them have *he*, representing the person concerned, as the subject; the other two have the impersonal *it* as the subject, and indicate the person concerned by *him*, used as an indirect object. You will notice that *pleases* can be used either way, but *likes* can now have only the personal subject, and *suits* (in this sense) only the impersonal one.

In Chaucer's time, with the word order still unfixed and the inflections more important, it was possible to say either "If it please him" or "If him please." Anybody could see that *him* could not be the subject, and the impersonal subject *it* could be omitted. And when *ye* was strictly the subject form and *you* the object

form, "If *you* please" was clearly parallel to "If *him* please." But
when *you* came to be used for all purposes and the modern
word-order became normal, *you* looked like the subject of *please;*
and a little later *him* in such a sentence began to seem unnatural,
and was replaced by *he.* Now if we want to keep the expression
impersonal we have to use four words instead of three and say
"If it pleases him." We usually don't do this with *please;* and
with *like,* and a number of other verbs, we never do; but Chaucer
and his contemporaries did, and we have to be alert for such
expressions as *him list* (it pleases him), *him repenteth,* and *me
thinketh,* (It seems to me).

With this much general preparation it should be possible to
read the next eighty-two lines with slighter notes.

> Bifil that in that seson on a day,
> In Southwerk at the Tabard as I lay   20
> Redy to wenden on my pilgrymage
> To Caunterbury with ful devout corage,
> At nyght was come into that hostelrye
> Wel nyne and twenty in a compaignye,
> Of sondry folk, by aventure yfalle   25
> In felaweshipe, and pilgrimes were they alle,
> That toward Caunterbury wolden ryde.
> The chambres and the stables weren wyde,
> And wel we weren esed atte beste.
> And shortly, whan the sonne was to reste,   30
> So hadde I spoken with hem everichon
> That I was of hir felaweshipe anon,
> And made forward erly for to ryse,
> To take oure wey ther as I yow devyse.
> But nathelees, whil I have tyme and space,   35
> Er that I ferther in this tale pace,
> Me thynketh it acordaunt to resoun
> To telle yow al the condicioun
> Of ech of hem, so as it semed me,
> And whiche they weren, and of what degree,   40
> And eek in what array that they were inne;
> And at a knyght than wol I first bigynne.
> A KNYGHT ther was, and that a worthy man,
> That fro the tyme that he first bigan

To riden out, he loved chivalrie,   45
Trouthe and honour, fredom and curteisie.
Ful worthy was he in his lordes werre,
And therto hadde he riden, no man ferre,
As wel in cristendom as in hethenesse,
And evere honoured for his worthynesse.   50
At Alisaundre he was whan it was wonne.
Ful ofte tyme he hadde the bord bigonne
Aboven alle nacions in Pruce;
In Lettow hadde he reysed and in Ruce,
No Cristen man so ofte of his degree.   55
In Gernade at the seege eek hadde he be
Of Algezir, and riden in Belmarye.
At Lyeys was he and at Satalye,
Whan they were wonne; and in the Grete See
At many a noble armee hadde he be.   60
At mortal batailles hadde he been fiftene,
And foughten for oure feith at Tramyssene
In lystes thries, and ay slayn his foo.
This ilke worthy knyght hadde been also
Somtyme with the lord of Palatye   65
Agayn another hethen in Turkye.
And everemoore he hadde a sovereyn prys;
And though that he were worthy, he was wys,
And of his port as meeke as is a mayde.
He nevere yet no vileynye ne sayde   70
In al his lyf unto no maner wight.
He was a verray, parfit, gentil knyght.
But, for to tellen yow of his array,
His hors were goode, but he was nat gay.
Of fustian he wered a gypon   75
Al bismotered with his habergeon,
For he was late ycome from his viage,
And wente for to doon his pilgrymage.
    With hym ther was his sone, a yong SQUIER,
A lovyere and a lusty bacheler,   80
With lokkes crulle as they were leyd in presse.
Of twenty yeer of age he was, I gesse.
Of his stature he was of evene lengthe,
And wonderly delyvere, and of greet strengthe.
And he hadde been somtyme in chyvachie   85
In Flaundres, in Artoys, and Pycardie,

And born hym weel, as of so litel space,
In hope to stonden in his lady grace.
Embrouded was he, as it were a meede
Al ful of fresshe floures, whyte and reede.   90
Syngynge he was, or floytynge, al the day;
He was as fressh as is the month of May.
Short was his gowne, with sleves longe and wyde.
Wel koude he sitte on hors and faire ryde.
He koude songes make and wel endite,   95
Juste and eek daunce, and weel purtreye and write.
So hoote he lovede that by nyghtertale
He sleep namoore than dooth a nyghtyngale.
Curteis he was, lowely, and servysable,
And carf biforn his fader at the table.[7]   100

    20.   *Tabard:* an inn.

    23.   *was come:* In Middle English, as in French and German, *be* rather than *have* is the auxiliary used with verbs of motion and change of condition.

    25.   *aventure: chance* rather than *adventure.* Many of Chaucers' borrowings from French have meanings which have been retained in that language but lost in Modern English.

    29.   *atte:* a contraction of *at the.*

    31.   *everichon:* every one.

    33.   *forward:* agreement for future action.

    34.   *ther:* where. The originally demonstrative pronoun forms (beginning with /ð/) were all used in a relative sense before the originally interrogative forms (beginning with /hw/) took over this function.

    37.   *Me thynketh:* not baby talk, but an impersonal construction meaning literally "it seems to me." In Old English *þencean* (think) and *þincean* (seem) were distinct verbs, but they became homonyms in Middle English.

    48.   *ferre:* farther.

    51–59.   The knight had fought in all the most distant campaigns available in Chaucer's time. Place names are among the most reasonable words to forget.

    52.   *the bord bigonne:* sat in the place of honor at a banquet.

    54.   *reysed:* traveled.

    55.   *degree:* rank.

[7] F. N. Robinson, *The Complete Works of Geoffrey Chaucer,* 2nd Edition (Houghton Mifflin Co., Boston, 1957).

60. *armee:* a military expedition rather than organization.

63. *lystes:* single mounted combat. Literally, the enclosed space in which combats took place.

67. *sovereyn pris:* a high reputation, not a prize worth $2.80.

68. *worthy:* brave; *wys:* prudent, the opposite of reckless.

69. *port:* way of carrying himself.

70. *vileynye:* churlish talk.

72. Notice the comma after *verray.* At this period *very* was simply an adjective, meaning *true.* Since it was often, as here, used as the first adjective in a series, it gradually came to be understood as an adverbial intensifier of the following adjectives.

74. *hors:* unchanged plural.

75. *fustian:* coarse cloth; *gypon:* tunic.

76. *bismotered:* besmutted; *habergeon:* coat of chain mail.

80. *lusty bacheler:* happy young aspirant for knighthood.

81. *crulle: curly.* Notice the metathesis.

83. *evene:* average.

84. *delyvere:* agile.

85. *chyvachie:* approximately "rough-riding." Like *chivalrie* this comes from a late Latin word for *horse.* The noble class did their fighting on horseback. *Chivalrie* refers to the ethical and social implications of this fact, *chyvachie* to the physical.

88. *lady grace: lady* is genitive, but this word had not yet fallen into the *stone* declension.

89. *Embrouded:* with all the bright colors of embroidery; *meede:* meadow.

91. *floytynge:* whistling, or perhaps playing the flute.

95. *make:* compose the tunes; *endite:* compose the words.

96. *Juste:* practice mounted combat with a spear.

97. *nyghtertale:* night time.

100. *fader:* not a corruption, but the original form. The /ð/ in the modern word is not a result of Grimm's Law, but of two other changes which happened to work out to the same result.

98. THE MORTE DARTHUR. Sir Thomas Malory's romance *The Morte Darthur* is the only long prose work in Middle English that is still widely read. The syntax is often, by modern standards, regrettably loose; but though many of the sentences would be hard to parse, their meaning is usually clear. Students may find it helpful to review the section on Middle English spelling (pages 133–135) before attempting this passage. Here as elsewhere

many words that seem strange to the eye become clear when read aloud in context.

And thus they fought all the longe day, and neuer stynted tylle þe noble knyȝtes were layde to the colde erthe. And euer they fought stylle tylle hit was nere nyȝt, and by than was þere an hondred thousand leyde dede vppon the erthe. Than was kynge Arthure wode wrothe oute of mesure, whan he saw hys people so   5
slayne frome hym. And so he loked aboute hym and cowde se no mo of all hys oste and good knyȝtes leffte, no mo on lyve but two knyȝtes: the tone was sir Lucan de Buttler and hys brother sir Bedwere; and yette they were full sore wounded.

'Jesu mercy!' seyde the kynge, 'where ar all my noble knyȝtes   10
becom? Alas, that euer I shulde se thys doleful day; for now,' seyde kynge Arthur, 'I am com to myne ende. But wolde to god,' seyde he, 'that I wyste now where were that traytoure sir Mordred that hath caused all thys myschyff.'

Than kynge Arthur loked aboute and was ware where stood   15
sir Mordred leanyng vppon hys swerde amonge a grete hepe of dede men.

'Now gyff me my speare,' seyde kynge Arthure vnto sir Lucan, 'for yondir I haue aspyed þe traytoure that all thys woo hath wrought.' 'Sir, latte hym be,' seyde sir Lucan, 'for he ys vnhappy.   20
And yf ye passe this vnhappy day, ye shall be ryȝt well revenged. And, good lord, remembre ye of your nyȝtes dreme and what the spyryte of sir Gawayne tolde you tonyȝt, and yet god of hys grete goodnes hath preserved you hyddirto. And for goddes sake, my lorde, leve of thys; for, blyssed be god, ye haue won the fylde. For   25
yet we ben here three on lyve, and with sir Mordred ys nat one on lyve. And therefore if ye leve of now, thys wycked day of desteny ys paste.'

'Now tyde me dethe, tyde me lyff,' seyde the kyng, 'now I se hym yondir alone, he shall neuer ascape myne hondes! For   30
at a bettir avayle shall I neuer haue hym.' 'God spyede you well!' seyde sir Bedyvere.

Than the kynge gate his speare in bothe hys hondis, and ran towarde sir Mordred, cryyng and saying: 'Traytoure, now ys thy dethe-day com!' And whan sir Mordred saw kynge Arthur, he ran   35
vntyll hym with hys swerde drawyn in his honde, and þere kyng Arthur smote sir Mordred vndir the shylde with a foyne of hys speare, thorowoute the body more than a fadom. And whan sir

Mordred felte that he had hys dethys wounde, he threste hymselff
with the myȝt that he had vpp to the burre of kyng Arthurs speare,   40
and ryȝt so he smote hys fadir, kynge Arthure, with hys swerde
holdynge in both hys hondys, vppon the syde of the hede, that
the swerde perced the helmet and the tay of the brayne. And
þerewith Mordred daysshed downe starke dede to the erthe.

And noble kynge Arthure felle in a swoughe to the erthe,   45
and þere he sowned oftyntymys; and sir Lucan and sir Bedwere
offtetymys hove hym vp. And so waykly betwyxte them they lad
hym to a lytyll chapell nat farre frome the see; and whan the
kyng was there, hym thought hym resonabely eased. Than harde
they people crye in the fylde. 'Now go thou, sir Lucan,' seyde   50
the kyng, 'and do me to wyte what betokyns that noyse in the
fylde.' So sir Lucan departed; for he was grevously wounded
in many placis; and so as he yode he saw and harkened by þe
moonelyȝt how that pyllours and robbers were com into the fylde
to pylle and to robbe many a full noble knyȝt of brochys and   55
bees and of many a good rynge and many a ryche juell. And who
that were nat dede all oute, þere they slew them for their harneys
and their ryches.

Whan sir Lucan vndirstood thys warke, he cam to the kynge
as sone as he myȝt, and tolde hym all what he had harde and   60
seyne. 'Þerefore be my rede,' seyde sir Lucan, 'hit ys beste that we
brynge you to som towne.' 'I wolde hit were so,' seyde the kynge,
'but I may nat stonde; my hede worchys so. A, sir Launcelot,'
seyde kynge Arthure, 'thys day haue I sore myssed the! And alas,
that euer I was ayenste the! For now haue I my dethe, where-of   65
sir Gawayne me warned in my dreame.'

Than sir Lucan toke vp the kynge the tone party and sir
Bedwere the othir parte, and in the lyfftyng vp the kynge sowned,
and in the lyfftynge sir Lucan felle in a sowne, that parte of hys
guttis felle oute of hys bodye, and þerewith þe noble knyȝt hys   70
harte braste. And whan the kynge awoke, he behylde sir Lucan,
how he lay fomyng at the mowth and parte of his guttes lay at
hys fyete.

'Alas,' seyde the kynge, 'thys ys to me a fulle hevy syȝt,
to se thys noble deuke so dye for my sake; for he wold haue   75
holpyn me that had more nede of helpe than I! Alas, that he
wolde nat complayne hym, for hys harte was so sette to helpe me.
Now Jesu haue mercy vppon hys soule!' Than sir Bedwere wepte
for the deth of hys brothir. 'Now leve thys mournynge and wep-

yng, jantyll knyʒt,' seyde the kyng, 'for all thys woll nat avayle   80
me. For wyte thou well, and I myʒt lyve myselff, þe dethe of sir
Lucan wolde greve me euermore. But my tyme passyth on faste,'
seyde the kynge. 'Þerefore,' seyde kynge Arthur vnto sir Bedwere,
'take thou here Excaliber, my good swerde, and go wyth hit to
yondir watirs syde; and whan thou commyste þere, I charge the   85
throw my swerde in þat water, and com agayne and telle me what
thou syeste þere.' 'My lorde,' seyde sir Bedwere, 'youre commaundement shall be done, and lyʒtly I brynge you worde
agayne.'

So sir Bedwere departed. And by the way he behylde that   90
noble swerde, and the pomell and the hauffte was all precious
stonys. And than he seyde to hymsellf: 'If I throw thys ryche
swerde in the water, þereof shall neuer com good, but harme and
losse.' And than sir Bedwere hyd Excalyber vndir a tre, and so
as sone as he myʒt he cam agayne vnto the kynge and seyde he   95
had bene at the watir and had throwen the swerde into the watir.

'What sawe thou þere?' seyde the kynge. 'Sir,' he seyde, 'I
saw nothyng but wawis and wyndys.' 'That ys vntruly seyde
of the,' seyde the kynge. 'And þerefore go thou lyʒtly agayne,
and do my commaundemente! As thou arte to me lyff and dere,   100
spare nat, but throw hit in!'

Than sir Bedwere returned agayne, and toke the swerde in
hys honde; and yet hym thought synne and shame to throw away
that noble swerde. And so effte he hyd the swerde and returned
agayne and tolde the kynge that he had bene at the watir and   105
done hys commaundement.

'What sawist thou þere?' seyde the kynge. 'Sir,' he seyde, 'I
sy nothynge but watirs wap and wawys wanne.' 'A, traytour vnto
me and vntrew,' seyde kyng Arthure, 'now hast thou betrayed
me twyse! Who wolde wene that thou that hast bene to me so leve   110
and dere, and also named so noble a knyʒt, that thou wolde betray
me for þe ryches of thys swerde? But now go agayn lyʒtly; for
thy longe taryynge puttith me in grete jouperte of my lyff, for
I haue takyn colde. And but if thou do now as I bydde the, if
euer I may se the, I shall sle the myne owne hondis, for thou   115
woldist for my rych swerde se me dede.'

Than sir Bedwere departed and wente to the swerde and lyʒtly
toke hit vp; and so he wente vnto the watirs syde. And þere
he bounde þe gyrdyll aboute the hyltis, and threw the swerde
as farre into the watir as he myʒt. And þere cam an arme and   120

an honde aboue the watir, and toke hit, and cley3t hit, and
shoke hit thryse and braundysshed, and than vanysshed with
the swerde into the watir.

So sir Bedyvere cam agayne to the kynge and tolde hym
what he saw. 'Alas,' seyde the kynge, 'helpe me hens; for I   125
drede me I haue taryed ouer longe.' Than sir Bedwere toke
the kynge vppon hys bak and so wente with hym to the watirs
syde. And whan they were þere, evyn faste by the banke hoved
a lytyll barge wyth many fayre ladyes in hit; and amonge hem
all was a quene. And all they had blak hoodis; and all they wepte   130
and shryked, whan they saw kynge Arthur.

'Now put me into that barge,' seyde the kynge. And so he
ded sofftely; and þere resceyved hym three ladyes with grete
mournyng. And so they sette hem downe, and in one of their
lappis kyng Arthure layde hys hede. And than the quene sayde: 135
'A, my dere brothir! Why haue ye taryed so longe frome me?
Alas, thys wounde on youre hede hath caught ouermuch coulde!'
And anone they rowed fromward the londe.

And sir Bedyvere behylde all tho ladyes go frowarde hym.
Than sir Bedwere cryed and seyde: 'A, my lorde Arthur, what   140
shall becom of me, now ye go frome me and leve me here alone
amonge myne enemyes?' 'Comforte thyselff,' seyde the kynge,
'and do as well as thou mayste; for in me ys no truste for to
truste in. For I muste into the vale of Avylyon to hele me of
my grevous wounde. And if thou here neuermore of me, pray for   145
my soule!'

But euer the quene and ladyes wepte and shryked, that hit
was pite to hyre. And as sone as sir Bedwere had loste the
sy3t of þe barge, he wepte and wayled; and so toke the foreste,
and wente all that ny3t. And in the mornyng he was ware be-   150
twyxte two holtis hore of a chapell and an ermytage. Than was
sir Bedwere fayne, and thyder he wente; and whan he cam into
the chapell, he saw where lay an ermyte grovelynge on all four,
faste þereby a tumbe was newe gravyn.

Whan the ermyte saw sir Bedyvere, he knewe hym well, for   155
he was but lytyll tofore bysshop of Caunturbery that sir Mordred fleamed. 'Sir,' seyde sir Bedyvere, 'what man ys þere
here entyred, that ye pray so faste fore?' 'Fayre sunne,' seyde
the ermyte, 'I wote nat veryly but by demynge. But thys same
ny3t at mydny3t here cam a numbir of ladyes and brought here   160
a dede corse, and prayde me to entyre hym. And here they

offird an hondred tapers, and they gaff me a thousande besauntes.'
'Alas,' seyde sir Bedyvere, 'that was my lorde kynge Arthur,
whych lyethe here gravyn in thys chapell!'

Than sir Bedwere sowned; and whan he awooke, he prayde 165
the ermyte that he myȝt abyde with hym stylle, þere to lyve with
fastynge and prayers. 'For from hens woll I neuer go,' seyde sir
Bedyvere, 'be my wyll, but all the dayes of my lyff here to pray
for my lorde Arthur.[8]

   1.   *stynted:* stopped
   5.   *wode:* wild
   8.   *the tone:* that one
 13.   *wyste:* knew
 14.   *myschyff:* much stronger than the modern word
 20.   *vnhappy:* unlucky
 27.   *of:* off
 29.   *tyde:* betide
 37.   *foyne:* thrust
 40.   *burre:* the protective enlargement just before the grip
 43.   *tay:* case
 45.   *swoughe:* swoon
 46.   *sowned:* swooned
 49.   *hym thought hym:* it seemed to him (or perhaps *them*)
that he was
 51.   *do me to wyte:* let me know
 53.   *yode:* old past tense of go, with the meaning *walked*
 56.   *bees:* armbands
 61.   *rede:* advice
 81.   *and:* if
 88.   *lyȝtly:* quickly
 91.   *pomell, hauffte:* the *pommel* is the knob at the end of the
haft (grip)
 98.   *wawis: waves*
100.   *lyff:* lief, synonymous with *dear*
104.   *effte:* again
108.   *watirs wap and wawys wanne:* waters quivered and
waves turned white
110.   *wene:* think
121.   *cleyȝt:* gripped
125.   *hens:* the final *s* is voiceless

[8] Kaiser, p. 561–563.

150. *wente:* walked
151. *holtis hore:* ancient groves
152. *fayne:* glad
154. *gravyn:* dug
157. *fleamed:* put to flight
158. *entyred:* interred
159. *demynge:* judging
162. *besauntes:* gold coins

CHAPTER SIX

The English Renaissance

99. EARLY MODERN ENGLISH. The period from 1500 to 1650 is often called the English Renaissance, and the language of this period is known as Early Modern English. The dates are of course arbitrary, but they will do as well as any others to bound the era during which our language took on most of its present characteristics. Most modern students simply cannot read the language of 1450 without either special training or considerable editorial assistance, but before 1550 they can find a good deal of material which they can handle without difficulty. We cannot reasonably suppose that during the intervening century the language habits of the whole country changed quite so rapidly as the differences in the preserved writing seem to indicate, but a number of forces were working together to cause a rather decided break about this time. These include the rapid spread of education, a loosening in the class structure of society, the introduction of printing, and the growing belief that the development of the language could and should be controlled. The first three of these we can consider only very briefly, but we must examine the last more carefully, since it added a new dimension to the language. It is not much of an oversimplification to say that during the Old and Middle English periods the language

just happened, while during the entire Modern period its development has been considerably modified by efforts (sometimes misguided) at conscious direction. From this time on it is necessary to consider attitudes toward the language as a part of its functioning machinery, along with the more obvious elements such as sounds and inflections.

During this period the changes in inflections were comparatively slight, but the changes in pronunciation were considerable, and the enlargement of the vocabulary was enormous. There were also some very important developments along what might be called the borderline between grammar and rhetoric. As English became a more responsible language the habit of using more sophisticated and better articulated sentences became fairly general. It is very difficult to decide how far changes of this last sort should be attributed to the language itself, and how far simply to the skill of particular writers in using it; for habits of sentence construction are likely to vary more from person to person than any other element of a language. In order to communicate at all we have to stay pretty close together in our pronunciation, our vocabulary, and those inflections which have an actual signalling value; but the skill with which we fit our words together in order to convey the relations between ideas varies enormously — and of course depends at least as much on our ability to grasp complex relations as on our facility with words.

Another important development was the gradual emergence of a single, generally accepted system of spelling, which has remained in effect ever since with only a few slight modifications. It was a poor system at the time, and has become more and more unsatisfactory as our pronunciation has changed since; but it has had a very strong unifying effect on the language. The fact that we tend to think of the written form of a word as the real form has, as we have seen, some serious disadvantages; but it does make it easier for us to think of an unfamiliar pronunciation as a comprehensible variant rather than as something completely and arbitrarily different.

100. THE GREAT VOWEL SHIFT. The most important development
in the sound system of English that took place during this period
was a change in the values of all the long vowels, usually called
"the great vowel shift." It is here described in a simplified form,
with a footnote for those who want more details. For some reason
people started pronouncing the long vowels with their tongues
higher in their mouths. When the front part of the tongue was
raised, /ɑ:/ changed to /e:/ and /e:/ to /i:/; when the back part
was raised, /ɔ:/ changed to /o:/ and /o:/ changed to /u:/. The
vowels /i:/ and /u:/ were already pronounced with the tongue
so high that any further raising would have resulted in consonant
rather than vowel sounds, so people backed up and made the
diphthongs /ɑi/ and /ɑu/ instead.[1] The whole process sounds
most unlikely, especially the last part. Nobody knows why it
happened, so there is no use worrying about that. We have very
convincing evidence that it somehow did, and at least it explains
one of the main peculiarities in English spelling.

Exact dating of the shift is impossible, partly because of scanty
and sometimes conflicting evidence, partly because some people
were slower than others in following the new tendency. It apparently began in the fifteenth century, and is sometimes called
the "fifteenth century vowel shift." The evidence of spelling suggests that the main development was rather later. There is some

---

[1] Actually there were two long *e*'s in Middle English: the open *e*,
[ɛ:], which is a prolongation of the vowel sound in *met*, and the close *e*,
[e:], which is a prolongation of the first element of the diphthong in *bait*.
The open *e* sound was often spelled *ea*, and the close *e* sound *ee*, though
there is a good deal of inconsistency. During the great vowel shift [ɛ:]
was raised to [e:], and [e:] to [i:]. Immediately after this *clean* rhymed
with *plain* rather than *keen,* and *tea* with *day* rather than *see.* This explains some of Pope's rhymes, and also the conservative pronunciation of
some proper names, such as *O'Dea.* However, early in the eighteenth century the new [e:] shifted further to [i:], so that the result indicated in the
text was eventually attained. The difference between the two *e* sounds in
Middle English has hitherto been disregarded in this book simply because
Chaucer, who is the only Middle English writer that most people are likely
to be concerned about pronouncing, often rhymes the two sounds. It could
not be disregarded in a more searching study of the language.

doubt that the modern diphthongs in such words as *bite* and *mouse* had been fully developed in Shakespeare's time, but they must have been well on their way. The evidence for the pronunciation at various times is of several kinds, of which the most obvious are English attempts at phonetic spelling of foreign words, and foreign attempts at phonetic spelling of English words. We also have some evidence from rhymes, some from nonstandard dialects which developed differently, and a few contemporary comments.

The following words indicate the changes:

Vowel	Word	Chaucerian pronunciation	Shakespearean pronunciation
/ɑ:/	place	/plɑsə/	/ple:s/
/e:/	feet	/fe:t/	/fi:t/
/i:/	bite	/bi:tə/	/bait/
/ɔ:/	stone	/stɔ:n/	/sto:n/
/o:/	fool	/fo:l/	/fu:l/
/u:/	mouse	/mu:s/	/maus/

As mentioned in the preceding chapter, Chaucer's vowels had approximately the same values as those in modern Spanish and Italian, and each pair of short and long vowels had approximately the same quality. The difference between the short and long *e*, for instance, was simply in the length they were held, and not in a different placement of the tongue. If the shift had happened a century or two earlier our spelling would probably have reflected it; but since it occurred only after some of our spelling conventions had at least begun to solidify, it left us with our very curious habit of using the same letters to indicate phonetically unrelated vowel sounds. Our ancestors simply continued to spell with the letters they were used to, even when they had greatly changed their habits of pronunciation. The shift does not explain all our odd spellings of vowel sounds, since other factors are involved in many words; but it does account for the greatest single peculiarity.

101. THE SHORT VOWELS. There was no general shift in the short vowels, but /æ/ was changed to /ɑ/, and in many words /u/ was changed to /ə/. However, the later development of both these vowels has been so varied in different phonetic environments that it is not practicable to consider them thoroughly here.

102. CONSONANTS. The only general change in the consonant system during this period was that /x/ (spelled *gh*) either changed to /f/ as in *cough* and *enough* or disappeared entirely as in *thought* and *bough*. The tendency was for it to change to /f/ when final and disappear when followed by a *t;* but this tendency was often disturbed by analogies too complicated to go into here.

Toward the end of the period /i/ changed to /j/ when it was preceded by a consonant and followed by a lightly stressed vowel. This accounts for our present pronunciation of words like *special* and *ambitious,* which often (but not always, because the change was then under way) have an extra syllable in Shakespeare.

The only other changes that need be mentioned are the shifts between /d/ and /ð/ in the neighborhood of /r/. Thus *fader* and *moder* changed to *father* and *mother,* while *burthen* and *murther* changed to *burden* and *murder.* Once again the full statement would be very complicated, and there are a number of irregularities. For most purposes it will be sufficient to remember that such changes were possible.

103. CHANGES IN INFLECTION. The changes in inflection during this period were comparatively slight, but the following should be noticed:

Nouns

Constructions like "the King of England's crown," known as the *group genitive* replaced the older "the King's crown of England."

The ordinary *-es* genitive ending was often written as *-is* or *-ys,* and probably usually pronounced /iz/, as it generally is today.

"Charles's book" therefore sounds exactly like "Charles his book" if both phrases are pronounced casually; and the idea that the second phrase is the original one and the first a mere contraction, became widespread during this period. (There are occasional examples of it even in Old English.) This idea has no historical justification, and could hardly explain such combinations as "the lady's dress," but it was held for centuries, and is taken for granted by many people today, though the "correct" form now seldom appears except in bookplates. The apostrophe which we still use in the genitive is due to this misunderstanding.

Pronouns

In older English *his* had been the genitive form of *it* as well as *he;* but in the neuter it was now supplanted, first by *it,* then by *its* (usually written *it's* until about 1800). The use of the forms *ye* and *you* in the singular when addressing superiors had begun in the thirteenth century. It later became normal among equals unless they were particularly intimate, and during the Renaissance the singular forms dropped out almost entirely in the standard language. Moreover, the original distinction between the nominative *ye* and the objective *you* became so blurred that either form could be used for all purposes, with *you* gradually gaining.

The use of *who* and *which* as relative pronouns became common during this period, though there are occasional examples earlier. It is generally believed that this construction developed in three stages, something like this: First, the direct question, "Who was there?" Second, the reported question, "He asked who was there." Finally, the statement, "I know the man who was there."

Since there are some grammarians who seem to believe that the *wh-* relatives are the only fully legitimate ones, it is well to remember that "the man *that* I saw" was in use for centuries before "the man *whom* I saw." "The man I saw" is still earlier — and still good.

Adjectives

Double comparatives and superlatives (*more nobler, most unkindest*) were used freely, but not by everybody. In other words, the permissible feeling that such expressions are redundant had not been put into a rule making them criminal. Also, long adjectives were often compared by *-er* and *-est*.

Verbs

By far the most important changes in inflection took place among the verbs. The drift of the originally strong verbs into the weak class continued. Such verbs as *bide, crow,* and *dread,* among others, show the weak preterites *bided, crowed,* and *dreaded* along with the older *bode, crew,* and *drad.* In fact the drift was so strong that a number of weak forms which have since been outlawed were in respectable use, such as *blowed, growed,* and *shrinked.*

In the third person singular the -(*e*)*s* ending, which in Middle English occurred only in the Northern dialect, began to compete with the -(*e*)*th* ending which had been in use throughout the rest of the country, and eventually drove it out. Shakespeare used both, frequently in the same sentence, and presumably chose whichever form he thought sounded better in a particular place. But in the first half of the seventeenth century the -(*e*)*s* ending apparently became universal in speech, though many writers continued to spell it as -(*e*)*th*. There are a number of comments on this inconsistency.

The Midland plural ending in -(*e*)*n* and the Southern one in -(*e*)*th* both dropped out of the standard language, leaving the uninflected form that we have today. But rather curiously, the -(*e*)*s* ending which had been used in the plural as well as the singular in the Northern dialect, now appeared for the first time in the plural in other areas. Though it is not nearly as common as the uninflected form, it appears so often in careful writing, and in verse where the extra syllable fits the meter, that it is generally accepted as a recognized variant rather than a mistake in agreement.

The -(e)n ending dropped out completely in the infinitive, and in most past participles except those in which it is still preserved.

We may summarize by saying that as far as inflections are concerned most verbs had reached the forms that they have now, except that the -(e)th third singular was still fairly common throughout most of the period, and the second singular -(e)st ending was still possible, though becoming infrequent. But our now rather rigid system of verb phrases had not fully developed. In questions Shakespeare could say "Goes he?" where we must use either "Does he go?" or "Is he going?" And in negative statements he could say either "He not goes" or "He goes not" where we have to use "He does not go" or "He is not going." On the other hand, he could say "I do go" without implying the special emphasis that such a sentence would now have.

On the whole the progressive forms (*is going*, etc.) were comparatively uncommon, partly because they were not needed in questions and negations, and partly because the simple forms could still be used to describe immediate action.

The most important difference in the "perfect tenses" is that *be* rather than *have* was used with verbs indicating change of condition or location — roughly the same kinds of verbs that require *être* rather than *avoir* in French, or *sein* rather than *haben* in German. We have preserved this tendency only very erratically. Thus in the sixteenth century the regular expressions were *is come* and *is gone*, rather than *has come* and *has gone*. We can now say either *is* or *has gone*, but only *has come*.

104. THE SPREAD OF EDUCATION. So far we have considered only what might be called the automatic changes in the language. Before turning to those that owe at least something to theory we must consider some of the nonlinguistic developments which made efforts at deliberate improvement far more effective than they could have been in the Old and Middle English periods.

During most of the Middle Ages education had not only been completely controlled by the church but directed very largely toward ecclesiastical ends. The language taught was Latin, and one of the chief reasons for sending boys to school was to train them to sing in choirs. The connection between the two meanings of *clerical* now found in *clerical job* as opposed to *clerical collar* was so close that anybody who could read was entitled to "benefit of clergy," which removed him from the jurisdiction of the secular courts, and was often very convenient if he didn't want to be hanged. Of course, not every student had a deep commitment to the church. Some education was obviously necessary for the law and certain other careers. But on the whole even bare literacy was comparatively rare, and not universally admired. Many of the noble class clearly regarded writing as a rather menial occupation, distinctly beneath their dignity; and most of their inferiors seem to have considered it as a mystery with which there was no reason for them to be concerned.

Both the spread and the secularization of education were gradual and complicated processes, but it is clear that they made considerable progress during the fifteenth century. A good many middle class people, including women, were now learning at least to read and write English as part of the natural order of things. One result of this was that when printing was introduced during the latter part of the century there was a very much greater market for books, and especially for books in English, than there would have been even a hundred years earlier; and their effects on the language as well as the life of the times were consequently more widespread and very much faster. It has been estimated that by Shakespeare's time between a third and a half of the population of London could read — a situation which in Chaucer's age would have seemed absolutely incredible.

105. WEAKENING OF CLASS DISTINCTIONS. One important reason for the spread of education was that hereditary class distinctions were losing some of their rigidity, so that the chance of rising in the world (as distinct from the church) was a good deal more

promising than it had been. We need not here go into the causes of this change, but we should notice two of the more obvious results. The first was simply that with the possibility of rising from one class to another a great many more people found it worth while to educate their children in order to prepare them for the new opportunities. The same situation is paralleled on a higher level today, when the concept of a "working class" has practically disappeared, and a college education is coming to be regarded as almost indispensable for a satisfactory life. The second was more complicated. When class lines are fixed, a man might as well behave naturally, because imitating his "betters" is more likely to bring him ridicule than rewards. But when it becomes possible to move from one class to another it is important for an ambitious man to learn to behave, linguistically and otherwise, like the members of the class into which he hopes to move. At the same time there is a tendency for those in the higher orders, no longer automatically protected from invasion, to become rather more careful in their own use of language as a sign of their continued superiority. The upshot is that class dialects are likely to become both more distinct and more important just at the time when a too simple analysis of the situation might suggest that they would break down.

It apparently took the schools of England a long time to adjust themselves to the problem of teaching "good English" to everybody who wanted to learn it; but ambitious people could read as well as listen, and there is no reasonable doubt that the written form of the language began to have a stronger effect on the spoken than it had ever had before.

106. Introduction of Printing. William Caxton set up the first printing press in England about 1476, and others soon followed. Looking back, it would be hard for us to pick a more strategic date for the invention to have its maximum effect. Books could now be reproduced for a very small fraction of their former cost, and exact duplicates could be made in any numbers desired. The spread of education was therefore greatly accelerated, and the

whole nature of the spread of knowledge — in and out of school — changed in many ways. It is easy for us to appreciate the effects of the economy brought about by printing, but it takes much more thought to realize how uniformity and immensely faster distribution affected the language.

On pages 122–124 we considered the extreme diversity of English manuscripts. An author might weep at the changes in his text made by a careless or independent copyist, but most people could not have had a very reliable idea of what the true text of even a single work was, to say nothing of an established set of conventions which should govern all works. Printing not only eliminated most of the diversity between copies but contributed greatly to the establishment of general conventions. It did not bring about any miraculously rapid change. A printer can make as many mistakes as a scribe, and it took some generations to develop the tools, the techniques, and the professional attitude which all seem so obvious once they have been achieved. But from the first, printers were forced by the very size of the audience at which they aimed to face some problems to which scribes had never had to pay much attention. And from the first the audience was presumably somewhat affected by the "authority of the printed page," which still has a powerful influence on most people — much in the way that a blueprint, which is merely an inexpensive reproduction of an architect's drawing, is likely to impress them with a feeling of inevitability that they never get from the drawing itself. The fact that London was the center of printing enormously reinforced the prestige of London English throughout the entire country. It no longer seemed reasonable for a northerner to translate a work from Southern English into his own dialect. Printed English was obviously for everybody.

Another effect of printing was to encourage writing as a way of making a living. Earlier authors were sometimes supported by patrons, but they could not possibly live on the sales of their work. Now printers and booksellers were willing to pay (in moderation) for copy, so that a career in letters was open to many more people than ever before. It is impossible to estimate how many books have been written primarily in the hope that they would be printed and sold, but at the most moderate guess the number is astronomical. Even if we consider only those both written and printed during the English Renaissance, the number is considerable, and many of these were either composed in or translated into English because writers and printers wanted to take advantage of the larger market in that language.

107. DEVELOPMENT OF SPELLING CONVENTIONS. Even today English spelling is notoriously confusing. Its general inconsistencies are so well known that there is no need to go into them here. Moreover, there are a number of characteristic differences between American and British practices, some of them affecting large classes of words (*-or* and *-our,* *-er* and *-re,* etc.), others only specific words (*tire* and *tyre,* *curb* and *kerb,* etc.). And finally, there are a fair number of words in which variant spellings are current and acceptable in each country. But at least the whole subject has been thoroughly surveyed, the results published, and for the vast majority of words a definite agreement has been reached. Most of us at least try to use the spellings authorized by the dictionaries; and if we get into print our publishers take a good deal of care to see that we do.

At the beginning of the Renaissance period there was not a single word with a definitely established spelling. Even the indefinite article *a* and the pronoun *I* might be spelled *o* and *y.* About the most that can be said is that words taken directly from Latin (which did, of course, have a long orthographic tradition) were spelled with a much greater approach to uniformity than those from other sources.

A good many people, naturally enough, were fairly consistent in their own habits, and a number of them proposed reformed spelling systems for general use. Some of the proposals were for purely phonetic spelling. One Thomas Smith extended the alphabet to thirty-four letters, and in addition marked the long vowels. William Bullokar, objecting to the arbitrary new symbols, took only the familiar letters as his base; but he showed variations in sound with such a bewildering collection of accents, apostrophes, and what he called "hooks and strikes" that his material is extremely hard to read even after careful study. It is too bad, however, that we could not have adopted his Rule 17, which might be called the philosopher's stone of orthography. It is given here without the diacritical markings:

> And this stryk ($_{\prime}$) is excepcion general
> Too spel wordz truly when thæz rulz fail al.

I haven't the faintest idea how this result was to be obtained.

Fortunately or unfortunately, such radical systems received no general support. Richard Mulcaster, in his *Elementarie* (1582), took an entirely different approach. He did not consider that truly phonetic spelling was possible, since pronunciation was constantly changing. He even doubted that it was greatly to be desired, since the use of one letter to indicate more than one sound seemed to him no worse than the use of one word to indicate more than one meaning — a variation which is inevitable unless we are to insist on a vocabulary far too large for any human memory to master it. Moreover, he was convinced that any attempt at a wholesale revolution was so hopeless as to be a complete waste of time. He therefore wanted to start with whatever nucleus of general agreement he could find, make such minor improvements as might be accepted without too much resistance, and — above all — make the point that it is more important for everybody to spell in the same way than it is to find a theoretically perfect system.

His work was often quoted with approval and undoubtedly had some effect, though not all his specific recommendations were followed. By the end of the period most of our spellings had become pretty well standardized, and we have made few changes since except in some of the commonest endings. For instance, we now use *-y* instead of *-ie*, *-al* instead of *-all*, *-ess* instead of *-esse*, and *-ic* instead of *-ick*. Since the modern forms all remove silent letters, we may consider them improvements. At any rate, since the seventeenth century we have been spelling words borrowed (not too early) from Latin and Greek with fair consistency, though with some pedantic complications. For instance, we use the *-ant* ending for words derived from Latin verbs of the first conjugation, and the *-ent* ending for those from other conjugations. Such etymological precision probably seemed reasonable enough to a generation of Latinists; but most people today would certainly vote for the French practice of using *-ant* for them all.

A minor complication resulted from occasional efforts to bring words borrowed from French closer to the original Latin forms. Thus *debt, doubt,* and *fault* come from the French *dette, doute,* and *faute.* The restoration in the first two of the *b* from Latin *debitum* and *dubitum* did nothing but make them harder to spell, but for some reason the restored *l* in *fault* eventually came to be pronounced.

Doubtless[2] the printers had more to do with the development of uniform standards than the scholars did. As anybody who has ever had much to do with them knows, they are likely to have a passion for consistency in detail, though during the early years of printing they were tempted in the other direction. They had to "justify" their lines — that is, make them come out even at the right hand margins. They could do this by inserting little wedges to vary the spaces between letters, but it must have been a great convenience to use a variable spelling to gain the same end even more neatly. Eventually, however, it seemed even more convenient to spell everybody's writing the same way, and disregard the peculiar preferences of erratic authors. Nobody really knows who was responsible; but on the simple grounds that an approximate agreement was reached in only one hundred and seventy-five years, I am inclined to give most of the credit to the printers.

108. ENGLISH AND LATIN IN THE RENAISSANCE. We are now rather generally accustomed to thinking of English as a living language,

---

[2] In academic writing the word *doubtless* generally means that the writer is bringing forth an opinion for which he has no real evidence.

and of Latin as not only a dead one, but one that has been dead
since about the fifth century. Of course we have heard of medieval Latin, but most people seem to think of it as a comparatively small and decidedly gloomy appendix to classical Latin,
consisting mostly of things like official charters and probably in-
comprehensible theology, all rather painfully and artificially
translated from the languages in which it must have been originally conceived. It is in those languages that they expect to find
all the really vivid impressions of medieval life and thought.

This evaluation would have seemed fantastic to the Middle
Ages. To them Latin was, like Greek and Hebrew and a few
others, a legitimate language going back to the Tower of Babel;
and as the official language of Christendom it was ordained to
last as long as the world. Though it was no longer the first
language for anybody, educated people still spoke it as a matter
of course — in casual conversation, not merely in set pieces; and
much of the time they automatically thought in it. They were
naturally inclined to write in it whenever they were addressing
their peers, and their writing is amazingly varied, including fine
drinking songs as well as magnificent hymns, and sophisticated
satire along with sober history. English, on the other hand, was
merely a "vernacular" — a corrupt form of speech with no particular future. A thirteenth century scholar (or even schoolboy)
would have taken the idea that it could supplant Latin for all
purposes about as seriously as a twentieth century scholar would
take the suggestion that Pennsylvania Dutch would drive out
Standard English as the future language of literature, learning,
and government in this country.

There is some very fine Middle English poetry, but most of
the prose and a great deal of pedestrian verse was written in a
definitely missionary spirit, "for the common people to understand" — and to understand in a rather limited way. The laity
were expected to *believe* the doctrine handed down to them
rather than to analyze its structure. In other words, the audience
was being talked down to — not contemptuously, but in a way

that called for simplicity, and certainly discouraged any effort
to "enrich and improve the language" in order to give them all
the confusing details.

During the Renaissance translations and compilations from
Latin sources were undertaken in a very different spirit. On one
side, there was a much greater effort to give the full intellectual
context; on the other, there was a growing respect for the capabilities of English, and a conscious and widespread effort to
develop those capabilities. The result was an enormous increase
in the vocabulary and a considerable development in the characteristic sentence structure. By the end of the period English was
firmly established as adequate for all purposes.

109. THE DEBATABLE IMPORTANCE OF AUTHORS. Since some
readers will feel that the preceding paragraph attributes far too
much importance to the efforts of individual authors, it will be
well to consider the question carefully. It used to be rather generally taken for granted (by such as had any opinion at all on the
subject) that a language was formed by its great writers; and
Chaucer, living at a critical time, was given especial importance.
As late as 1932 G. K. Chesterton began a book on this poet with
an almost casual assertion that he would be writing in French
if Chaucer had not chosen to write in English. It is now more
usual for linguists to hold the directly contrary opinion that language develops among the mass of the people, with writers
simply using the medium as they find it, and affecting it very
little. Both attitudes are exaggerated, but it is not very satisfactory to toss them aside with a sentence to the effect that "there
is much to be said on both sides, and the truth no doubt lies
somewhere between these two extremes." Conditions vary so
much that any single operating formula is hopeless, but we can
occasionally learn something by considering the evidence in
specific cases.

There can be no doubt of Chaucer's influence on literature.
All through the fifteenth century he was widely imitated and

enthusiastically praised, and the following passage from Caxton's preface to his second edition of the *Canterbury Tales* (1484) will give some idea of the esteem in which he was held:

> Grete thankes, laude, and honour ought to be gyuen vnto the clerkes, poetes, and historiographs, that haue wreton many noble bokes of wysedom of the lyues, passions, and myracles of holy sayntes, of hystoryes, of noble and famous actes and faittes, and of the cronycles sith the begynnyng of the creacion of the world vnto thys present tyme, by whyche we ben dayly enformed and have knowleche of many thynges, of whom we shold not haue knowen, yf they had not left to vs theyr monumentis wreton. Emong whom and inespecial to-fore alle other we ought to gyue a synguler laude vnto that noble and grete philosopher Gefferey Chaucer, the whiche for his ornate wrytyng in our tongue may wel haue the name of a laureate poete.
>
> For to-fore that he by hys labour enbelysshyd, ornated, and made faire our Englisshe, in thys royame was had rude speche and incongrue, as yet it appiereth by olde bookes, whyche at thys day ought not to haue place ne be compared emong ne to hys beauteuous volumes and aournate writynges, of whom he made many bokes and treatyces of many a noble historye as wel in metre as in ryme and prose, and them so craftyly made, that he comprehended hys maters in short, quyck, and hye sentences, eschewing prolyxyte, castyng away the chaf of superfluyte, and shewyng the pyked grayn of sentence, utteryd by crafty and sugred eloquence. . . .[3]

We may cheerfully grant everything that Caxton says about the quality of Chaucer's writing; and for the sake of the argument we may even accept the contrast with all that had been written in English before as "rude speche and incongrue," though if Caxton had seen and been able to read all that is now available he might not have made his statement quite so strong. But the fact that Chaucer did wonderful things *with* the language does not in itself prove that he did anything *to* it. His influence does not, for instance, seem to have had the effect of making Caxton's

[3] Kaiser, p. 566, 11. 118–136.

own sentences particularly short and quick. It was not sufficient to keep the London dialect from changing markedly soon after his death, and losing most of the Southern forms in which his work abounds; and the best of his followers wrote in their own quite different Scottish dialect. We don't even know definitely that he added a single word to the vocabulary. He certainly contributed to the preservation of some that might otherwise have dropped from the language, but this was largely the result of later antiquarianism rather than of immediate contact. On the whole we must accept the belief that during the manuscript age the general drift of the language was not much influenced by literature.

But with the introduction of printing and wider education there was a much greater possibility of the language changing from the top down as well as from the bottom up. From Caxton's time on we find evidence of a growing desire to improve English, and to establish it as an adequate language for all purposes, on a par with Greek and Latin. Many of the workers had contradictory aims, and much of the effort may seem misdirected, but the total effect on the language was certainly considerable. Most of us can recognize that our own usage is heavily influenced by the books we have read and the instruction we have received, and even a complete illiterate today speaks differently from the way he would if Shakespeare had never written a play or Lowth a grammar.

110. INCREASE IN VOCABULARY. The most conspicuous change in the language during the Renaissance was the enormous growth of the vocabulary — a growth of which the literate public was well aware, and about which writers held strong though conflicting views. Some of them were simply against it. They saw no reason why the words already in the language should not be enough for anybody who took the trouble to use them effectively, and ridiculed all innovations. The borrowings from Latin they called "inkhorn terms"; those from the other modern tongues

"oversea language"; and the revivals of obsolete English words "Chaucerisms." Some of the innovators certainly gave them targets for legitimate ridicule, but the opposition to all changes now seems petty as well as absurd. Directly opposed to these conservatives was a group who believed in enriching the language by borrowing from all available sources; and in between was a third who were opposed to foreign borrowings, but believed the language could be improved not only by reviving old words but by making new compounds from native elements.

It is perhaps misleading to speak of the adherents of these three attitudes as groups. There was no movement in England with a unity or organization comparable to the school of poets known as the Pléiade, which at the same period was fighting a carefully planned campaign for the enrichment of the French language. But though the debate was less thoroughly organized, it was quite as vigorous, and even more interesting because there were no party lines to tone down individual differences of opinion.

111. THE CONSERVATIVES. A blow-by-blow account of the controversy would be long and confusing. Here we need only attempt to see the main issues in relation to their eventual effect on the language. We may begin by examining the position of a man who was quite satisfied with the language as it stood, and thought it only needed to be used more skilfully. In his *Arte of Rhetorique* (1553) Thomas Wilson has a famous passage on "Plainness what it is," which includes an imaginary "inkhorn letter" supposed to be written by a clergyman to a friend who might be able to help him get a position. It is here annotated rather thoroughly, partly because it illustrates some of the printing conventions of the times, and partly because many of the words differ from their modern equivalents either in having been formed with different suffixes from those that are now used, or in more closely preserving the literal meaning of their Latin originals. It will be noticed that the punctuation differs from ours about as much as the spelling.

Emong al other lessons this should first be learned, y^t we neuer
affect any strauge ynkehorne termes, but so speake as is commonly
receiued: neither sekyng to be ouer fine, nor yet liuyng ouer care-
lesse, vsyng our speache as most men do, & ordryng our wittes,
as the fewest haue doen. Some seke so farre for outlādishe Eng-   5
lishe, that thei forget altogether their mothers lāguage. And I dare
swere this, if some of their mothers were aliue, thei were not able
to tell, what thei say, & yet these fine Englishe clerkes, wil saie
thei speake in their mother tongue, if a mā should charge thē for
coūterfeityng the kynges English. Some farre iorneid ientlemē at   10
their returne home, like as thei loue to go in forrein apparell, so
thei wil pouder their talke w^t ouersea lāguage. He that cometh
lately out of France, wil talke Frēche English, & neuer blushe at
the matter. Another choppes in with Angleso Italiano: the lawyer
wil store his stomach with the pratyng of Pedlers. The Auditour in   15
makyng his accompt and rekenyng, cometh in with sise sould, and
cater denere, for vi. s. iiij d. The fine Courtier wil talke nothyng
but Chaucer. The misticall wise menne, and Poeticall Clerkes, will
speake nothyng but quaint prouerbes, and blynd allegories, de-
lityng much in their awne darkenesse, especially, when none can   20
tell what thei dooe saie. The vnlearned or foolishe phantasticall,
that smelles but of learnyng (suche felowes as haue seen learned
men in their daies) will so latine their tongues, that the simple
cannot but wonder at their talke, and thynke surely thei speake by
some Reuelacion. I know them that thynke Rhetorique, to stande   25
wholy vpon darke woordes, and he that can catche an ynke horne
terme by the taile, hym thei compt to bee a fine Englishe man,
and a good Rhetotician [*sic*] And the rather to set out this folie,
I will adde here suche a letter, as Willyam Sommer himself, could
not make a better for that purpose. Some will thinke and swere to,   30
that there was neuer any suche thyng writtē, well I wil not force
any man to beleue it, but I will saie thus muche, and abide by it to,
the like haue been made heretofore, and praised aboue the Moone.

An ynkehorne letter

Pondering, expēding, and reuoluting with my self your ingent   35
affabilitie, and ingenious capacitee for mundane affairs: I cannot
but celebrate and extolle your magnificall dexteritee, aboue all
other. For how could you haue adepted suche illustrate prerogatiue,
and domenicall superioritee, if the fecunditee of your ingenie had
not been so fertile, & woūderfull pregnaunt. Now thefore beeyng   40
accersited, to suche splendent renoume, & dignitee splendidious:

I doubt not but you will adiuuate suche poore adnichilate
orphanes, as whilome ware cōdisciples with you, and of antique
familiaritie in Lincolne shire. Emong whom I beeyng a Scholas-
ticall panion, obtestate your sublimitee to extoll myne infirmitee.   45
There is a sacerdotall dignitee in my natiue countrey, contiguate
to me, where I now contemplate: whiche your worshipfull benigni-
tee, could sone impetrate for me, if it would like you to extend
your scedules, and collaude me in them to the right honorable
lorde Chauncellor, or rather Archigrãmacian of Englande. You   50
knowe my literature, you knowe the pastorall promocion, I obtestate your clemencie, to inuigilate thus muche for me, accordyng
to my confidence, and as you knowe my condigne merites, for
suche a compendious liuyng. But now I relinquishe to fatigate your
intelligence with any more friuolous verbositie, and therefore he   55
that rules the climates be euermore your beautreux, your fortresse,
and your bulwarke.
       Amen[4]

1. y^t: that. A carelessly made thorn (þ) looked rather like
a y, and early printers often abbreviated *the* as y^e and *that* as
y^t. The pronunciation of this y^e as *ye* is a purely modern error.

1. *neuer*. The letters u and v were originally merely different
forms of the same letter, which could be used to indicate either
the vowel or the consonant sound. Printers generally adopted the
practice found here, of using v for either sound initially, and u for
either sound in all other positions.

2. *straũge*. In manuscripts a macron (ˉ) or tilde (˜) over a
vowel indicated that a following m or n had been omitted to save
space. This practice is followed rather erratically here, and in
many other early books.

6. *mothers*. The convention of using an apostrophe to indicate
the genitive had not yet been developed.

10. *iorneid ientlemē:* journeyed gentlemen. The practice of
using i for initial j is very common. It is not so often used instead
of g, as here.

12. w^t: with. This abbreviation is not nearly so common as y^t.

15. *pratyng of Pedlers*. Underworld slang.

17. *vi. s. iiij d*. Six sous and four deniers (French coins) for
six shillings and sixpence. The modern abbreviation for English

⁴ J. L. Moore, *Tudor-Stuart Views on the Growth, Status, and Destiny
of the English Language* (Halle, 1910), pp. 91–93.

money, £–s–d, are from the same source, with £ standing for *livres* (pounds).

20. *awne:* own.

29. *Sommer.* Author of a Saxon-Latin-English dictionary, and thus well supplied with all sorts of words if he wanted to use them.

35. *expēding:* weighing out. The modern meaning skips to the logical next step of paying out.

35. *reuoluting.* Many Latin verbs had in the past participle an -*at*-, -*et*-, or -*ut*- element which did not appear in the infinitive. French verbs are regularly taken from the infinitive form, and many English verbs are taken from the French. But English verbs borrowed directly from the Latin are regularly based on the past participle. Thus we say *celebrate* and *contemplate* (both of which occur in this passage) where the French have *célébrer* and *contempler*. *Revoluting* is thus as reasonable a form as *revolving*, though it does not happen to have survived (except as a playful expression for "making a revolution").

35. *ingent:* enormous. Probably dropped because it didn't sound big enough.

37. *magnificall.* After all, we say *beneficial* as well as *beneficent*.

38. *adepted:* attained. An *adept* has obtained a good deal of skill.

39. *domenicall:* Lordly, though we now use this word only in connection with the Lord's day (*dimanche* in French).

39. *ingenie:* intellect. From *ingenium*, and better etymology than our *ingenuity*.

41. *accersited:* brought.

42. *adiuuate:* aid. From the past participle *adiuvatus*.

42. *adnichilate:* reduced to nothing. A variant (on good authority) of *annihilate*, though here not quite as strong in meaning. Here, as in a few other words, the implication of the past participle is preserved without the addition of the -*d* ending. Compare *finite, destitute,* and so forth.

45. *panion.* From *panis*, meaning *bread*. We now say *companion*, or fellow bread-eater.

45. *obtestate:* call upon for testimony.

46. *sacerdotall dignitee:* priestly position.

46. *contiguate.* Change -*ate* to -*ous*.

48. *impetrate:* obtain by request.

49. *collaude.* The prefix which was omitted from *companion* is added here to *laud.*

52. *inuigilate:* look out for.

53. *condigne:* worthy.

54. *compendious.* Here, simply *convenient,* because so close at hand.

56. *beautreux:* buttress.

The gist of his argument is the sound Aristotelian advice that we should depend on our brains and skill rather than on our vocabularies for rhetorical effect; and it is presented so skilfully that unless we are very careful we may overlook its two serious defects. The first is that it simply assumes that the language is already completely adequate for all purposes; the second, that it considers only the practices of fools and a straw man set up to be conveniently demolished, and makes no attempt to consider what might be done by sensible men using the practices it opposes.

Obviously anybody who seriously wrote such a letter as the one presented would be an ass (unless he happened to know that the man he was addressing was one, and proceeded accordingly). But possibly he would have been an ass in any language, and a good many of the words that Wilson ridicules have not only passed into everyday use, but would be very hard to do without today. We may grant Wilson's principle that it is always bad to use a fancy word when a simple one will do the job as well; but we shall soon find evidence that some of the new words were being introduced because they could demonstrably do the job better. Wilson does go on to say that some borrowings are legitimate "either for lacke of store, or els because wee would enriche the language"; but since he excepts them from the charge of affectation only when "all other are agreed to folowe the same way," it is hard to see how anybody could legitimately introduce them.

Nearly forty years later (1592) Thomas Nash echoes Wilson, offering a "patheticall posie" of inkhorn words and phrases, including such (to him) obvious absurdities as *conscious mind, ingenuity, rascality, artificiality, addicted to theory, perfunctory discourses, amicable terms, extensively employed, notoriety,* and *negotiation.* But perhaps the most delightfully innocent summary of the conservative position is the following sentence from Samuel Daniel's *A Defence of Ryme* (1603):

> And I cannot but wonder at the strange presumption of some men that dare so audaciously aduenture to introduce any whatsoeuer forraine wordes, bee they neuer so strange; and of themselues as it were, without a Parliament, without any consent, or allowance, stablish them as Free-denizens in our language.

It would be nice to know what *past Parliament* he thought had had the *strange presumption* to give *consent* or *allowance* to such *forraine* words as *stablish, audaciously,* and *aduenture,* and to *introduce* them as *denizens* in our *language.*

112. THE ENTHUSIASTS FOR NATIVE RESOURCES. Wilson's remark that "The fine Courtier wil talke nothyng but Chaucer" is tantalizing. We don't know how much exaggeration it contained, nor how long the fad lasted. The movement to revive old terms, and to make new combinations of old elements, had a much slighter permanent effect on the language than borrowings from outside sources; but courtiers were not the only ones engaged in it. A number of poets, with Spenser as the most determined as well as the most distinguished example, were naturally enough delighted with Chaucer, and felt free to reintroduce any words that he had used — or that they thought he had or might have used. (It is quite unreasonable, but it is almost inevitable for a student of Middle English to wish that Spenser had been a better linguist. Obviously false antiques have a singular lack of charm for anybody who recognizes their synthetic quality.) And finally there were scholars like Sir John Cheke, interested not so much in the flavor of antiquity as in the theoretical purity of the language. In a letter to a friend (1557) he says:

> I am of this opinion that our own tung shold be written cleane and pure, vnmixt and vnmangeled with borowing of other tunges, wherein if we take not heed bi tijm, euer borowing and neuer payeng, she shall be fain to keep her house as bankrupt. For then

doth our tung naturallie and praisablie vtter her meaning, when
she bouroweth no conterfeitness of other tunges to attire her self
withall, but vseth plainlie her own with such shift, as nature
craft, experiens, and folowing of other excellent doth lead her
vnto, and if she want at ani tijm (as being vnperfight she must)
yet let her borow with suche bashfulnes, that it mai appeer, that
if either the mould of our own tung could serue vs to fascion a
woord of our own, or if the old denisoned wordes could content
and ease this neede we wold not boldly venture of vnknowen
wordes. . . .[5]

Whatever we may think of the argument as a whole, the paragraph is a beautiful example of the difficulty of expressing a
puristic attitude without doing violence to it in the very expression. We should write English clean and pure, unmixed and
unmangled. Good enough. But while *cleane* and *vnmangeled*
follow the precept in which they appear, *pure* is not pure in this
sense, and *vnmixt* is decidedly mixed, since it contains a Latin
root and an English prefix. In fact a sixth of all the words in the
paragraph have foreign roots, which seems rather a high proportion for the "bashful" borrowing which Cheke condones since
the language is "vnperfight." A great many later objections to
borrowings, whether of Latin words, Americanisms, or slang
terms, have been marked by the same kind of inconsistency.

Cheke did follow his expressed principles to the extent of coin-
ing such words as *hundreder* for *centurion* and *gainrising* for
resurrection; but most of them failed to stick, and it seems likely
that similar ones would fail in the same way today. It is a very
curious fact that we seem to regard the roots and prefixes of
Greek and Latin as the natural building blocks of new words,
to be used with complete freedom, but are extremely conservative about making any combination with their English equivalents
that are not already authorized by the dictionary. In this respect
English is in strong contrast with German, which still compounds
native elements so freely that no dictionary pretends to list all
the legitimate combinations.

[5] Moore, p. 94.

But curiously enough there was not in the Renaissance, and there is not now, any hesitation about the use of native suffixes, inflectional or otherwise, to shift borrowed words to new functions. As Richard Carew points out:

> For our owne partes, we imploye the borrowed ware soe far to our advantag that we raise a profitt of new woordes from the same stock, which yeat in their owne countrey are not merchantable; for example, wee deduce diuers wordes from the Latine which in the Latyne self cannot be yealded, as the verbes To *Aire, beard, cross, flame,* and their deriuations *ayring, ayred, bearder, bearding, bearded,* &c., as alsoe *closer, closely, closnes, glosingely, hourely, maiesticall, maiestically.* In like sort wee graffe vpon Frentch wordes those buddes to which that soyle affordeth noe growth, as *cheifly, faulty, slauish, precisenes.* Diuers wordes alsoe wee deriue out of the Latyne at second hand by the French and make good English, though both Latyne and French haue their handes closed in that behalfe, as verbes *Praye, Pointe, Paze, Prest, Rent,* &c., and alsoe in the aduerbs *carpingly, currantly, actiuely, colourably,* &c.[6]

Half a century later Richard Verstegan was carrying on Cheke's argument, and showing the same sort of inconsistency. He tells us that English is a branch of Teutonic, and traces Teutonic back to the Tower of Babel, thereby putting it on a par with Latin, Greek, and Hebrew. He even finds etymological evidence that Teutonic rather than Hebrew (as was generally believed) was the original, pre-Babelian language of all mankind. The argument is that the name *Adam* is cognate with the Teutonic word for breath (German *atem*), and *Eve* with *even,* as in "even the same" — Adam having been changed from clay to man by the Lord's breath, and Eve having been made even the same as her husband. Verstegan does not insist on this theory, taking the stand that its originator's "opinion exceeded his proofs"; but he puts it in for whatever it may be worth. After several pages of demonstration that a language of such antiquity

[6] *The Excellency of the English Tongue* — Moore, 114.

needs no help from strangers, he sums up his argument in the following words:

> For mine owne part, I hold them deceived that thinke our speech bettered by the aboundance of our daily borrowed words, for they being of an other nature, & not Originally belonging to our language, do not neyther can they in our tongue, beare their naturall, and true derivation . . .[7]

Counting the Scandinavian pronoun forms, exactly one-fourth of these words are of foreign origin.

113. THE TRAVELERS: OVERSEA LANGUAGE. Foreign travel was very fashionable, and apparently most of the travelers thought it was worth advertising. The young man who returned from the continent wearing strange clothes and filling his talk with foreign phrases is a popular object of Elizabethan ridicule. Borrowing from French, of course, was nothing new, and most of us would find it impossible to distinguish between the words taken in at this time and those imported earlier, though contemporaries could recognize their novelty. Italian and Spanish words had a much more exotic flavor, especially in their -*a* and -*o* endings (which the Elizabethans frequently confused). Many of these other words have now lost their endings, and their flavor with them. *Barricade, cavalier, duel,* and *grenade* have nothing like the exotic effect of *barricado, cavaliero, duello,* and *grenado.* Other words have retained their endings but become commonplace through everyday use — *banana, potato, tobacco,* for instance. But we still have many that retain some of their original tang, though we might disagree about just which these are. *Bastinado, bravado, cupola, desperado, embargo, peccadillo,* and *sombrero* are examples.

114. SCHOLARLY INNOVATORS: INKHORN TERMS — AND OTHERS. Much more important than either the Chaucerisms or the oversea language were the thousands of words taken from the classical

---

[7] From *A Restitution of Decayed Intelligence,* Moore, 128.

languages. Some of these were taken directly from Greek; but since many Greek words had already been borrowed by Latin, and reached English through this language, they will here be lumped together as Latin borrowings. They differed from earlier ones from the same source in two important ways. In the first place, a much higher proportion of them were learned rather than popular, since learned borrowings now had a much better chance of becoming permanent. A word borrowed earlier in a manuscript might easily be replaced the first time that manuscript was copied, if the scribe happened to dislike it or fail to understand it; and in any case its spread into general use was necessarily slow — often a matter of generations. But a word borrowed in print could get to thousands of readers in a very short time, and therefore had an excellent chance of being used again and again until it was generally accepted, and used in speech as well as in other books. The delight in words, of which we find so much evidence in Elizabethan literature, made the chances of survival greater than they would have been somewhat earlier. This delight was not, as we have seen, shared by everybody; but the general climate was decidedly favorable to rapid growth. No impersonal way of evaluating this growth is possible. An inkhorn term might be defined as a newly imported polysyllable that you don't happen to like. There is therefore no reliable way of determining exactly which of the new words could legitimately be called inkhorn, but we should all now agree that at least a good many of the imports were valuable.

In the second place, many of the new additions were the result of a conscious, and to some extent concerted, effort to improve the language. The Renaissance had made available a great many Latin works which had been unknown in England during the Middle Ages, and the spread of education had created a large new class of readers who knew no Latin, or at least not enough to allow them to use it with comfort. Both writers and publishers were tempted by this public. As a result there was great activity in both translation and the compilation of new works based largely on Latin sources. Translators and compilers almost inevitably borrowed freely. Often there were no English words in existence which could render a technical term or an unfamiliar shade of meaning. Even if such words existed, they might not occur to the writer who had the Latin words right before his eyes, or might not seem to him either sufficiently precise or sufficiently dignified. Intellectual snobbery, on the part of authors and readers alike, certainly played its part, but many of the new words were so useful that we can now hardly imagine being without them.

Perhaps the most interesting of these innovators was Sir Thomas Elyot. In the "proheme" to *The Knowledge that Maketh a Wise Man* (1533) he says:

> His highnesse benignely receyuynge my boke which I named the Gouernour, in the redynge therof sone perceyued that I intended to augment our Englyshe tongue, wherby men shulde as well expresse more abundantly the thynge that they conceyued in theyr hartis (wherfore language was ordeyned) hauynge wordes apte for the pourpose: as also interprete out of greke, latyn or any other tonge into Englyshe, as sufficiently as out of any one of the said tongues into an other. His grace also perceyued that through out the boke there was no terme new made by me of a latine or frenche worde, but it was there declared so playnly by one mene or other to a diligent reder that no sentēce is therby made derke or harde to be understande.[8]

Some examples of the ways in which he "declared" his new terms follow:

> to *deuulgate* or sette fourth some part of my study
> shulde *animate* or gyue courage to others
> the beste fourme of *education* or bringing up of noble children
> shall be *appoynted* or chosen by the soueraigne gouernour
> without *adminiculation* or aid
>
> made his exile to be more *facile* and easy
> *inclination* and towardnes to vertue
> *agilitie* and nymblenesse
> *Affabilitie* . . . where a man is facile or easy to be spoken unto

[8] Moore, 82.

Metamorphosios, whiche is as moche to saye as, chaungynge of
men in to other figure or fourme
Wherefore I am constrained to usurpe a latine worde, calling
it *maturitie* . . . that word *maturitie* is translated to the actis of
man . . . reseruyng the wordes rype and redy to frute and other
thinges
wisdome, in a more elegant worde called *Sapience*[9]

These examples have been chosen to illustrate the whole range
from those like *devulgate* and *adminiculation,* which are likely
to strike us as purest inkhorn, to ones like *appoint* and *education,*
which we can hardly imagine doing without. It is just as well to
bear in mind that our immediate reactions to strange words are
not necessarily sound. *Devulgate* — to make common — has not
stuck, possibly because *divulge,* with a somewhat different implication, has; but the word itself seems in no way inferior to
popularize. Adminiculation for *aid* (presumably only a little of it)
strikes me as ridiculously overanalytical; but no more so than
thousands of words which are current today — and perhaps a few
that I use myself.

Another comment in much the same spirit as Elyot's is this
from Richard Eden (1562):

> And whereas the Master of Savoye tolde me that your Honour
> sumwhat Doubted that the booke coulde not be translated into
> the Englysshe toonge, I assure you Honour that this I Dare saye
> without arrogancie, that to translate the variable historie of Plinie
> into our toonge, I wolde be ashamed to borowe so muche of the
> Latine as he Dothe of the Greke, althowgh the Latine toonge be
> accompted ryche, and the Englysshe indigent and barbarous, as
> it hathe byn in tyme past, muche more than it nowe is, before
> it was enriched and amplified by sundry bookes in manner of all
> artes translated owt of Latine and other toonges into Englysshe.[10]

115. COPIOUSNESS. One of the particular aims of the borrowers
was to make English *copious* — that is, to provide it with a
wealth of approximate synonyms which would serve to express

[9] Moore, 83–86.
[10] Letter to Sir W. Cecil, Moore, pp. 94–95.

exact shades of meaning. Elyot's *maturity* is an obvious example of this effort. He wants to use this word for a distinctly human quality, confining *ripeness* to things like fruit. There can be no doubt that a high degree of copiousness was obtained. It is often said that no other language is as rich as English in the ability to express fine distinctions; and it is sometimes added that there are no exact synonyms in the language.

The first of these statements is, to the best of my knowledge, true. The second is a half truth. There is probably no word which can satisfactorily be exchanged for any other in all positions; but it certainly cannot be proved that one of a set of synonyms is inevitably best in any position, and that the substitution of any other will necessarily take something from the sentence. Any word that we encounter often will build up a set of associations; and if we attempt to communicate above a very simple level we must gamble that our audience will have a fairly similar set. But, as in any gamble, we will sometimes lose. The distinction that Elyot makes between *ripe* and *mature,* and their corresponding nouns, is of course sometimes followed today. We are probably more likely to speak of *ripe fruit* and a *mature man* (or *plan*) than the other way around. But we can also speak of *mature fruit;* and (unless I am losing this gamble) we can speak only of a *mature tree,* not a *ripe* one. On the other hand, a man may be either *ripe* or *mature,* with or without an intended difference of meaning. If Shakespeare had said "maturity is all" the line would probably never have been quoted — except perhaps by psychologists.

116. COMPENDIOUSNESS. Another aim often expressed was to make English *compendious* — that is, compact and economical. If we tried to write English now without using any of our Latin borrowings, we would often have to use four or five words in place of one. To consider only a few of the words introduced at this time, take *absurdity, analogy, compatible, contradictory, democracy,* and *education.* If we tried to paraphrase a passage containing several of these words, using only native words to

do so, the result would inevitably be much longer than the original, and would probably seem almost childish in its simplicity. (And if we tried to write that last sentence without using *paraphrase, native, result, inevitably, original, probably,* and *simplicity* we would have another — well, *task* is not quite as good as *problem* here, but it will have to do.)

We have all been advised so often to write simply and use concrete terms whenever we can that we may be tempted to think that all polysyllables are always inferior, but this is not so. It is a sound rule never to use a long and comparatively fancy word when it says no more than a short, everyday one (unless you are saying so little that you have to depend on sound rather than sense to make any impression at all). In most sentences, and to most people, *remuneration* means no more than *pay*. The language could spare it without much loss. But when a long word not only takes the place of several short ones, but sums up their relationship in a familiar arrangement that can be grasped as a unit, it can be very useful.

Such words, sensibly used, are abstractions in the best sense, because they abstract the particular features of a complicated situation which we want to consider at a given time. They have the same sort of value as the simple symbols which mathematicians use to sum up complicated equations when they want to move into still higher orders of complexity; or that the term *field army* has to a soldier, who knows that it means an organization composed of several corps, each composed of several divisions plus supporting artillery, and so on all the way down the line. The advice so often given to young writers to "avoid abstractions" would, if taken literally, reduce us all to a kindergarten level. What is actually meant is something like this: "Avoid using abstract terms unless you have a very clear idea of what they stand for, and can convey that idea to your intended audience."

The two preceding paragraphs may seem to belong to a freshman English text rather than a history of the language; but it is impossible to consider Renaissance borrowings intelligently without giving some thought to their possibilities, both good and bad.

The translations and much of the new literature needed many new abstract terms unless they were to be intolerably wordy.

117. OTHER REASONS FOR BORROWING. The workmanlike and demonstrable qualities of copiousness and compendiousness were not the only ones sought in the development of the vocabulary. Such terms as *choice, sweet,* and *elegant* occur again and again in the discussions. It would be silly to deny the importance of the qualities indicated by these words; but it would be just as silly to pretend that we can examine them with impersonal accuracy. They did not mean the same thing to everybody, and we can never be sure that we know exactly what they meant to anybody. Our esthetic reactions to words are based on a mixture of immediate sense-impressions and past associations which it is simply impossible to separate. Even when we hear a word for the first time, the effect it has on us depends partly on the way we subconsciously associate it with other words we have known.

Of course many people have complete faith in the absolute validity of their own reactions, and we hear confident assertions that such and such words are "the most beautiful in the language." But beauty contests among words are no more conclusive than they are among women. I recall a student who was perfectly sure that she reacted simply to the sounds, not to the associations, but believed that it was a natural, if somewhat mysterious process, for us to give beautiful names to beautiful objects. For her prize example she chose *ermine,* a word as lovely as the fur it names. To prove that this was not an accident, she pointed out that the French word for the mysterious medieval fur, *vair,* was equally beautiful. She repeated both words aloud, several times, and they certainly sounded fine. But when it was suggested that an even more beautiful word, combining the qualities of the first two, was *vermin,* we had to change the subject.

It is natural that some of the words borrowed for esthetic reasons have not pleased enough people to remain in the language. Even when the aim was copiousness or compendiousness it often happened that competing words or competing forms of words were borrowed by different people to meet the same purpose. Sometimes these were later differentiated in meaning, to give a still more copious effect, as in the pairs *continuous-continual* and *beneficial-beneficent,* but naturally some of the words simply dropped out of use. Thus *obtestate* seems to have gone completely, *splendent* has given way to *splendid* (though we still have *resplendent*), *magnifical* to *magnificent,* and *contiguate* to *contiguous.* No principle of choice in such cases seems to be discoverable.

Many borrowings from Greek and Latin have lost much of their effectiveness with the general decrease in the knowledge of these languages. *Conflagration,* for instance, conveys to a ready Latinist the idea of a number of fires burning together and reinforcing each other. It is thus a fine term, significant as well as resounding, when used among Latinists. But to most people now it means simply "big fire"; and though it has the apparent advantage of being one word against two, it has the more important disadvantage of being four syllables against two, and those syllables less meaningful. Nobody ever seems to speak of the "San Francisco conflagration," or even "the great conflagration of London." It therefore seems to be approaching the end of its usefulness. Perhaps the moral is that we can afford to be compendious only about situations that arise again and again. It is easier to be a little diffuse now and then than to control too enormous a vocabulary.

Considered simply as a debate, the long argument about improving the language did not get anywhere in particular. At the very end of the period we still find adherents of the three main theories — for enrichment, for purification, and for a more careful use of the language as it was — stating their positions as strongly as ever. As Edward Phillips wrote in *The New World of English Words* (1658): "Whether this innovation of words deprave, or enrich our English tongue is a consideration that admits of

various censures, according to the different fancies of men." But
when we turn from theoretical discussions to observable facts,
there can be no doubt that the vocabulary was enormously increased during the period, and that the methods of addition were
so well established that it has been increasing on the same lines
ever since. It is also clear that much of the enlargement was
due to conscious effort rather than passive absorption, and that
far more people than ever before developed a lively interest in
the quality of the language, and took pride in trying to use it well.

Men still have different fancies, but now that three centuries
have passed since Phillips wrote, very few of them would argue
that this particular issue "admits of various censures." Most of
us would agree with what George Pettie wrote in the preface to
a translation in 1581:

> There are some others yet who will set light by my labours,
> because I write in English: and those are some nice Trauailors,
> who retourne home with such queasie stomachs, that nothing
> will downe with them but French, Italian, or Spanish, and though
> a worke bee but meanelie written in one of those tongues, and
> finelie translated into our Language, yet they will not sticke farre
> to preferre the Originall before the Translation: . . . For the
> barbarousnesse of our tongue, I must likewise saie that it is much
> the worse for them, and some such curious fellowes as they are:
> who if one chance to deriue anie word from the Latine, which
> is insolent to their eares (as perchance they will take that phrase
> to be) they forthwith make a iest at it, and tearme it an Inkhorne
> tearme. And though for my part I vse those wordes as little as
> anie, yet I know no reason why I should not vse them, and I find
> it a fault in my selfe that I do not vse them; for it is in deed
> the readie waie to inrich our tongue, and make it copious, and it
> is the waie which all tongues haue taken to inrich themselues;
> For take the Latine wordes from the Spanish tongue, and it shall
> bee as barren as most part of their Countrie; take them from the
> Italian, & you take away in a manner the whole tongue: take
> thē frō the French, & you marre the grace of it: yea take from
> the Latine it selfe the wordes deriued from the Greeke, & it shall
> not be so flowing & flourishing as it is. Wherefore I meruaille
> how our English tōgue hath crackt it credit, that it may not

borrow of the Latine as wel as other tongues: and if it haue
broken, it is but of late, for it is not vnknowen to all men, how
many wordes we haue fetcht from thence within these few
yeeres, which if they should be all counted inkpot tearmes, I
know not how we should speak anie thing without blacking our
mouths with inke: for what word can be more plaine thā this
word (plaine) & yet what can come more neere to the Latine?
What more manifest than (manifest)? & yet in a manner Latine:
What more commune than (rare), or lesse rare thā (commune) &
yet both of them comminge of the Latine? But you will saie, long
vse hath made these wordes currant: and why may not vse doe
as much for these wordes which we shall now deriue? Why should
not we doe as much for the posteritie, as we haue receiued of
the antiquitie? and yet if a thing be of it selfe ill, I see not how
the oldnesse of it can make it good, and if it be of it selfe good,
I see not how the newnesse of it can make it naught: wherevpon
I infer, that those wordes which your selues confesse by vse to
be made good, are good the first time they are vttered, and
therefore not to be iested at, nor to be misliked. But how hardlie
so euer you deale with your tongue, how little so euer you es-
teeme it, I durste my selfe vndertake (if I were furnished with
learning otherwise) to write in it as copiouslie for varietie, as
compendiouslie for breuetie, as choicelie for words, as pithilie
for sentences, as pleasantlie for figures, & euerie waie as elo-
quentlie, as anie writer should do in anie vulgar tongue what-
soeuer.[11]

118. Renaissance Neglect of Grammar. In an age like ours,
when "good grammar" and "good English" are generally regarded
as synonymous terms, it may seem curious that grammar got so
little attention during a period so greatly concerned with the
language; but there seems to have been quite general agreement
with the famous remark of Sir Philip Sidney which has convinced
so many modern students that he was indeed the flower of his
age:

Nay truly, it [English] hath that prayse, that it wanteth not
Grammer; for Grammer it might haue, but it needs it not; being

[11] Moore, pp. 103–104.

so easie of it self, and so voyd of those cumbersome differences
of Cases, Genders, Moodes, and Tenses, which I thinke was a
peece of the Tower of Babilons curse, that a man should be put
to schoole to learne his mother-tongue.[12]

This is of course a naive statement. The fact that English is
comparatively "voyd of those cumbersome differences" does not
mean that English has less grammar than more highly inflected
languages, but only that its structural patterns are of a different
sort; and Sidney found it "easie of it self" simply because he had
grown up with it. No Frenchman forced to learn the language
would have agreed with him. Communication is possible only
when a group of speakers have a similar reaction to patterns of
arrangement as well as to individual words. Whether these patterns have been explicitly described and formally taught is a
secondary, though not a trivial, matter.

Nevertheless, Sidney had a point that is worth emphasizing
because it is hard for most people today to believe that the situation he took for granted could ever have existed. In matters of
syntax and accidence the "don't do this" age had not yet arrived.
Toward the end of the period we find a few attempts to explain
the structure of English to foreigners, and a few others aimed at
teaching children, in English, those principles of grammar which
they would later need in studying Latin; but it is not until a
century later that we find any serious efforts to teach native
speakers the grammar of English for its own sake. Those critics
who accuse Shakespeare of being ungrammatical are a trifle
anticipatory, since the rules he broke had not yet been either
formulated in books or arrived at by tacit agreement.

119. DEVELOPMENT OF SENTENCE STRUCTURE. But even without
a formal theory there was a remarkable change in the standards
of sentence construction. It seems to have come mostly from an
increased respect for the language and a greater sense of responsibility about using it. Here again the influence of Latin was of

[12] Moore, pp. 105–106.

great importance. It cannot be proved by any such definite evidence as we have for the borrowing of words, and the opinions expressed in this section are certainly open to argument. But since the matter is too important to be passed over, they are given for whatever they may be worth.

For centuries students had been trained in the exact analysis of Latin sentences, as some are still being trained today. They were required to identify the precise form in which each word appeared, explain why it was in that form, and exactly what function it performed. It was assumed that any sound sentence could meet the test of such analysis — that its total meaning was the inevitable result of all the detailed interrelations within it. The structure of most Classical Latin sentences can, in fact, be analyzed as definitely and finally as algebraic equations — though it is not unlikely that this is true of some of them only because they have been emended by centuries of scholarship. And students were sternly encouraged to compose sentences of their own that could meet the same tests.

It is only since the middle of the eighteenth century that any such analysis has been applied to English. Its value is open to question, and will not be debated here. The point we are concerned with is that though in Old and Middle English comparatively short grammatical patterns were as definite and significant as ours, there were no strict and generally recognized standards for combining them. There was a tendency to join the clauses of a long sentence loosely by a series of *and*'s, rather than precisely by the appropriate subordinating conjunctions. It was very common to change the construction in the middle — to start out in one person and finish in another, to shift from one number or tense to another, or to mix direct and reported statements. The result is that many sentences are ambiguous. And often even when we are quite sure, from the context or by intuition, that we know what an author meant by a sentence, we can't prove it — or anything else — by the most careful analysis. The sentence simply does not hang together as we have been taught that it should.

As we have already seen, one reason for the lack of discipline
in English sentences was the fact that so many books were composed in an effort to meet uneducated people on their own
ground. A writer was likely to take the attitude expressed in the
explanation of why *The Castle of Love* (which is moralistic
rather than romantic) is put in English for those who know no
other language:

> Þauh hit on Englisch be dim and derk
> Ne nabbe no sauur bifore clerk,
> ffor lewed men that luitel connen
> On English it is thus bigonnen.[13]

If this attitude seems curious, we must remember that in the
Middle Ages the laity were often asked to believe rather than
understand, and it may have seemed more important to address
them in the comfortable rhythms of familiar speech than to confuse them with exact reasoning. But a Renaissance man, writing
for his peers and taking pride in his language, was naturally inclined to attempt a higher standard of performance. Translators
and compilers, for instance, were no longer content to make the
English a loose equivalent of the Latin; they felt responsible for
preserving the precise relations between ideas. There was a good
deal of difference of opinion as to how far this was possible. Even
at the beginning of the period we find some writers arguing that
the language is already fit for the highest tasks. Even at the end
we find others scorning its attempts to compete with its natural
betters. But all the way through we find still others holding the
view that it can be made better than it is, and working to make
it so. Some would be content to put it on a par with the other
modern or "common" languages; others saw no reason why it
should not rival or even surpass the classical or "learned" languages. Among them, they established the English sentence as
a solid and coherent unit.

This is not to argue that the basic structure of the language
was changed because a few writers were handling it more care-

---

[13] Kaiser, p. 243.

fully. The point is rather that the whole literate population was exposed to more carefully constructed English than their ancestors could have encountered, and that this exposure had a very perceptible effect on their own use of it.

120. THE STATUS OF LOCAL DIALECTS. The spoken language of the uneducated classes still varied greatly in different parts of the country, as the following quotation from Richard Verstegan's *A Restitution of Decayed Intelligence* will illustrate:

> . . . in some severall parts of *England* it selfe, both the names of things, and pronountiations of words are somewhat different, and that among the Country people that never borrow any words out of the *Latin* or *French,* and of this different pronountiation one example in steed of many shall suffice, as this: for pronouncing according as one would say at *London I would eat more cheese if I had it,* the Northern man saith, *Ay sud eat mare cheese gin ay hadet,* and the Westerne man saith, *Chud eat more cheese an chad it.*[14]

But although such departures from the London usage had once been perfectly respectable, they were now regarded as "uplandish" or countrified. Sir Walter Raleigh, in spite of his learning and position at the court, is reported to have spoken broad Devonshire to his dying day. The interesting thing about this is not that it shows his independent spirit, but that it was considered worth mentioning as something remarkable.

In written, or at least in published English, all the local dialects practically disappeared except for the Scottish. This had once been simply a subvariety of the Northern dialect; but its use had gradually become a national rather than a geographical habit, and its distinct qualities were patriotically preserved.

121. THE QUALITY OF RENAISSANCE ENGLISH. An adjective often applied to Renaissance English is *luxuriant* — a term which suggests both the richness of the language and its freedom from the

[14] Moore, p. 126.

sort of restrictions that later came to be applied to it. Although
Court English had become a national standard, it was in itself
not nearly so rigid as it later became. Grammarians and school-
masters had not yet begun the attempt to "ascertain" it — that is,
to decide which of the various ways of saying anything was right,
and to outlaw all the others. The general feeling of guilt about
the language which has plagued most educated speakers for the
past two hundred years had not yet been aroused. Some people
had strong objections to borrowing words from other languages,
but everybody seems to have felt free to use whatever words he
regarded as English however he liked — with reasonable attention to their meaning, of course, but with no fear of misusing a
part of speech, and little concern about which was the accepted
idiom. Among the unsettled questions that are likely to strike us
most forcefully were the forms of many verbs and the idiomatic
uses of prepositions and the articles.

As for the richness of the language, we have been talking about
it ever since; and in spite of those traveled show-offs who sneered,
it seems to have been quite generally appreciated at the time.
Choosing from the many glorifications of the state of the tongue,
we may close the chapter with this from William L'Isle:

> . . . our language is improued aboue all others now spoken by
> any nation, and became the fairest, the nimblest, the fullest; most
> apt to vary the phrase, most ready to receiue good composition,
> most adorned with sweet words and sentences, with witty quips
> and ouer-ruling Prouerbes: yea able to expresse any hard conceit
> whatsoeuer with great dexterity; waighty in weighty matters,
> merry in merry, braue in braue. Tell me not it is a mingle-
> mangle; for so are all: but the punishment of confusion we
> marke not so much in other tongues, because wee know not
> them and their borrowing so well as our owne; and this also is
> delightfull to know.[15]

15 Moore, p. 139.

CHAPTER SEVEN

The Authorities Step In

122. THE DESIRE TO REGULATE THE LANGUAGE. The exuberant English Renaissance ended in eighteen years of exhausting struggle, running from the first Civil War in 1642 to the Restoration in 1660. It was followed by an age of more orderly and much more regulated progress, which it is convenient to call the eighteenth century. The period from 1660 to about 1800 was by no means uniform. There was a considerable difference in tone between the Restoration and the Age of Johnson, not to mention the intervening Age of Pope and the succeeding Age of the Precursors of Romanticism, or whatever we choose to call these generations. And in each of these ages there were of course strong differences of opinion on practically all important questions, including the nature of language and what should be done about it.

Grammarians and pedagogues have never been able to establish the complete control over the language that some of them have wished, but for the past two centuries they have exerted at least a modifying influence of a kind that was previously lacking. Throughout the Old and Middle periods English had developed with practically no attention to academic theory, partly because it had always been overshadowed by Latin, and for several centuries by French as well. During the next century and

207

a half it had come to be recognized as the primary language of England, and the feeling had grown that it was adequate for all purposes. We find different degrees of enthusiasm for its new status expressed — that it could at last hold its own with the other modern languages (all, by nature, inferior to the classical ones); that it was comparable to Latin and Greek themselves; and even that it was — or could be made — the finest language ever known. There had been a definite movement to enrich it by systematic borrowings and coinings, but comparatively little interest in regulating it.

Some progress toward regularity in the conventions of writing had certainly been made, and there had been some tentative efforts to set up guides in the way of dictionaries and grammars. But the dictionaries were merely lists of "hard words" — recent borrowings, technical terms in special fields, and puzzling archaisms; and the grammars, mostly intended either to introduce foreigners to English or to prepare schoolboys for the later study of Latin, had made practically no impression on the general public. Most people seem to have felt (like Sidney) that they could use their mother-tongue without instruction. A writer might criticize the vocabulary or the rhetorical taste of another writer, but he was no more likely to find fault with the other man's "grammar" than to doubt the soundness of his own.

Shortly after the Restoration we find a very different atmosphere. It was by now generally agreed that the resources of English were up to any demands that could be made on them; but there was a growing feeling that even "the best authors" were often regrettably deficient in their practice, and that explicit guides were needed to help them out. Thus John Dryden complains that ". . . we have as yet no prosodia, not so much as a tolerable dictionary, or a grammar . . ."; and in another place, ". . . I am often put to a stand, in considering whether what I write be the idiom of the tongue, or false grammar." Having no English grammar to help him, he sometimes solved a problem by translating a sentence into Latin, and then putting it back into English in the light of what he had discovered. He was particularly shocked to find that he (like practically all writers of English up to his time) was in the habit of using prepositions at the ends of sentences — a practice that conflicted both with the habits of Latin authors and with the etymology of the word *preposition,* which means something placed before. He not only revised some of his own writings to remove this supposed fault but established a shibboleth that has been bedeviling the language ever since. Of course terminal prepositions are sometimes awkward; but to change a sentence like "You are just the man I am looking for" to "You are just the man for whom I am looking" is, to put it mildly, very dubious progress. Unfortunately, Dryden's rule is exactly the sort that delights a certain kind of pedant. After all, there is not much satisfaction in being able to recognize and correct mistakes that educated people seldom commit. To make a really pleasurable career of your superiority it is necessary to find something wrong with their habitual practices.

It was to be a long time before the effective guides that Dryden wanted were to be actually produced, but the feeling that they were needed was widely shared. It was quite generally accepted (in some circles) that Man, after a long struggle through the hopeless valley of medieval ignorance, had finally reached the plateau on which he was henceforth to dwell. There was still work to be done in order to make this plateau a second Eden, but not a great deal, and the blueprints for it were pretty well in hand. Thus we find Dryden writing in his "Essay of Dramatic Poesy":

> Is it not evident, in the last hundred years, when the study of philosophy has been the business of all the Virtuosi in Christendom, that almost a new nature has been revealed to us? That more errors of the school have been detected, more useful experiments in philosophy have been made, more noble secrets in optics, medicine, anatomy, astronomy discovered, than in all those credulous and doting ages from Aristotle to us? — so true

it is, that nothing spreads more fast than science, when rightly and generally cultivated.[1]

Dryden's uncertainty about his own grammar is an unhappy portent of a kind of anxiety that has afflicted many if not most educated speakers of English (and particularly American English) ever since, though it seems to be almost unknown among their opposite numbers in other countries. Most of us take it for granted that a French doctor speaks "good French," and a German banker "good German" — and the doctor and banker agree with us completely. But American doctors, bankers, and even university professors in other departments are very likely to confess (often quite cheerfully) that "good English" is beyond them. Since there is no particular reason to believe that we are the most modest of all nations, the likeliest explanation is that there is a greater gulf between school theory and normal usage here than elsewhere. It is in the period we are now studying that this gulf developed. Caxton's uncertainty, expressed nearly two centuries earlier (see page 7 above) was natural enough, for he was a businessman who had grown up in Kent, and then spent most of his life abroad before he began his literary career. But Dryden was the most distinguished professional man of letters of his time; and the fact that he felt uncertain foreshadows the belief that good English is not a normal practice but a sort of Holy Grail, to be pursued but not attained.

123. "UNIVERSAL GRAMMAR." Dryden's trick of translating an English sentence into Latin in order to find its true structure was obviously based on a belief in universal grammar. This is a question on which the linguists of today are sharply divided. Some of them hold that behind the obvious diversity of known languages there are certain basic similarities, and that these must be accurately charted before we can make really adequate analyses of the structure of individual languages. Others believe that each language must be studied in and for itself, and that any

[1] Ed. Thomas Arnold, 1903, p. 18.

resemblances in structure are best considered simply as coincidences. Bloomfield, for instance, says: "The only useful generalizations about language are inductive generalizations. Features which we think ought to be universal may be absent from the very next language that becomes accessible."[2] Both sides, however, now believe that differences in structure should be considered impartially, and that changes are both inevitable and legitimate. The eighteenth century idea was rather that all changes were corruptions of the original true structure, which was pretty well preserved in Latin but badly eroded in most modern languages, particularly English. This theory crops up again and again throughout the period, sometimes explicitly stated, more often apparently assumed; and it brought into our grammatical tradition a number of concepts from Latin grammar that could never have been derived from the study of English alone.

Even in the eighteenth century the theory was by no means universally accepted. There was much support for the contrary "doctrine of usage," which held that the only reasonable criterion of language is simply the established "custom" of its speakers, and that any theoretical considerations which conflict with this custom are nonsensical. And finally, since usage on many points was so obviously divided that no simple description of it seemed possible, there were plenty of people willing to accept any set of rules, even perfectly arbitrary ones, in the hope that they would settle matters once and for all.

124. THE IDEA OF AN ACADEMY. In 1635 Cardinal Richelieu had founded the French Academy, a self-perpetuating group of forty members charged with the tasks of compiling an official dictionary, grammar, rhetoric, and prosody, and in general with assuming control of the language. Shortly after the Restoration the idea of founding a somewhat similar institution in England received a good deal of support. We do not know who first proposed it, but Dryden was its most important advocate up to

[2] Leonard Bloomfield, *Language* (New York, 1933), p. 20.

the time of his death in 1700. Thereafter Dean Swift headed the movement, and there is reason to believe that an English Academy might indeed have been established if Queen Anne had not died in 1714. But the German George I, who succeeded her, was not sufficiently interested in the English language even to learn to speak it himself. The movement accordingly died, and it has never been seriously revived since.

125. THE INCUBATING PERIOD. The aims proposed for the abortive academy had been to "ascertain" the language by settling all disputed questions; to free it from all impurities (which might be defined as those features to which any particular pundit particularly objected); and to stabilize it so as to prevent any future changes. Even after the idea of an academy had died there was a great deal of interest in attaining the same ends by unofficial means; and a modern writer is under a strong temptation to "trace the development of the eighteenth century tradition" as if this had been an orderly, cumulative process. Actually it was nothing of the sort. It is true that the makers of dictionaries generally used and enlarged upon preceding efforts, but the growth of such works was influenced at least as much by commercial as by intellectual considerations; and theorists about the structure of the language for the most part beat their own lonely drums and got nowhere in particular. As an active force, our grammatical tradition began in 1762 with Lowth's *Short Introduction to English Grammar* — a book that could just as well have been written, with little change except in the illustrative quotations, at least a century earlier. What had happened in between was not the development of a foundation on which he could build, but simply a growing demand for some guiding authority. There were now millions of people who wanted (though perhaps not very badly) to be told how to use the language correctly; and there were thousands of school-teachers who wanted a basis for telling them — definitely and without hesitation or qualification. My own opinion, though I can't prove it, is that the thousands were more influential in this respect than the millions. A teacher of

Latin knew exactly where he stood. There was a definite rule for everything, and anybody who questioned it could be smacked. Those who had to teach English — and there were more of them every year — must have longed for comparable security.

126. THE EARLIEST ENGLISH DICTIONARIES. Most of us seem to have grown up with a vague but nonetheless powerful idea that The Dictionary was somehow dictated shortly after the Ten Commandments, and with approximately the same moral authority. It must therefore contain all the legitimate words in the language, with their pronunciation, spellings, grammatical classifications, and exact meanings, along with a little etymology which it is usually convenient to skip. If anybody uses a word that we cannot find in the sacred list we say it is not a real word; and if anybody questions any of the dictionary's statements we are likely to regard him as either intolerably conceited or a dangerous radical.

Now, a good dictionary is an extremely valuable as well as interesting work; but anybody who regards it with superstitious veneration not only loses much of its usefulness but puts an unnecessary obstacle in the way of his own understanding of the language. To get the full benefit from such a work it is necessary to understand its limitations as well as its achievements; and the best way to do this is to consider both the gradual steps in the development of lexicography and some of the conflicting demands which make anything like a perfectly satisfactory all-purpose dictionary impossible even today. The first steps were taken before the period we are now discussing, and very important advances have been made since the end of it. But since it was in the eighteenth century that dictionaries first became a really important influence on the development of the language, it seems reasonable to discuss them here.

During the medieval period a reader who found an unusual word in a manuscript might write an explanation of it, called a *gloss,* in the margin — a practice which most students will recognize as natural. Eventually it occurred to somebody that it would be convenient to collect all the glosses in his small library into a single list, called a *glossary.* The next step was to combine several glossaries into a longer list. When such lists became too long to be scanned at a glance it seemed helpful to group the words by subjects. Then some unknown genius decided it would be still more convenient to put together all those that began with the same letter. It took a surprisingly long time for the completely alphabetical order which we now take for granted to develop.

The earliest glossaries were in Latin. Next came bi-lingual ones — Latin-English, English-Latin, and so forth. These tended to be more inclusive than the older type, since even the simplest words in one language might be unfamiliar to a speaker of the other. Not until 1604 was the first attempt at a purely English dictionary published. This was Robert Cawdrey's "*A Table Alphabeticall,* conteyning and teaching the true writing and understanding of hard usuall English wordes, borrowed from the Hebrew, Greeke, Latine, or French, &c." Though a step forward in one way, this is obviously a step back in another, since only the "hard" words are included. Cawdrey's book was soon succeeded by others of the same sort, each claiming to have longer and more complete lists than any of its rivals.

Next to the hard words derived from foreign languages perhaps the most obvious sources of difficulty are archaic words and the array of technical terms we encounter in fields with which we are not familiar; and such terms were soon added, by no means silently. The blurb on the title page of Blount's *Glossographia* (1656), though comparatively short and modest, may be taken as sufficiently illustrative:

GLOSSOGRAPHIA
OR A
DICTIONARY
Interpreting all such
HARD WORDS,

Whether *Hebrew, Greek, Latin, Italian, Spanish, French, Teutonick, Belgick, British* or *Saxon;* as are now used in our refined *English Tongue.*

Also the Terms of *Divinity, Law, Physick, Mathematicks, Her-*
aldry, Anatomy, War, Musick, Architecture; and of several other
Arts and *Sciences* Explicated.

With *Etymologies, Definitions,* and *Historical Observations* on
the same.

Very useful for all such as desire to understand what they read.

There is of course a sort of superficial logic in limiting a dictionary to the hard words. You explain them by the easy ones —
and if the reader doesn't already know *them,* he can't use the
book anyhow. However, even the simplest words do bring up
a number of questions, and it eventually became obvious that
a dictionary including the ordinary basic vocabulary would be
very useful. The first considerable attempt in this direction was
made in 1706, in John Kersey's edition of Edward Phillips' *The*
New World of English Words, the best of the hard-word dictionaries. By adding ordinary words chosen from "the best authors" Kersey increased the vocabulary of this work from 17,000
to 38,000 words. In 1721 Nathan Bailey published *An Universal*
Etymological English Dictionary. This work was carefully compiled from most of its best predecessors, and remained popular,
in many editions, throughout the century. It is, on the whole, a
very competent work, considering the state of linguistic knowledge then available; but a modern school-teacher might be
shocked to discover that in the most authoritative work of the
time a good many of the definitions begin "is when."

Up to this point the growth of dictionaries had been largely
a matter of what might be called incremental plagiarism. Each
compiler took what he wanted from his predecessors, often ver-
batim. He might or might not acknowledge these debts. Then he
added something of his own, either additional words or special
features, ranging from common proverbs to mythology, to support his claim that his was the best dictionary yet offered to the
public. Such a process involved the perpetuation of many errors,
and particularly encouraged the continual listing of words which
had never been used enough to have any reasonable claim to be
considered as being in the language. In fact, it has often been

suspected that some of them had never been used at all, but were simply borrowed or adapted from foreign sources to increase the lists.

127. JOHNSON's DICTIONARY. In 1747 Samuel Johnson, whose reputation in the world of letters was already considerable, was engaged by a group of booksellers to undertake the preparation of a new dictionary. He completed the task in eight years, with no other help than that of half a dozen copyists who transcribed passages that he had marked in books. When we compare this with the seven hundred fifty-seven editorial years needed for the preparation of Webster's Third, the accomplishment seems almost incredible; yet during these same years Johnson found time for other work which so increased his reputation that he came to be regarded as a sort of semi-official one-man academy who should be entrusted with the regulation of the language. His preface suggests that he began the work with very much this idea. What he learned during the process convinced him that the prevention of change was impossible, and that established customs must be respected even when they were not reasonable; but he retained a firm belief that a lexicographer (at least one named Johnson) had a definite responsibility for improving the language, and the authority to do so.

This preface should emphatically be read as a whole, both as admirable prose and as one of the most enlightening discussions of the language ever published;[3] but the paragraphs quoted below will give some indication of the task that he saw confronting him and the way he proposed to go about it.

> When I took the first survey of my undertaking, I found our speech copious without order, and energetick without rules: wherever I turned my view, there was perplexity to be disentangled, and confusion to be regulated; choice was to be made out of boundless variety, without any established principle of

[3] It is most readily available in *Johnson's Dictionary, A Modern Selection,* E. L. McAdam, Jr. and George Milne, New York, 1963. The page references are to this book.

selection; adulterations were to be detected, without a settled test of purity; and modes of expression to be rejected or received, without the suffrages of any writers of classical reputation or acknowledged authority.

Having therefore no assistance but from general grammar, I applied myself to the perusal of our writers; and noting whatever might be of use to ascertain or illustrate any word or phrase, accumulated in time the materials of a dictionary, which, by degrees, I reduced to method, establishing to myself, in the progress of the work, such rules as experience and analogy suggested to me; experience, which practice and observation were continually increasing; and analogy, which, though in some words obscure, was evident in others.[4]

An incredibly difficult job could hardly be described more modestly. What Johnson proposed to do was to list the words of the language as he found them in his enormous reading; to define them as he found them actually used; and to support his definitions by actual quotations from his sources. Thus his book would be derived directly from the language rather than from earlier compilations which, whether good or bad, offered no evidence in support of their statements. He was prepared to use earlier dictionaries as checklists to make sure that he did not leave out any important words, but not as reliable sources. This is essentially the process that was actually followed, over a century later, in the making of the Oxford English Dictionary; and which then required nearly seventy years and hundreds of skilled workers. Johnson, working with only half a dozen copyists, soon had to modify his plan, but with characteristic honesty he made his deviation from the ideal clear:

Many words yet stand supported only by the name of Bailey, Ainsworth, Phillips, or the contracted *Dict.* for Dictionaries subjoined: of these I am not always certain that they are read in any book but the works of lexicographers. Of such I have omitted many, because I have never read them; and many I have inserted, because they may perhaps exist, though they have escaped my notice: they are, however, to be yet considered as

[4] *Ibid.*, p. 4.

resting only upon the credit of former dictionaries. Others, which
I considered as useful, or know to be proper, though I could not
at present support them by authorities, I have suffered to stand
upon my own attestation, claiming the same privilege with my
predecessors of being sometimes credited without proof.[5]

It is so easy to miss the significance of this paragraph that a
rather insistent repetition may be forgiven. It implies that a dictionary is primarily a record of the language — a list of the words
actually used, and an explanation of the meanings actually intended by the users. The statements of the lexicographer are
properly based simply on his understanding of what past usage
was, not on any theory of what it should have been; and they
should be supported as far as possible by actual examples of
usage, which the reader can examine for himself. Anything other
lexicographers have said should be repeated only with an appropriate warning, so that possible errors may not be reinforced
and perpetuated; and unsupported opinions should be given only
as a last resort.

Johnson thus laid the foundation for the "dictionary on historical principles" which (in theory) aims simply to record usage,
not to judge it; but he obviously did not feel that a simple record
of past events would entirely fulfill his duty. The following sentence occurs in a paragraph describing his treatment of spelling,
but is a fair description of his attitude toward every aspect of
language:

> Every language has its anomalies, which though inconvenient,
> and in themselves once unnecessary, must be tolerated among the
> imperfections of human beings, and which require only to be
> registered, that they may not be increased, and ascertained, that
> they may not be confounded; but every language has likewise its
> improprieties and absurdities, which it is the duty of the lexicog-
> rapher to correct or proscribe.[6]

The debate on whether it really is the duty of a lexicographer
to correct or proscribe has been extremely lively in this country

[5] *Ibid.*, pp. 12–13.
[6] *Ibid.*, p. 4.

since the publication by the Merriam-Webster Company of the third edition of Webster's New International Dictionary. I shall not attempt to settle that debate here; but it is worth pointing out that most dictionaries are actually intended to perform two not entirely compatible functions, and that their compilers almost inevitably aim directly at only one, and treat the other as secondary. To oversimplify somewhat, we may say that a dictionary must be aimed either at readers or at writers.

A reader's main interest is in knowing what the words he encounters mean. If he meets one that he doesn't know, he looks it up. If he is a good reader and has a good dictionary he will not be satisfied with the most obvious or common meaning, but will want to find out what the writer probably meant in the particular sentence he is investigating. On the same principle, he will often look up words which are quite familiar in some meanings, but which do not seem to fit the sentences in which they occur. Suppose he encounters the word *disinterested* used in a sentence where there seems to be no implication of lack of bias. He looks it up, finds it can also mean *uninterested,* decides that that is what it means here, and goes on with his job. He does not particularly care whether the word in this sense is used "loosely" or even "erroneously." He simply wants to understand the sentence. Maybe he is a Frenchman, and feels no responsibility toward English.

On the other hand, a writer wants to use words that will not only express his meaning, but impress his readers favorably. If he has heard both *uninterested* and *disinterested* used to express boredom, he wants to know (even if he is a Frenchman) which one he should choose; and he will be grateful for any labels which indicate that one is better for his purpose than the other.

Of course, with the cost of bookmaking what it is, all actual dictionaries aim at both readers and writers, and all lexicographers must make some kind of choice (which will not please everybody) about how far they should go in indicating the status of words, and how insistent they should be. If they go lightly they will be accused by some critics of abdicating their responsibilities. If they take a strong stand they will be accused by others of assuming a kind of authority to which they have no right whatever. It seems rather silly to be dogmatic in either direction about what all dictionaries should do. There are now a number of good dictionaries, and they vary. The best way to use them is to find out what each one attempts, and make allowances.

Since Johnson does not point out the exact borderline between anomalies which must be tolerated and improprieties which should be proscribed, we may assume that he located it about where most of us do — between those irregular expressions we happen to use ourselves, and those we have somehow been trained to avoid. His division is likely to strike us as especially arbitrary in his assignment of such classifications as *low, cant, burlesque language,* and *not used* to words he felt to be less than standard. Thus he doubly condemns *fun* and *stingy* as both low and cant, though he lists a number of well-known four-letter words with no suggestion that they are not respectable. To *progress* is "not used," though *myropolist* ("one who sells unguents") apparently is. But if we are tempted to make too much of these and many similar peculiarities, we may be restrained by rereading the sentence in which he remarks that "a few wild blunders, and risible absurdities, from which no work of such multiplicity was ever free, may for a time furnish folly with laughter, and harden ignorance in contempt."

A dictionary two hundred years old is bound to be hopelessly out of date. Thus many of Johnson's statements, while accurate at the time, have been invalidated by later changes. Others were always highly personal, or even eccentric; and some, as he foresaw, were wildly wrong. His book is now read mostly as a curiosity, with more attention to its lapses than to its virtues. This is probably inevitable; but we should remember that Johnson not only made a better dictionary than had existed before, but gave it a new status. Chesterfield had suggested that Johnson should be accepted as the dictator of the language. This could hardly be done officially, but to a very considerable extent it was done

unofficially. To the best of my belief, our tradition of reverence
for "the dictionary" goes back to Johnson's work, and no further.

128. THE BEGINNINGS OF OUR TRADITIONAL GRAMMAR. The first
attempt at an English grammar of which we have any record was
the *Bref Grammar* of William Bullokar, printed in 1586. During
the next hundred and seventy-five years about twenty others
appeared, varying greatly in purpose, quality, basic assumptions,
and method of analysis. The one valid generalization that can be
made about them is that they had very little influence either in
their own time or on the later development of grammatical
theory. The most convincing testimony on this point is that of
Samuel Johnson, who certainly knew the field as well as any man
of his time. Presumably at the insistence of his publishers, he
preceded his dictionary with what he called a grammar. He
begins with the following statement: "Grammar, which is *the art
of using words properly,* comprises four parts: *Orthography,
Etymology, Syntax,* and *Prosody.*" His treatment of all four is
contained in thirteen pages (admittedly large ones), and is
divided as follows: orthography, four pages; etymology, seven;
prosody, two pages; and syntax, twenty-three lines, including the
following paragraph:

> The established practice of grammarians requires that I should
> here treat of syntax; but our language has so little inflection, or
> variety of terminations, that its construction neither requires nor
> admits of many rules. Wallis therefore has totally omitted it; and
> Johnson [*sic,* but he is referring to Ben Jonson], whose desire
> of following the writers upon the learned languages made him
> think a syntax indispensably necessary, has published such petty
> observations as were better omitted.[7]

His own observations can hardly be considered a step forward.
He does not, for instance, formally list the parts of speech, though
he makes a few comments about some of them. Perhaps his most

---

[7] This and the following quotation are taken from the 8th edition (1790),
in which the grammar has no pagination.

significant sentence is the one which concludes his treatment of adjectives:

> Some comparatives and superlatives are yet found in good writers formed without regard to the foregoing rules; but in a language *subjected so little and so lately to grammar* such anomalies must frequently occur.

The italics are mine. I do not know whether Johnson intended the phrase to mean that the true rules of grammar had not been adequately discovered and stated, or that arbitrary ones had not been invented and accepted. Possibly he had not made up his mind. In any case, he obviously felt that it was not worth his while to make any serious attempt to fill the gap.

129. THE LOWTH TRADITION. Not all of Johnson's contemporaries were so willing to accept "anomalies" cheerfully. In an age so devoted to reason and authority there were strong theoretical reasons for organizing the language. Moreover, the rise of a new middle class and the trend toward universal education were proceeding simultaneously. One of the principal reasons for going to school was to learn to talk, not like your old neighbors, but like the new ones you hoped to acquire. It would obviously be convenient if they could be persuaded to talk with some regularity. In any case, definite and dependable rules were needed.

Under these circumstances it was inevitable that systematic grammars designed for school use should be written and adopted; but the question of what form they would take was still open. In 1761 Joseph Priestley, better known as a chemist, published an English Grammar which, if it had been successful, might have given us a very different tradition from that which actually developed. It was based quite consistently on actual usage, allowed for a reasonable degree of variation, and insisted throughout that there were many more important things in life than a pedantic concern with trifles. Perhaps it was these virtues that prevented its academic success. The demand was for yes-or-no answers.

The man who did most to meet the demand was Robert Lowth,

who published his *Short Introduction to English Grammar* in 1762. At this time he had already been a professor of Hebrew poetry at Oxford for many years, and he was later to become Bishop of London, and to be offered (though he declined it) the archbishopric of Canterbury. With such a background he naturally had a strong belief in order and authority — not to mention a reasonable confidence in the soundness of his own opinions.

I do not wish to imply that he had no basis for his confidence. He was a competent scholar in Hebrew and the classical languages, at home in several modern languages, and had a surprising (for his time) knowledge of Old English. It would be hard to find a man of his period whose knowledge better qualified him for the task of "ascertaining" English grammar. But his authoritarian attitude and his concern for regularity set an unfortunate tone, which was exaggerated by some of his much less qualified followers. His book was immediately successful in the schools. More than twenty editions appeared during the eighteenth century; and simplifications, modifications, and expansions began to appear almost at once. The most influential was that of Lindley Murray, a retired Philadelphia lawyer who happened to be bed-ridden in England. He was approached by the headmistress of a girls' school who wanted a text for her pupils and convinced Murray that he had nothing better to do than to write one. The work he produced, which might be described as the logical expansion of Lowth worked out by a well-informed but petty mind, became the bible of most schools in both England and America for several generations.

130. LOWTH'S PREFACE. Lowth's grammar is such a pivotal document that it is worth while examining in some detail the preface in which he gives his view of the state of the language and explains what he proposes to do about it. A condensed version is therefore given here:

> The English language hath been much cultivated during the last two hundred years. It hath been considerably polished and

refined; its bounds have been greatly enlarged; its energy, variety, richness, and elegance, have been abundantly proved, by numberless trials, in verse and prose, upon all subjects, and in every kind of style; but, whatever other improvements it may have received, it hath made no advances in Grammatical Accuracy. . . .

The Construction of this Language is so easy and obvious, that our Grammarians have thought it hardly worth while to give us anything like a regular and systematic Syntax. The English Grammar, which hath been last presented to the public, and by the person [Johnson] best qualified to have given us a perfect one, comprises the whole syntax in ten lines. . . .

It doth not then proceed from any peculiar irregularity or difficulty of our Language, that the general practice both of speaking and writing it is chargeable with inaccuracy. It is not the Language, but the practice, that is in fault. The truth is, Grammar is very much neglected among us . . . . a faculty, solely acquired by use, conducted by habit, and tried by the ear, carries us on without reflection; we meet with no rubs or difficulties in our way, or we do not perceive them; we find ourselves able to go on without rules, and we do not so much as suspect, that we stand in need of them.

A Grammatical Study of our own language makes no part of the ordinary method of instruction, which we pass through in our childhood; and it is very seldom that we apply ourselves to it afterwards. Yet the want of it will not be effectually supplied by any other advantages whatsoever. Much practice in the polite world, and a general acquaintance with the best authors, are good helps; but alone will hardly be sufficient. . . . Much less then will what is commonly called Learning serve the purpose; that is, a critical knowledge of antient Languages, and much reading of antient authors. . . .

But perhaps the Notes subjoined to the following pages will furnish a more convincing argument, than anything that can be said here, both of the truth of the charge of Inaccuracy brought against our Language, as it subsists in Practice; and of the necessity of investigating the Principles of it, and studying it Grammatically, if we would attain to a due degree of skill in it.

It will evidently appear from these Notes, that our best authors have committed gross mistakes, for want of a due knowledge of English Grammar, or at least of a proper attention to the rules of it. The examples given . . . might easily have been increased in number. . . . However, I believe they may be sufficient to answer the purpose intended: to evince the necessity of the Study of Grammar in our own language; and to admonish those, who set up for authors among us, that they would do well to consider this part of Learning as an object not altogether beneath their regard.

The principal design of a Grammar of any Language is to teach us to express ourselves with propriety in that Language; and to enable us to judge of every phrase and form of construction, whether it be right or not. The plain way of doing this is, to lay down rules, and to illustrate them by examples. But, beside shewing what is right, the matter may be further explained by pointing out what is wrong. I will not take it upon me to say, whether we have any Grammar, that sufficiently instructs us by rule and example; but I am sure we have none, that, in the manner here attempted, teaches what is right by shewing what is wrong; though this may perhaps prove the more useful and effectual method of instruction.[8]

It does not seem quite fair to call the views here expressed "the eighteenth century attitude," since Lowth is obviously dissatisfied with his century and wants to change its ways. But they are the very fountainhead of a schoolroom attitude that is still common, particularly in the patronizing admonishment to "those who set up for authors among us" that they would do well to pay less attention to earlier authors, even the best of whom have committed gross mistakes, and more to the teacher and the text. There is (he says) absolutely no substitute for a formal study of grammar, which alone can teach us to express ourselves with propriety, and "to judge of every phrase and form of construction, whether it be right or not." I am willing to believe that by this last Lowth meant "whether it be right *for us to use* or not"; but the other possible interpretation has proved more attractive. Only by studying grammar can we prepare for a lifetime of pleasure in pointing out the mistakes of practically everybody else. Unfortunately, we may have to pay for this pleasure by a tense and defensive concern about our own use of language.

[8] Ed. of 1775, pp. viii–xi.

131. Lowth's Grammar. When we turn from Lowth's preface to his text we find on the first page two definitions which neatly conceal a basic paradox:

> Grammar in General, or Universal Grammar, explains the principles, which are common to all languages.
> The Grammar of any particular Language, as the English Grammar, applies those principles to that particular language, according to the established usage and custom of it.

This pair is easy enough to swallow if we take it fast; but if we stop to wonder just how far the usage and custom of two different languages may diverge without either one of them doing violence to the "common principles," a definite answer is hard to find, and "universal grammar" becomes a rather vague term. On the other hand, if we try to base our grammar simply on established usage, we are immediately faced with the question of "whose usage?" It can't be everybody's usage, because the reason for writing the grammar is a conviction that much usage is wrong. The best usage, then — but whose usage *is* best? A conscientious grammarian may find a temporarily satisfactory answer in "the usage of our best authors." But when he examines these authors more carefully, he finds "gross errors" even in them. For a really satisfactory standard he has to look higher — not at the actual sentences the authors wrote, but at the sentences they would have written if they had understood grammar better, and practiced it more carefully — if they had, in fact, studied and followed the book he is in the process of composing. To a non-grammarian this reasoning may seem a little peculiar, but neither Lowth nor his followers seem to have been bothered by it.

In laying down his rules Lowth did not ordinarily pay much attention to universal grammar, which was usually believed to be best exemplified in Latin. Thus (unlike most of his successors) he rejected Dryden's theory that terminal prepositions were basically incorrect. On the contrary, "This is an idiom, which our language is strongly inclined to: it prevails in common conversation, and suits very well with the familiar style in writing. . . ." And on various other attempts to model English grammar on Latin we find such comments as "This comes of forcing the English under the rules of a foreign language, with which it has little concern. . . ."

But he likewise had some reservation about accepting "custom" as a satisfactory basis. Complaining about the corruption by which the past tenses of some strong verbs were substituted for the past participle, he says: "And in some of these, Custom has established it beyond recovery: in the rest it seems wholly inexcusable. The absurdity of it will be plainly perceived in the example of some of these Verbs, which Custom has not yet so perverted." The *yet* in the last clause is most revealing. In fact, his whole book is quite as much an attempt to reform custom as to expound it.

On the whole he seems to have depended largely on his own ear and judgment — the latter sometimes expressed modestly, sometimes simply announced as absolute. (Remember, he was already a professor, and was soon to become a bishop.) Thus he says, simply and firmly: "Two negatives in English destroy one another, or are equivalent to an affirmative." He illustrates the point by a single quotation from Milton:

> *Nor* did they *not* perceive the evil plight
> In which they were, or the fierce pains *not* feel.

This might strike some of us as a rather cloudy way of explaining that "they" really suffered, while the five examples he gives of incorrect usage all seem perfectly clear; the negatives obviously reinforce rather than cancel each other. Yet his statement was quite generally accepted as revelation, and most educated people have been carefully avoiding double negatives from this time on.

Lowth either invented or gave general currency to a number of other shibboleths that have been taking up a great deal of time in schools ever since, such as the distinction between *will* and *shall*, the proper use of *who* and *whom* in the most complicated situations, the theory that *as* and *than* should never be used as prepositions, the distinction between *lie* and *lay*, the theory that adjectives with an absolute meaning (such as *extreme* and *straight*) can have no comparative or superlative degrees, and so forth. His followers sometimes rejected some of his rules; more often they expanded them to cover finer and finer points, or made new ones in the same spirit. The result was that in many school-rooms the study of grammar became an exercise in fault-finding; and a great many of the people who had suffered through it became so nervous about possible criticism that their own writing became labored and colorless.

Nevertheless, the tradition that Lowth founded had a distinct value. The time had come when the English-speaking world badly needed school grammars of some sort; and if Lowth's analysis was not entirely satisfactory, it was more usable than any that had been available before. Many of the constructions he criticized were in fact awkward or ambiguous; and most of the rules he laid down are reasonably sensible if not pushed too far. The main trouble with our traditional grammars is not so much in the books themselves as in the way they are often used. This subject will be discussed in Chapter 9.

132. Sound Changes. During the eighteenth century, as in all other periods, some developments simply happened with no guidance from academic theory. Changes in the sound system were few. The long vowels /e:/ and /o:/ became the diphthongs /ei/ and /ou/ as they are today. The /w/ disappeared from the initial combination /wr/, so that originally contrasting pairs like *wring* and *ring*, *wreak* and *reek* became homonyms. In some dialects /r/ disappeared finally and before consonants. Americans are likely to consider this feature as a characteristic of the "southern accent," but it appears also in the Received Pronunciation of Britain and in the dialect of Eastern New England. And a large number of words in which the spelling *ea* represents an original long open *e* changed their vowel sound from /ei/ to /i:/. Pope, for instance, is very consistent in rhyming words like *tea* and *obey*, *ear* and *repair*; but by the end of the century such rhymes

have practically disappeared, and the modern phonemic system is pretty well established.

There have, of course, been many changes in the pronunciation of individual words, but these are very hard to date, because different pronunciations often compete for a long time; and even the most careful poets are likely to take advantage of them. Thus Pope rhymes *none* with *own* and *alone,* but also with *sun* and *upon;* and he shows the same sort of variety in his treatment of many other words.

133. DEVELOPMENT OF PROGRESSIVE AND "EMPHATIC" CONSTRUCTIONS. One of the most unusual features of contemporary English is that we can use expressions like *I am going* (often called the progressive form) and *I do go* (often called the emphatic form) along with the simple *I go.* Most languages have only the equivalent of *I go* for all purposes. We can find examples of both the other types in earlier English; but the extensive and fairly systematic use of them is an eighteenth century development. As late as Shakespeare's time *do go* is used simply as a variant of *go,* with no suggestion of emphasis; and *go* is often used where we should now expect *are going.*

Though *going* in such constructions is now considered a participle, it was originally a verbal noun. In its earliest stage the expression was *he was on going* — that is, in the act of going. This shortened first to *he was a going,* then to *he was going. Is going* and *was going* appear with increasing frequency during the Middle English period, but such combinations as *will be going, had been going,* and *will have been going* are not found until much later, and it is only at the very end of the eighteenth century that the "progressive passive" appears in such phrases as *is being built.* For many years this was criticized by purists as an unnecessary complication, on the grounds that the active construction meant the same thing, and was both older and simpler. Like most puristic theories, this works only on selected samples. *Dinner is cooking* is, indeed, equivalent to *dinner is being cooked;*

but *he is being cheated* means something quite different from *he is cheating*.

It has often been pointed out that "emphatic" does not indicate the most important uses of the *do* phrases. In expressions like "I *did* finish it" it is not the word *did* but the heavy stress that makes the emphasis, and the result is no more emphatic than "I *have* finished it," or even "I *finished* it," though the implications may be slightly different. Though Shakespeare could use such expressions as "Goes he?" and "He goes not," we must now say "Does he go?" and "He does not go." The most reasonable explanation of these new constructions is that verb-phrases gradually became so common in questions and negations that they, rather than simple verbs, eventually came to be regarded as the typical pattern. Our ears have grown used to expressions like the following:

> Will he go?
> Can he go?
> Has he gone?
> Is he going?

Consequently the old expression "Goes he?" seems to lack something, and we supply the deficiency by saying "Does he go?" In the same way we say "He does not go" to be consistent with the pattern of "He will not go" and so forth.

CHAPTER EIGHT

English Spreads Out

134. THE DOUBLE EXPANSION OF ENGLISH. In 1800 the population of the British Isles was about fifteen million, but nearly a third of them, including most of the Irish and many of the Scotch and Welsh, spoke little or no English. The combined population of the United States and Canada (both much smaller in area than they are now) was between five and six millions, and many of their inhabitants had their roots in France, other European countries, and Africa. None of the other British colonies had yet attracted much emigration. Altogether there were perhaps fifteen million native speakers of English; but a good many of them knew only their local dialects, some of which differed enough to interfere seriously with mutual understanding. At this time horses and sailing vessels were still the fastest means of communication as well as travel. Steam had not yet been put on wheels or keels, and the practical uses of electricity and electronics were not yet dreamed of. Even newspapers and the postal service were still too expensive to be parts of the lives of most people.

Today there are over three hundred million native speakers, much more widely distributed over the earth, plus a good many more millions who use English in their daily work; and practically all of them are exposed, by modern communications if not per-

sonal contact, to the main stream of the language. Dialectal differences still exist, but for the first time in history they seem to
be getting weaker instead of stronger.

The expansion of the English vocabulary has proceeded at least
as fast as the expansion in the number of speakers. Johnson's
dictionary contained about fifty thousand words, and was as
complete as he could make it. He even included a few at whose
meaning he could not even guess, simply to record their existence.
By contrast Philip B. Gove, the editor of *Webster's Third New
International Dictionary* claims for his book a vocabulary of over
450,000 words, and specifically denies that the coverage is complete. He says in the preface: "The number of words available is
always far in excess of and for a one-volume dictionary many
times the number that can possibly be included."

135. TRADE AND THE BRITISH EMPIRE. The two kinds of expansion
were of course closely related. As the British people spread over
the world they came into contact with all sorts of things their
ancestors had never encountered at home, and they needed new
words to designate them. The goods they brought home, the new
foods they learned to eat, the new plants, animals, geographical
features, and customs they encountered — all these things inevitably made their contributions. And the fact that English was
already a decidedly mixed language seems to have made it more
hospitable to additional foreign words than more homogeneous
languages such as French and German. New words do not stand
out so strongly against the already patchwork background, and
therefore are more readily acceptable. All the European languages were borrowing, but none — not even those of the other
powers that were competing for world trade and dominion —
nearly so freely as English.

It is a rather curious fact that words borrowed from distant
parts of the world were more completely naturalized than those
from European neighbors. They were spelled more or less
phonetically and took on the regular English inflections. But
European borrowings usually retained their original spelling, and

often developed a curious pronunciation, which might not be comprehensible in their land of origin, but at least marked them as expensive imports. (A Frenchman might shudder at our /tæbǝl dout/ — if he suspected that it meant *table d'hôte* — but at least we don't say /teibǝl dǝ hout/. The same Frenchman, if he has honored the English word *shocking* by admitting it to his language, spells it *schocking,* pronounces it — approximately — as *show can,* and is quite prepared to criticize an Englishman for getting it all wrong.) There was also a strong tendency, fortunately now diminishing, to insist on such foreign plural forms as *tableaux, banditti,* and *seraphim,* not to mention the even more confusing Latin and Greek ones.

136. THE INFLUENCE OF AMERICAN ENGLISH. The British colonies that contributed most to the expansion of the language were of course the ones that broke away and became the United States. By 1840 the population of this country had passed that of England, and at present about two-thirds of all native speakers of English are Americans. Their numbers alone would have made a sizable contribution inevitable. In addition there was a new continent which invited new ways of living, and an enormous polyglot immigration.

No attempt will be made here to consider in detail the differences between the British and American varieties of English, or the specifically American contributions to the common language. There is a fascinating treatment of these subjects in H. L. Mencken's *The American Language,* recently (and admirably) abridged and revised by Raven I. McDavid, Jr. In fact this book is so good that I am delighted that lack of space makes it impossible for me to offer a competing treatment, or even a digest. The main point I want to make here is that English is no longer the language of part of an island, with somewhat debased extensions in other parts of the world. It is now the established language of one entire continent, most of another, and considerable areas in other parts of the world, as well as all of the original island. And in spite of all local differences, it is used with an amazing approach to uniformity throughout all this enormous territory. If the colonization had taken place a few centuries earlier, American might well have become as different from English as French is from Italian. But the earliest settlements were made well after the invention of printing, and the growth took place through a period when the idea of educating everybody was making rapid progress. For a long time most of the books in America came from England, and a surprising number of people read those books, in or out of school. Moreover, before the Revolution most of the colonists felt a strong tie with England. In this they were unlike their Anglo-Saxon ancestors, who apparently made a clean break from their continental homes.

Nevertheless, some differences did develop. The earliest settlers borrowed from the Indians words like *hickory, moccasin, moose, opossum, powwow,* and *wigwam* — all (except possibly *powwow*) new and strange things for which they had no existing words. A little later they were borrowing from other colonists: words like *chowder, levee,* and *portage* from the French, *boss, cookie,* and *sleigh* from the Dutch. At the same time they were making new combinations of English words, such as *backwoods, bullfrog, catbird,* and *eggplant;* and using old words in new ways, such as *creek* for a running stream instead of a tidal inlet, and *lumber* for timber rather than miscellaneous junk. They were also developing new habits of pronunciation, intonation, and sentence construction. The same sort of thing was happening in the other colonies; but because their ties with England were more enduring, their population much smaller, and their political and economic influence less significant, their influence on the whole language was much weaker.

There was little objection in England to borrowings for entirely new things — after all, what can you call a moose but a moose? But all the other kinds of change were frequently and bitterly criticized. A good many conservative Englishmen felt that Americans were debasing the language; and — above all — that any Americanisms which showed any signs of taking root in England should be resisted with all necessary violence. Their attitude was perfectly natural, if not entirely reasonable. They considered that colonials were, in the nature of things, an inferior class of people, who should at least have the decency to try to preserve the traditions of their homeland. And ungrateful colonials who rebelled and broke away were essentially traitors as well as barbarians. Nothing good could come out of Nazareth. Of course this attitude was far from universal, as the continual and still growing influence of American on British English clearly shows; but the opponents of change were much more vocal than the receptive ones, who simply took what they wanted.

Not all the conservatives lived in England. There were many Americans (there are still a few) who believed that "Americanisms" were somehow inferior, even in America. Undoubtedly the name of the language is an important factor in this belief. If we called it something else — say *Jutish* — there would be no reason to feel that the variety spoken in Ohio was inferior to that spoken in Devon. But the name *English* powerfully suggests that the English people still own the language, and have the exclusive right to guide its development. One interesting result is that many speakers of other languages, though they learn English primarily because of its importance as the language of America, would be shocked at the idea of learning it from American teachers, who could give it to them only in a corrupted form. They are, of course, no sillier than the Americans who insist on learning the "pure" Castilian Spanish in school, though their only reason for learning it is to do business in Latin America.

There are thousands of differences in detail between British and American English, and occasionally they crowd together enough to make some difficulty. If you read that a man, having trouble with his *lorry*, got out his *spanner* and lifted the *bonnet,* you might not immediately understand that the driver of the *truck* had taken out his *wrench* and lifted the *hood.* And since such differences stand out, while similarities remained unnoticed, their importance is often greatly exaggerated. Actually it is often very hard to decide whether a book was written by an American or an Englishman; and even in speech typically national differences are no greater than some local differences in either country. Moreover, the language habits of the two countries are clearly growing more, rather than less, alike, although some differences will undoubtedly remain, and some new ones will develop.

137. THE EXPANSION OF KNOWLEDGE. The development of modern science and technology has resulted in a much more detailed analysis of the universe, and a greatly increased ability to manipulate it. We need words for a great many things that our ancestors never heard of; and we meet this need partly by giving new meanings to old words, partly by creating new ones. Even those branches of knowledge which have not resulted in new inventions or physical discoveries have contributed great numbers of words for new, or at least newly defined, ideas — some of them useful, some merely pretentious. We can read a fair proportion of eighteenth century books with little trouble; but an eighteenth century reader would find in our books — even those dealing quite simply with everyday affairs — innumerable words which would either mislead him or mean nothing to him; and no dictionary could explain to him their meaning. He would need, at the very least, an encyclopedia to give him some idea of what they were about.

138. THE MAKING OF COMPOUNDS. The most obvious way of forming new words is to take old words or parts of words and put them together in new combinations, preferably self-explanatory. In some of the sciences, particularly chemistry, new words are literally formulated, so that a competent analyst can recognize the composition of an unknown substance by inspection of its name. Thus the *-ide* ending in such words as *oxide* and *chloride* indicates the presence of a simple element in a compound, while the *-ate* ending indicates the presence of a salt of that element. Even I can recognize that *carbon tetrachloride* must consist of molecules containing one atom of carbon combined with four of chlorine; and I am perfectly willing to believe that an expert can do equally well with *dichlorodiphenyltrichlorethane,* though I

am quite satisfied to call it DDT and hope that it will get rid of mosquitoes.

Laymen follow the same general process in making compounds like *workmanship* and *unworkable,* but their methods are less precise, and both the choice of affixes and the exact meaning assigned to them is often a matter of accident. We may carefully observe the distinction between *continual* (occurring with great frequency) and *continuous* (going on without interruption); but the two words could just as well have been reversed, and there is no obvious reason why we say only *contiguous* and *residual* instead of *contigual* and *residuous.* We have not always shown such restraint. The availability of both native and borrowed affixes of parallel meaning makes for a very large number of variants, some of which are not demonstrably useful. There is, of course, a well-known theory that there are no two exact synonyms in English, and it is possible to argue that any two competing forms *should* be used with some distinction in meaning; but it is not possible to prove that they always are so used; and it would take a good deal of ingenuity even to recommend a distinction between some pairs, which exist simply because they were brought into the language independently by different people. What is the useful difference between such pairs as *incontrovertibility* and *incontrovertibleness, incompetence* and *incompetency, incommode* and *discommode, inconformity* and *unconformity?* Yet one or both members of each of these pairs, along with a dozen others not here listed, occur on a single page, chosen completely at random, of the first desk dictionary at hand.

Our vocabulary has been enormously swollen by the convention that all legitimate compounds are permanent. In German, compounds are made even more freely than in English; but many of the self-explanatory ones are regarded as temporary creations, almost like sentences, and no lexicographer dreams of trying to list them all. Thus you can start out with an already compound word like *Gesellschaft* (*company*), combine it with another for insurance to make *Versicherungsgesellschaft,* limit it to fire insurance as *Feuerversicherungsgesellschaft,* and designate its chief

executive as *Feuerversicherungsgesellschaftpräsident.* There is
not, to the best of my knowledge, any particular place to stop.
Dictionaries list only those compounds which either occur very
frequently or have a special meaning which a reader might not
be able to get by examining the component parts. In English,
however, the feeling is that a word is a word; and any new
compound should either be denounced as incorrect or listed for
all to share.

139. SHORTENINGS. Since compounds are often inconveniently
long, we often shorten them in various ways. Thus *automobile* is
often reduced to *auto,* while *aeroplane* was first simplified to
airplane, and then shortened to simple *plane.* Such abbreviations
are often denounced as undignified, but many of them have become so well established that they have practically superseded
the original words. Even people who insist on *telephone* rather
than *phone* usually ride on a *bus* rather than an *omnibus.* The
shortened form may, as in *auto* and *plane,* be one of the original
elements of a compound; or it may be either more or less than
an independent element.

Another way of shortening words is by using the initials of
their component parts, or of the words in a phrase. If the result
is pronounced like an ordinary word, it is called an *acronym.*
Thus *NATO* is an acronym for *North Atlantic Treaty Organization, radar* (with an extra letter to make it pronounceable) is
formed from *r*adio *d*etection *a*nd *r*anging, and so forth. There is
no special name for terms like DDT and c.o.d. In fact, the
question of whether such combinations are really words is usually
silently avoided.

Then there are blends like *smog* from *smoke* and *fog, pulmotor*
from *pulmonary* and *motor,* and so forth; somewhat mangled
abbreviations like *bike* from *bicycle* and *pram* from *perambu-
lator;* back-formations like *opine* from *opinion* and *enthuse* from
enthusiasm. Since these last are presumably formed by mistake,
they are often denounced, though a few, like *beg* from *beggar,*
have been established for centuries.

140. OTHER SOURCES. Two other common sources are proper names and brand names, both of which often go beyond their original boundaries. Thus any raincoat may be called a *mackintosh,* and *Stetson* is often used to indicate the shape rather than the make of a cowboy hat. *Kodak* is often used for any small camera, and *coke* for any cola drink. Pure coinages are rare. Words come in from slang, the underworld, occupational terms, etc. But we often have no idea how they started in the first place.

141. WHAT IS A WORD? THE SIZE OF THE CURRENT VOCABULARY. There is no doubt that the English vocabulary is much the largest in the world, but it is impossible to determine even approximately just how large it is, since nobody has yet devised either a satisfactory all-purpose definition of a word or a precise way of determining just how and when one becomes a part of a language — whatever *that* is. *Webster's Third,* doing about as well as anybody, gives (among others) the following three definitions of a word:

1. *2a* (1): a speech sound or series of speech sounds that symbolizes and communicates a meaning without being divisible into smaller units capable of independent use

This sounds reasonable, but brings up some questions when we consider compounds containing two roots. Perhaps /poustmən/ (*postman*) is a single word, since the syllable /mən/ is not used independently, but /kɑubɔi/ (*cowboy*) is not, since either syllable can be used alone.

2. *2a* (2): the entire set of linguistic forms produced by combining a single base with various inflectional elements (as affixes) without change in the part of speech

This quite different definition shifts the emphasis from physical to theoretical considerations. Perhaps we can agree that *man, men, man's,* and *men's* are four forms of the same word rather than four different words; but if we do we should realize that this is an arbitrary convention, not a demonstrable fact. If we decided the other way, our vocabulary count would be several times larger. And perhaps we can agree with the implication that *work* is three different words when it is used as a noun, a verb, and an adjective. But this is also arbitrary, and if we decided the other way our count would be much smaller. And whichever way we decide these questions, so many complications arise that it is practically impossible to be entirely consistent. Thus dictionaries list only the base forms of regular nouns and verbs, but give (and count) separate entries for such irregular forms as *men* and *did*. This is entirely sensible, but not very logical, and it distorts the word-count one way or the other. They also have to decide, for each verb, whether the past participle is only a verb-form, or also an adjective, to be counted separately. The first three I look at agree (perhaps by coincidence) that *beaded* is an adjective, but indicate by omission that *blazed* is not. Yet *blazed trail* seems to me quite parallel to *beaded bag*. The three dictionaries also agree in having separate entries for *wrapping* but not for *rapping*. This again is sensible. Anybody who understands *rap* can understand "the *rapping* on the table"; but the fact that *wrapping* can mean the material in which a thing is wrapped as well as the act of wrapping makes a separate entry useful. But if an -*ing* form (gerund, if you like) is already a verbal noun when it names an action, should it be counted as a separate word when it shifts its meaning but not its part of speech? And if so, just how much difference in meaning is required before a noun splits into several?

   3.   *2b:* a written or printed character or combination of char-
         acters representing a spoken word: *esp.* any segment of
         written or printed discourse ordinarily appearing between
         spaces or between a space and a punctuation mark

The two parts of this definition are contradictory, and should be connected by something like *alternatively* rather than *especially*. The first part sticks to speech as the basis, and suggests that writing reflects it accurately; the second part shifts to our habits of writing as the basis, with no suggestion of how irregular these often are. Why do we write *bedroom* and *poolroom*, but *dining room* and *card room?* The fact that we usually write *milkman* but *egg man* might be explained as a matter of frequency of use; but we also write *milk shake,* though this combination must now occur much more often than *milkman.* In the same way we write (if we follow our dictionaries) *mainsheet* but *main deck; mailbox* and *mailcatcher* but *mail car; sidewalk, sidesaddle,* and *sideslip,* but *side street, side show,* and *side line.* Neither meaning nor pronunciation is a dependable guide. Any good dictionary must contain thousands of such entries; and the easiest — and usual practice — is to count them as entries, and pass over the question of how many of them are words.

These are only a few of the questions that arise. We don't have to settle them, but we should keep them in mind in order to understand how writers dealing with the same material can reach such apparently contradictory results. Thus, by using different definitions and assumptions, we could calculate the vocabulary of *Webster's Third* as either very much lower or very much higher than the "over 450,000 words" that Gove claims for it. But even if we accept his count as satisfactory (as I am perfectly willing to do) we are a long way from establishing the size of our vocabulary. He also says that the dictionary includes only a fraction of "the words available." How are we to decide whether the fraction is too large or too small?

142. WHEN IS A WORD IN THE LANGUAGE? The number of words that can be legitimately used in English sentences is enormous. There are said to be nearly a million scientific names for insects alone; and since most of them have no ordinary equivalents, an entomologist writing in English simply must use them. But very few are either used or understood by non-scientists. And even if we know that *anopheles* is the kind of mosquito that carries malaria germs we may differ about whether it is an English word or a Greek word used in English. Then there are the botanical terms, and the names (essentially spelled out formulas) for chemical compounds. No general dictionary has space for more than a small fraction of them, and no lexicographer would guarantee that he has listed exactly the right ones. His aim, of course,

is simply to list those that enough people will want to look up to make their inclusion worth while, and he can never know how well he has succeeded.

There are also an inestimable number of non-scientific words which are in daily use, but only in limited areas, occupations, and so forth. Some of them are listed only in special dictionaries, some not at all; but they are just as real as if they appeared in *Webster's Third* or the *Oxford*. A layman may think they are legitimate only if they are listed in a dictionary; but a lexicographer may want to list them only if they are legitimate. To consider just one type, here are the names of a few Mexican dishes: *frijole, tamale, tortilla, enchilada, taco, guacamole, quesetilla*. The first three have been listed in dictionaries for many years; the next three only quite recently; and the last, to the best of my knowledge, not at all.

To dwellers in the Southwest, *enchilada* and *taco,* as well as *tamale* and *tortilla,* have long been as natural a part of the everyday vocabulary as *potato* and *tomato.* They have probably spread to other parts of the country mostly by way of labels on cans and recipes in Sunday papers, and now seem to be established nationally. Moreover, they are irreplaceable, because if you want the foods you can find no other words for them. *Guacamole* and *quesetilla* are words of the same sort, though not as widely known, even in the Southwest. But *frijole* is merely the Spanish word for *bean,* and is generally pronounced *bean* by the customer, even when printed *frijole* on the menu. It is not needed in English, and in my opinion (which I should not dream of trying to prove correct) it does not exist in English, no matter how often it is used, either playfully or snobbishly, in otherwise English sentences.

There are similar borderline decisions to make when we consider dubious words of purely native origin, whether they are technical terms, dialect words spreading into general use, jive talk, or whatever. We use the word *language* with very different degrees of inclusiveness; and since we disagree passionately about how much territory the word ought to cover, there is very little chance of our ceasing to do so.

143. Advantages and Disadvantages of a Great Vocabulary. The size of our vocabulary is generally considered to be a reason for great pride; but (like the size of our population) it has a few drawbacks. We often hear that a man who writes in English has unparalleled resources at his command, since the language is copious, compendious, capable of innumerable fine distinctions, and so forth. Such statements are not false, but they are based on a hidden and dangerous assumption that a man's readers all know, or should know, all the words he chooses to use, and interpret them in the same way. If this were even remotely true a great many arguments would stop — and I suppose a great many English professors would be out of jobs.

It is very hard to make even an approximate estimate of the size of any one man's vocabulary — different tests give wildly different results — and even harder to discover how thoroughly he controls it. Suppose we take a vocabulary test based on the thirty thousand most frequent words in English (as determined by a very small sampling), and administer it to a student. The result indicates that he knows all the words selected from the first five thousand, 94 percent of those in the next five thousand, 88 percent of those in the third five thousand, and so on. By taking these samples as typical and doing a little arithmetic we can conclude that he has a vocabulary of 22,387 of the most common words, plus an undiscoverable number of rarer ones. But such tests are notoriously deceptive. In the first place, a student with a little knowledge of etymology may, by weighing the probabilities in multiple-choice questions, get credit for knowing many words which he is not conscious of ever having seen before, and which might mean nothing to him in context. In the second, most tests indicate nothing about the degree of acquaintance with a word. Nobody can be sure he knows all about any word; and certainly nobody knows all the words he uses equally well. On the whole, the results of our vocabulary testing seem to be very flattering. The student who is credited with knowing 22,387 words might be bewildered or misled by five thousand of them as he encountered them in reading, and incapable of using another five thousand in his own writing and conversation. But to take the most optimistic estimates, a recognition vocabulary of fifty thousand words, and an active vocabulary of half as many, are distinctly rare.

From these figures it might seem that the eighteenth century vocabulary was quite large enough, and that the growth since that time has been an impediment to mutual understanding rather than a glorious accomplishment. There is some truth in this: a great many unnecessary words have been added to the language by fools who thought that calling a familiar thing by a fancy name reflected credit on their intelligence. A great many others have been compounded in simple ignorance that slightly different compounds of identical meaning were already available. But many of the additions are indispensable, and others have a definite value in special areas, even though they may not be suitable for ordinary use.

Certainly the more specific and detailed our knowledge of the universe becomes, the more impossible it is for anybody to know it all, so that our areas of real competence become narrower and narrower. Physicists, botanists, psychologists, and other specialists need a constantly increasing special vocabulary — whether they add new terms or give new meanings to old ones. But for the ordinary affairs of life we need a more limited vocabulary — and the smaller it is, the more chance there is that everybody can master it. Disregarding formula words, we might get along very well with fifty thousand, and if we never encountered more than fifty thousand, some of us would get familiar with them all, and all of us would have a considerable stock in common. But if we encounter half a million, we actually learn fewer words, because we have less experience with each one; and we don't all learn the same ones. The theoretical effects of the two sizes might be something like this:

Total vocabulary of 50,000 words:
  Individual vocabularies: 20,000 to 50,000 words
  Number of words known to practically everybody: 15,000
  Number of words known to all well educated people: 40,000

Total vocabulary of 500,000 words:
  Individual vocabularies: 15,000 to 100,000
  Number of words known to practically everybody: 7,500
  Number of words known to all educated people: 20,000

The figures given are of course wild guesses. There is not enough evidence available to indicate whether the proportions are even approximately right. But it does seem obvious that there is an upper limit to the number of words that any one person can master; and equally obvious that we would all learn more words if we were not exposed to quite so many. It would therefore be profitable to cut a great deal of the deadwood out of the language. Unfortunately, there does not seem to be any practicable way to do this. When a word appears in print often enough, a dictionary will record it. Anybody who hears or sees it may use it again if he chooses to. We don't have a government bureau to decide just which words are legitimate, and most of us don't want one — just look at the kind of language that appears in most government bulletins. And several centuries of experience indicate that the self-appointed guardians of the sacred vocabulary are remarkably ineffective. But we might improve the situation a little by encouraging the beliefs that a rare word is better than a common one only when it will communicate an idea more precisely, and that there is no automatic virtue in polysyllabification.

144. CHANGES IN MEANING. Along with the creation of new words there has been at least an equally great change in the meanings of old ones. This process, sometimes called "semantic shift," has always occurred in all languages, and will obviously continue, in spite of objections. Those people who tell us we should use words only in their "true" meanings seem to have logic on their sides — how are we to communicate effectively

unless words stay put? — but they have all history and human nature against them. They also suffer from the delusion that the earliest meanings with which they happen to be acquainted are the original ones. The fact is that nobody knows what the original meaning of any of our really old words was. An etymologist can tell us that *digit* meant a finger or toe before it meant an Arabic numeral, but if he calls this the original meaning of the word he is simply guessing. We know quite well that *tête*, the normal and entirely respectable French word for *head*, began to be used in its present sense as a bit of slang; an earlier meaning was *pot*, and before that there may or may not have been others. We can trace the English word *head* to a hypothetical Indo-European form, from which Latin *caput*, French *chef*, Anglo-Norman *chief*, German *Haupt*, and various other cognates were derived by quite regular though complicated processes; but for all we know this hypothetical form may itself have been a slang or metaphorical transfer from a still earlier meaning.

The four kinds of semantic shift most frequently discussed are *specialization, generalization, elevation,* and *degeneration* (other terms, such as *narrowing, broadening, amelioration,* and *pejoration* are sometimes used). Thus *deer,* which used to mean any wild animal, has been specialized to mean only the kind that produces venison; while *horse* has been generalized to designate a mare or gelding as well as a stallion. A *governor* used to be a man who steered a ship. Now it may be one who steers the ship of state. (Of course it may also be a mechanical gadget that keeps an engine from running too fast — some words move in all directions.) An Old English *hūswīf* was presumably a respectable woman; but by the time the form of the word had contracted to *hussif* and then to *hussy* its meaning had become so uncomplimentary that the original elements in a later form had to be recombined to make *housewife*.

The four kinds of shift mentioned in the preceding paragraph are not the only ones that occur; in fact, their neat symmetry probably does more to conceal than to explain the ways words change their meanings. In general, a word may be shifted from one meaning to another whenever there is a resemblance between two things. To go back to the word *head,* its first known use is to name a part of the body. But it has been transferred to various other things which resemble this part in shape, as a *head of lettuce;* in position, as the *head of the stairs;* in function, as the *head of the company.* Sometimes there is a resemblance at two or more removes. Since the top part of almost anything can be called a head, the water kept high in a dam to supply power may be called a *head of water;* then steam, ready to work regardless of its position, may be called a *head of steam.* Such an expression as the dispute *came to a head* would be meaningless if we were not familiar with boils and pimples forming a recognizable head as they were about to pop.

Of course it could be argued that any extension of meaning is simply a kind of generalization; but sometimes the earlier meaning drops out of use, leaving a complete transfer. Very few people now use *digit* to refer to a finger, and no Frenchman uses *tête* to refer to a pot.

We sometimes call the supposedly original meaning of a word its *literal* meaning, and all derived meanings *figurative;* but until we all become profound etymologists, such a distinction is not very useful. If the *head of a pin* is a metaphor, how are we to express the same idea literally? Our language is full of frozen metaphors. Many of them were deliberately created, proved attractive, and thus came into common use. Others came about simply because there are more things in the world than there are words in any conceivable human vocabulary. When we meet a new thing we have to call it something, and it is usually more convenient to modify the meaning of an old word than to invent a new one.

Changes in meaning are so fascinating that there is a strong temptation to go on discussing them for dozens or hundreds of pages, and to revel in all their historical, philosophical, and psychological implications. In this chapter we have room for only two more points. First, semantic shift has been unusually active during the past two centuries simply because our environment, both physical and intellectual, has been changing more rapidly than ever before. To my grandfather, who was born in Ireland, the "natural" meaning of the word *car* was a small horsedrawn vehicle; to my father, it was a railroad coach; to me, a street-car. Of course all of us had to recognize new meanings as conditions changed. To my son, the natural meaning is an automobile; and it is quite possible that to his son it may seem the obvious word for what we now call airplanes, especially if our roads get so full of automobiles that they can't move any more. And while all generations of our family have of course believed in the *rights of man*, the *principles of democracy*, and the advantages of a *liberal education*, the exact meaning to be assigned to these phrases might cause a bit of argument.

Second, the development of euphemisms was particularly extensive. The tendency to avoid the direct naming of things felt to be offensive, unpleasant, or dangerous has always existed, but has never been so widespread as in our recent history. The "four-letter words" dealing with sex and elimination became so disgraceful that they were not even listed in dictionaries, though most of them managed somehow to survive; and even quite innocent parts of the body, if they happened to be too near a danger area, had to be disguised in polite conversation. A lady might conceivably sprain an *ankle*, but she couldn't possibly bruise a *thigh* — in fact she was not supposed to know of the existence of this term for the upper joint of a *limb* (even furniture did not have *legs* as far as really particular people were concerned).

Euphemisms are not confined to "indecent" areas. There is also a marked tendency to avoid direct mention of death, certain diseases, things particularly holy or unholy, and so forth. Unfortunately, some subjects cannot be avoided entirely; and when a euphemism becomes fully established it becomes offensive to some ears and has to be replaced by a new one. Thus *powder room* may be substituted for *toilet*, which was originally of about the same degree of delicacy. The process could obviously go on forever, and perhaps it will; but the direction veers from time to time. On one hand, as a disapproving elderly lady once remarked,

"Young people nowadays talk about anything — in fact they don't talk about anything else." On the other, we seem to be verbally abolishing *old people* in favor of *senior citizens,* changing the *poor* to the *underprivileged,* and *relaxing our tensions* instead of merely *loafing.*

145. VARIETIES OF ENGLISH. It has already been mentioned that the three hundred million speakers of English, scattered all over the globe, use their language with a surprising approach to uniformity. A banker from London, a farmer from Alabama, and a mechanic from Sydney can, with a little adjustment, communicate quite readily and efficiently; while their opposite numbers from Lisbon, Andalusia, and Paris, though they live much closer together and speak languages of a common origin, would be helpless without interpreters. Nevertheless, there are many varieties and subvarieties of English, based on differences in location, education, occupation, and a number of other things; and the various differences intersect in such a complicated way that a complete analysis of them is utterly hopeless. We cannot even agree on the meanings of the various terms used to designate different kinds of English, as the following excerpt from *Webster's Seventh New Collegiate Dictionary* indicates:

dialect . . . . 1 a: a regional variety of language distinguished by features of vocabulary, grammar, and pronunciation from other regional varieties and constituting together with them a single language (the Doric *dialect* of ancient Greek) *b:* one of two or more cognate languages (French and Italian are Romance *dialects*) *c:* a regional variety of a language usually transmitted orally and differing distinctively from the standard language (the Lancashire *dialect* of English) *d:* a variety of a language used by the members of an occupational group (the *dialect* of the atomic physicist) *e:* the customary language of a social class (peasant *dialect*) . . .

syn DIALECT, VERNACULAR, LINGO, JARGON, CANT, ARGOT, SLANG mean a form of language that is not recognized as standard. [But dialect obviously does not mean that to everybody — see definitions *a, b,* and *d* above.]

DIALECT applies commonly to a form of language persisting

regionally or among the uneducated; VERNACULAR applies to the
everyday speech of the people in contrast to that of learned men;
LINGO is a mildly contemptuous term for any language not readily
understood; JARGON applies to a technical or esoteric language
used by a profession, trade, or cult; it may also be a stronger
designation than LINGO for language or usage that sounds out-
landish; CANT is applied derogatorily to language that is both
peculiar to a group or class and intrinsically lacking in clarity or
precision of expression (journalistic *cant*); ARGOT is applied to a
peculiar language of a clique or other closely knit group (thieves'
argot); SLANG designates a class of mostly recently coined and
frequently short-lived terms or usages informally preferred to
standard language as being forceful, novel, or voguish.

I have no wish to criticize these definitions, since I couldn't
hope to do any better in the same space — or perhaps in ten
times as much. It is obvious that the terms overlap, that they
are used differently by different people, and that it is extremely
hard even for one man to use any one of them with complete
consistency. Even if we got ten competent linguists to agree exactly on the precise meaning of each term (which seems a remote
possibility) they would get into endless arguments as soon as
they began to classify particular expressions. The best I can do
is to try to explain how I use the terms in this book, without pre-
tending either that my way is the best way or that I am perfectly
consistent.

First, I shall not use the terms *lingo, cant,* and *argot* at all
(though I have no objection to their use by others); and I shall
have no further use for the term *vernacular,* which appeared
earlier as a term to distinguish the modern languages from Latin
and Greek. By *jargon* I mean any group-usage which I consider
conspicuously pretentious, conveniently vague, or lazily poly-
syllabic, as "the *jargon* of government bureaus." The only helpful
things I can say about *slang* are that I consider some slang terms
much more useful and attractive than others, and that neither I
nor anybody else can determine exactly when a widely accepted
term ceases to be slang and becomes something else.

This leaves two terms to be considered — *dialect* and *standard*. The second is used in the quoted excerpt without explanation, but is defined elsewhere in the same book as "substantially uniform and well-established by usage in the speech and writing of the educated and widely recognized as acceptable and authoritative." Many people consider the two terms mutually exclusive: standard is the "good" English used by educated everywhere, while dialect "persists" (a revealing term) only "regionally or among the uneducated." But many linguists consider that even the best-educated people must speak one dialect or another, and that a given dialect may therefore have both standard and non-standard forms. And some linguists consider standard to be merely one dialect, enjoying greater prestige than the others, but not intrinsically better. I use *dialect* simply in the regional sense; and I use *standard* rather loosely, because it is such a slippery term that I have never been able to do any better. It is easy enough to talk about what is "well established and widely recognized," but we disagree widely and violently not only about whether many usages are in fact established, but about what principles to use in judging them. There will be more on this point in the last chapter. Meanwhile, I use *standard* for usage that I think is generally respected, and I am reasonably broadminded about variations, regional and otherwise.

146. "FORMAL ENGLISH." Writing is naturally far more uniform than speech for several reasons. In the first place, it conceals many differences in pronunciation, intonation, etc. In the second, it is a much slower process, so that there is time for some editing before even the first draft of a sentence goes down on paper. Many little peculiarities and inconsistencies can therefore be eliminated; and at least some of them should be. No competent writer, even when he is trying to achieve a very personal flavor, writes exactly as he talks. But the degree of separation between the spoken and written forms of languages can vary enormously. In English, the differences concealed are comparatively minor. In

the Mohammedan world they are so great that classical Arabic
is an efficient means of written communication among people
who find each other's spoken dialects completely unintelligible.
During the past two centuries our schools have made a tremen-
dous effort to keep the language uniform, primarily by insisting
on the writing of "formal English," secondarily by trying to make
the students talk as they were learning to write. It is impossible
to say how much they are responsible for the degree of uniformity that has been preserved. It can be argued that printing and
better communications have been more effective than the schools;
but without the schools our books and so forth would themselves
have been far more diverse.

Those linguists who insist that writing is merely a representation of speech are likely to regard the schoolroom reversal of the
"natural order" as both vicious and hopeless. It is of course true
that English has continued to change, though more slowly than
it would have under other circumstances; and it is equally true
that the kind of English taught in the schools was not based
entirely on the way even the best educated people actually used
the language, but partly on some rather peculiar theories of how
they ought to use it. Logic — or what passed for logic — was
often considered more important than even the most thoroughly
established custom, so that schoolroom English became a somewhat artificial jargon, usually admired in theory, but considerably modified in practice by all but the most docile.

But even the rebels usually regarded "formal" English as the
only really legitimate form. They had been brought up to believe
that all contractions and other shortcuts (such as incomplete
comparisons) were essentially sinful; that *colloquial* was practically equivalent to *illiterate;* that correctness was more important than force, grace, or even comprehensibility; and (perhaps
most unreasonable of all) that whoever had written "the book"
knew what he was talking about. Some excellent books were in
fact written, but they had very little influence on instruction.
Most school texts were compiled by men whose main qualification was an ability to find a publisher; and the sort of progress

they represented was mainly in the direction of finer and finer theoretical distinctions. Analysis and diagramming became ends in themselves. Students spent month after month learning to distinguish not only between adjectival and adverbial clauses, but between adverbial clauses of time, manner, condition, concession, and a number of other things; and strong stands were taken about whether *while* could be used adversatively, or only temporally. Shibboleths multiplied, and were almost never abandoned. I once traced a rule, illustrated by the same sentence, through thirty grammars published over a period of a hundred and fifty years. No writer admitted that he had taken it from an earlier book, and no writer ever changed the illustration, because the point at issue was so artificial that it was almost impossible to find another sentence that contained it. Unfortunately (if you are curious) a war came along about then and I lost my notes. But perhaps it is just as well I have forgotten the point at issue. Somebody might take it up again.

The result of this attitude was not, of course, entirely calamitous. A good teacher can get good results from even a bad textbook by using it with some discretion; and the contribution to uniformity was worth a fairly stiff price. Many people learned to use the language admirably, whether in or out of school. But the situation was definitely unhealthy (as every English teacher who is greeted with suspicion by all strangers knows), and we have reason to be glad that it is now being considerably modified.

147. Changes in the Verb System. The principal structural changes that have taken place since the eighteenth century concern the verbs, and they are of three sorts. In the standard language the tendency toward the simplification of inflections was arrested, and in a few cases reversed. Lowth's campaign to prevent any more verbs from shifting to the regular conjugation, or losing the old distinction between the past tense and past participle, has proved more successful than he would probably have thought possible, so that some of the forms to which he says regretfully that "our ears have grown accustomed" would now

strike most educated people as impossible, though they continue to be heard in popular speech. And we have come to insist on "you *were*" for both numbers, though "you *was*" in the singular seemed to be well established a hundred and fifty years ago.

The development of perfect and progressive systems has continued, so that now it is at least theoretically possible to say something like "By next month he *will have been being treated* for three years," and call it "third person singular future perfect indicative passive." Such expressions are fortunately rare, but we do frequently use combinations that would not have occurred to our ancestors. We have also extended the use of some additional auxiliaries, in such constructions as *got hurt, got moving, kept* (*on*) *doing it,* and so forth. In fact our system of verb-phrases has become so complicated that few grammarians have even attempted a systematic study of it, and no analysis has been generally accepted. The usual practice is either to oppose or ignore those that cannot be readily explained; but they continue to gain ground.

There has also been a great increase in what are now usually called verb-adverb combinations, such as *put away, put by, put down, put in, put off, put on, put out,* and *put up.* Many of us used to be taught that these were deplorable, and that it was much better to use a specific word for each purpose, and not to overuse the common ones. This advice ignored the fact that the preferred words were usually Latin compounds of no greater variety — *appose, compose, depose, expose, impose, interpose, oppose, propose,* and so forth (the two lists are typical rather than parallel). The fact that the Latin compounds have the modifying element first and are written solid, while the English ones have it second and after an intervening space, is interesting, but hardly proves that the English ones are inferior. At any rate, we may rejoice that we are not afflicted with the German mixture of the two systems, which calls for saying "Wollen sie hereinkommen?" (Will you enter?), but "Er kam herein."

CHAPTER NINE

The Background of Traditional Grammar

148. Some General Remarks About Grammar. We have now reached the contemporary period, and in the next chapter we shall consider the current state of our knowledge of the language and some of the forces which are affecting our treatment of it in our schools. But before we do so it will be well to examine with some care the grammatical tradition to which we have all been exposed, and which most of us have been inclined to accept as beyond question, whether or not we have ever been able to understand it.

Grammar is notoriously the most widely and deeply hated of all studies, at least in English-speaking countries. Several reasons, each containing at least some truth, have been advanced to explain this fact. One is that the kind of grammar that has been traditionally taught in our schools is based on Latin, and fits English so loosely that considerable parts of it can be understood only as an act of faith, with a distinct element of mysticism. Another is that the subject is often taught not as a body of information but as a system of morals, toward which we often have a split reaction. While one side of our minds tells us that we ought to obey the rules because they must somehow be right, the other tells us that if we do we'll lose many of our friends, and feel like prigs in the process. And finally there is the widespread suspicion that the whole subject is unnecessary — an imposition foisted on us by schoolteachers and their ilk. If somebody would just shoot all grammarians, honest men could live in peace. "Why," asks young Tommy, "have any parts of speech at all? What are they good for? Why don't they just let us talk sense?"

Such questions are often dismissed as silly or rebuked as impertinent, but they are important and deserve honest and careful answers. As a professional grammarian I am not inclined to underrate the importance of my subject; but if we are to continue to insist that everybody study it, we ought to be able to explain clearly what it consists of, and how it can be profitably used.

One reason for the general confusion is that we use the term *grammar* in a number of incompatible ways, and we often shift from one meaning to another without realizing that we are changing the subject. We cannot solve this problem by defining the term to indicate that only one meaning is legitimate; but we can clarify it by getting a firm grasp of the more important meanings, and keeping them distinct in our own minds.

1. The *study* of the structural patterns which are used to put words or morphemes together into meaningful sentences. The exact boundaries of this study have never been settled, but this meaning causes comparatively little trouble.

2. The *patterns themselves*. Here we run into a very real difficulty which is often disregarded. We are tempted to say that *the* grammar of a language is the set of patterns that actually exist in it, built into the minds of the speakers, and that *a* grammar is a particular attempt to describe them. But if the language is composed of dialects, subdialects, and finally idiolects, no two quite alike, the "set of patterns that actually exists" becomes a rather vague (though impressive) term. A grammarian can describe only those patterns that he has observed — inevitably a limited

sample, seen from a particular point of view. Conceivably the time may come when all competent grammarians will agree on at least the major points of their descriptions. At present they do not.

3. A *set of rules* which everybody ought to follow. Grammars which lay down such rules are called *prescriptive* or *normative,* and many linguists feel that they are illegitimate — that a grammarian has no more right to legislate about his phenomena than a chemist has; his "laws" should be merely generalizations about what he has observed. Most laymen, on the other hand, think of prescriptive grammars as the only possible kind. Some of them assume that the rules are based on the same sort of inevitable relations as those that underlie the rules of arithmetic; others that they are an arbitrary set of regulations, like traffic laws, but that they are necessary to make accurate communication possible. In either case, they consider that any utterance that does not comply with the rules is ungrammatical, though by definition (2) above it would be simply based on a different kind of grammar.

It would be a waste of time to argue about which of these two attitudes is correct, because they are based on such different premises that they are not comparable. But we can probably agree that if we are to use prescriptive grammars in our schools they should be based on the best descriptive ones now available; and we should know what we are using them for. The idea that nobody can learn to handle a language competently without a thorough knowledge of grammatical theory, though firmly believed by many teachers, simply will not stand investigation. Grammars appeared so late in history that the authors of much of the great literature of the world could not possibly have been acquainted with any systematic descriptions of the structure of the languages in which they wrote. The first Greek grammar, for instance, was not composed until long after the great age of Greek literature. Dante could not possibly have seen an Italian grammar. Shakespeare could have seen an English grammar, composed by a crackpot named Bullokar; but it is hard to see how he could have profited by it, and there is certainly no evidence that he or anybody else ever did.

In fact, there is a great deal of evidence to indicate that anybody who grows up thoroughly immersed in *one socially satisfactory and fairly homogeneous dialect* can learn that dialect by simple exposure quite as well as he is at all likely to do by any system of structural analysis. But today few people in America are in a position to do this. How often do we hear mothers complain, "Rick used to talk so nicely until he went to school, and now he is an absolute barbarian"? For anybody who grows up in a socially unsatisfactory dialect, or in a confusing mixture of competing but not clearly differentiated dialects, a systematic description of how standard patterns differ from others can be very useful in saving time and increasing confidence — provided, of course, that the description is reasonably accurate, and is not offered for more than it is worth.

If it is offered and accepted as gospel it can lead to its own kind of trouble. People who have always received A's in grammar courses are often handicapped in a way of which they are quite unaware. Having accepted a particular set of conventions as universal truths, they are very comfortable in certain situations, but rather helpless in others, and the mixture of smugness and irritation which they often develop is not particularly attractive. I can make this statement with all the confidence of a reformed sinner. Grammar was always easy for me in school — so easy that I was in my middle thirties before I realized that I had been mistaking docility for intelligence. It was a severe shock when I was forced to realize that boys I had thought stupid when they said "I don't see it" were often on sounder ground than I had been in accepting everything that the books and teachers said.

149. STRUCTURAL PATTERNS. Speakers of any language somehow develop by tacit agreement (but never quite uniformly) a set of structural patterns; and the organization of these patterns, even in languages that we are likely to think of as primitive,

can be amazingly complex. Students who find the subjunctive mood confusing may be interested in learning that the Cree Indians in Canada have verbs with fifteen different moods; and a Turkish verb is said to have over three thousand possible terms. Moreover, recent investigations have shown that the structural differences among languages are far greater than used to be believed. Some languages do not have the subject-predicate sentences which are so important in our structure. Some do not even have permanent words, but rather word-sentences composed of such shifting arrangements and modifications of elements that at first meeting we find them absolutely incredible. These and other differences are so fundamental that we cannot satisfactorily treat them as variations within a single system, but as representing utterly different systems, each of which must be studied in and for itself.

There is no reason to believe that any of the speech communities who developed these amazing complications were more consistent than their descendants, nor can we reasonably assume that in the ages before written grammars the learning of any language was a systematic mastery of a completed structure. Presumably most people gave the patterns no particular thought, but simply assumed that they were among the laws of nature. Each speaker absorbed what he could of the conventions in which he was immersed, and perhaps made a few small contributions or modifications of his own. The language was therefore gradually but continually changing in its patterns as well as its vocabulary, and at no time was it ever quite uniform.

To suppose that behind this ever-shifting collection of imperfectly consistent habits there is somehow a "true" and logically consistent grammar now seems a little unreasonable; and such a supposition certainly cannot be proved. With a few million people talking as fast and as variously as they do, the obvious fact is that anybody who tries to make a comprehensive description — any grammarian — must first select a sample of language small enough for him to have time to examine and consider it

carefully. He must then find some way to classify his material —
a process which involves a number of arbitrary decisions about
which similarities and differences are significant and which are
negligible. And when he finds inconsistencies and outright contradictions, as he surely will if his sample is large enough, he
must either find ingenious ways of fitting them into his system
or throw them out as illegitimate. In other words, there is an
element of invention as well as of discovery in his grammar.
There is nothing shameful about this, and his grammar may be
valuable and useful; but it is inevitably limited. Some grammarians are abler and more sensible than others, but none of
them can approach the impersonal accuracy of physicists, because
the speech acts of people are more complicated and less regular
than the movements of particles. And even in physics it is now
realized that any description is an interaction between the
observer and what he observes.

We shall no doubt continue to talk about *the* grammar of a
given language, but we should realize that this is a convenient
rather than a precise use of the word. A grammar is an attempt
to describe the patterns which a particular student, called a
grammarian, has observed in a particular language, usually with
the aid of some earlier attempts, and necessarily from a particular
point of view. The enormous array of facts is always somewhat
contradictory, and different analyses and descriptions are always
possible. This statement annoys a few of the more zealous linguists, who are quite sure that they have found the one true
road to the truth. But they disagree forcefully about which road
is this true one. At least three approaches (each with variations)
are being used by able scholars in studying the patterns of English. Some features of the oldest one will be considered in this
chapter, and of the two newer ones in the next.

150. VARIATIONS IN TRADITIONAL GRAMMAR. Two things must be
emphasized here: First, that the word "traditional" is not used
as a term of reproach; second, that the tradition has never been

either static or uniform. Admirable scholars as well as bigoted pedants have used the traditional approach, modifying it in the light of new knowledge. Once we recognize the fact that it is an analysis based on certain assumptions and not a moral code, we can use it for what it is worth — which may be a good deal in certain circumstances. But the schoolroom version of it did, as it developed, become more and more Latinized, and this during a period when fewer and fewer students had any real knowledge of Latin. The result is that even people who have mastered the rules are often oppressed by a sense of mystery about the whole thing. It therefore seems worth while to run through the traditional parts of speech in an effort to show how certain concepts which are quite comprehensible when applied to Latin become almost mystical when transferred to English. The result is comparable to what we might get if we tried to indicate the political geography of Africa on an outline map of South America. The picture would not be utterly useless. After all, both continents are roughly triangular, and much wider at the top than at the bottom, so that the sizes and relative positions of the countries could be indicated after a fashion. But a good deal of distortion would be necessary — and instruction based on such a map would be better if this fact were continually borne in mind. Detailed argument about the exact and true locations of all the boundaries would be rather pointless.

151. NOUNS AND ADJECTIVES. Latin nouns are inflected much more fully than Modern English ones; and Latin adjectives have the same kinds of inflection as nouns. In fact the resemblance between Latin nouns and adjectives is so great that until the nineteenth century they were not usually classified as separate parts of speech. When a noun was used to name something it was called a *noun substantive;* when used to modify another noun it was called a *noun adjective.* (In both these phrases the second noun modifies the first.) Some nouns could be used either way. Others were restricted by their meaning (not by rule) to one

function or the other. Nouns adjective could also be inflected
in different degrees comparable to our *big, bigger, biggest*. There
doesn't seem to be any temptation to speak of *wolf, wolfer,
wolfest*.

A noun is now usually said to be the name of something, and
an adjective to be a word that modifies a noun. These two definitions carry the seeds of confusion, since nouns are defined in relation to the things of which we talk, but adjectives in relation to
other words rather than to things. They still work well enough
in simple cases, but lead to endless argument in others. Consider
the word *green* in the following sentences:

> *Green* is my favorite color. (Noun)
> The *green* grass grows all around. (Adjective)
> The grass is *green*. (Adjective)
> The color is *green*. (Debatable)
> I like *green* better than red. (Noun)
> I like the *green* better than the red. (Highly debatable. Is
> *green* an adjective modifying "a noun understood," an adjective
> used in place of a noun, an adjective that has become a noun
> by its use in the sentence, or a noun in its own right? And does it
> make any difference whether we are talking about two tubes of
> paint or two sweaters?)

Or consider the phrase "a stone fence." Is *stone* an adjective
modifying *fence* or is it an attributive noun, the phrase being
"a fence made of stone," and its real structure remaining unchanged in spite of the quite perceptible difference in form?
The fact that such questions have been argued with much
heat for many generations suggests that they cannot *within this
system* be settled by an appeal to evidence. They should therefore be classified as a philosophic diversion rather than linguistic
analysis. To provide a tangible basis for more limited discussions
we will now look at the forms of a Latin noun. Five of the
original eight cases of Indo-European are still in common use,

and their forms are still fairly, though not perfectly, distinct. This is the Latin noun for *wolf:*

	Masculine	
	Singular	*Plural*
Nominative	lupus	lupī
Genitive	lupī	lupōrum
Dative	lupō	lupīs
Accusative	lupum	lupōs
Ablative	lupō	lupīs

	Feminine	
Nominative	lupa	lupae
Genitive	lupae	lupārum
Dative	lupae	lupīs
Accusative	lupam	lupās
Ablative	lupā	lupīs

1. The set of forms of a noun is called its *declension* — an apparently mysterious term with a simple origin. In some early grammars the forms were shown in a diagram like this:

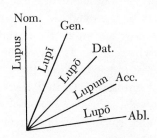

Here all cases but the nominative "decline," or fall away, from the vertical. They are therefore still often referred to as "the oblique cases."

2. There are five different declensions in Latin. Nobody knows why. *Lupa* belongs to the first and *lupus* to the second. The others are not illustrated here.

3. We have good reason to believe that originally all twenty of the forms listed above (as well as some others long lost) were different, but keeping them all straight had apparently been too much of a strain, and some of them had run together. Thus in the masculine singular the dative and ablative forms had both become *lupō,* and in the feminine singular the genitive and dative had both become *lupae.* In the plural the dative and ablative forms are not only identical with each other but are the same in both genders. Altogether we have only thirteen different forms where there ought to be twenty — the smallest number that could unambiguously indicate the three "properties" of gender, number, and case. *Property* is another term which often carries an aura of mystery. Its only discoverable meaning in grammar is a *restriction in use imposed by a certain form.* Modern English adjectives have completely lost these three properties, since one form can now be used for all purposes; and Modern English nouns have lost more of the properties than some grammars admit.

There is no justification for the idea that these properties are somehow inherent in all nouns, whether or not there is any tangible evidence of them. None of these limitations is necessarily shown by the forms of nouns, since other devices are available. And when any one of them is not shown by the form of a noun it ceases to be a property of that noun. Thus our word *sheep* has neither gender nor number, and the only limitation on its case is that it is not genitive. It is a reasonable, though not a necessary, fiction to consider it as sometimes singular and sometimes plural, since it can thus be treated as resembling most other nouns. But it is a completely useless fiction to consider it as sometimes nominative and sometimes objective, since no English nouns are now limited in this way.

152. NUMBER. The easiest of the three "properties" for us to grasp is number because, like the Romans, we not only think of things as being either singular or plural, but we indicate which almost every time we use a noun. This is not a matter of course. Some

languages have more than two grammatical numbers: for instance, one, two, and more than two. Other languages do not
bother with grammatical number at all, but use the equivalent
of *one man, two man, many man* with all nouns, whereas we do
it with only a few, like *sheep.* And many languages show number
in their adjectives as well as their nouns. The French, for instance, call a little boy *un petit garçon;* but two little boys *deux
petits garçons.* In other words, although arithmetical numbers
are international, grammatical number is an arbitrary device in
a given language. You will notice that in Latin number is not
expressed either separately or consistently by anything equivalent to the modern *-s* ending. Instead, number, gender, and case
are all indicated (though sometimes ambiguously) by a single
ending. This seems so complicated that we wonder how illiterate
people, including their small children, could have practiced it
for centuries, but they somehow managed, at least after a fashion.

153. GENDER. Gender is a grammatical device, very useful in
such synthetic languages as Latin because it helps to show which
adjectives modify which nouns, and which nouns particular pronouns refer to. In analytical languages, where these relationships
are indicated by a dependable word-order, it is a complicated
and almost completely useless nuisance inherited from the past.
In speaking French we must be careful always to call an old
man *vieux* and an old woman *vieille,* though one form would do
for both exactly as well as *old* does in English.

Some languages have as many as a dozen genders, which may
be based on any kind of distinction, such as animate against
inanimate, or even small against large; but the best-known
genders are based, though far from reliably, on sex. Thus both
Latin and Old English have three genders — masculine, feminine,
and neuter. Male beings are likely to be referred to by masculine
nouns, and female beings by feminine nouns, but there are some
conspicuous exceptions. It is hard to think of anything more pro-
fessionally female than a prostitute, yet the Latin word *scortum,*

which means one, is neuter. So was the Old English *wīf* (woman, later wife); and the Old English *wīfman* was masculine, because *man* was masculine, and remained so even in a combination that meant *woman*.

We can see gender in action by examining the French translations of three sentences:

> I saw the king, and he was happy.
> J'ai vu le roi, et il était heureux.
>
> I saw the queen, and she was happy.
> J'ai vu la reine, et elle était heureuse.
>
> I saw his majesty, and he was happy.
> J'ai vu sa majesté, et elle était heureuse.

It seems natural enough to use the feminine pronoun *elle* in the second sentence, because it is here the equivalent of our *she*. Using *la* and *heureuse* instead of *le* and *heureux* for *the* and *happy* may strike us (reasonably enough) as an unnecessary complication, but we can accept it without much concern. What most Americans find ridiculous at first meeting is the feminine forms in the third sentence. Why call a king *she?*

The answer is that while *elle* is often equivalent to *she*, there is an essential difference between the two words. In languages having gender, pronouns must be selected to agree with their antecedents. In English, pronouns must simply be appropriate to the people or things to which they refer. We call a woman *she* not because *woman* is a feminine word — it never has been — but because a woman is female.

It is often said that Modern English has "natural gender," but this curious statement only complicates the problem. Gender is a purely grammatical convention, and there is nothing natural about it. We can understand it more easily if we don't extend the term to cover something quite different. The fact that we use *cow* to refer to a female bovine has no more grammatical consequence than the fact that we use *calf* to refer to a young one.

154. CASE. A case is a special form used to show the noun's relation to other words in the sentence. To see how it works we can consider the following simple Latin sentences:

1. a. Lupus videt Marcum.   The wolf sees Marcus.
   b. Marcum videt lupus.   "
   c. Marcum lupus videt.   "
   d. Lupus Marcum videt.   "
   e. Videt lupus Marcum.   "
   f. Videt Marcum lupus.   "

Lupus is in the nominative case and is therefore the subject. *Marcum* is in the accusative case and is therefore the direct object. The different word orders give slightly different emphases, but cannot change the basic relations.

2. Lupum videt Marcus.   Marcus sees the wolf.

Now the cases have been reversed, and so has the meaning. Here again six different word orders would be possible.

3. Lupō Marcus carnem dedit.   Marcus gave the wolf meat.

Lupō is in the dative case, and is therefore the indirect object. *Marcus* is the subject and *carnem* (from a different declension) is the direct object. But I have no idea why Marcus gave him the meat.

4. Lupī Marcus carnem surripuit.   Marcus stole the wolf's meat.

Lupī is in the genitive case, which shows that the meat was already his. I hope it disagreed with Marcus.

An English-speaking child, meeting structures like this for the first time, finds them not only confusing but ridiculous. Take sentence (1b), for instance. If *Marcum* means *Marcus, videt* means *sees,* and *lupus* means *wolf,* how in the world can "Marcum videt lupus" mean anything but "Marcus sees the wolf?" The people who say it does — Romans and teachers alike — must be crazy, and the subject is obviously not worth pursuing. As a matter of fact a good many children give up the subject right here, and even if they are forced to sit in Latin classes for some years, and to memorize some words and some rules, they never learn anything of the slightest importance about the language.

Other children, with slightly more flexible minds, are willing to accept the rules, and to treat all Latin sentences as something like algebraic equations — puzzles which can be solved by application of the proper techniques, but which obviously have to be torn apart and re-assembled before they can be understood. Such children usually consider Latin a very learned subject, of which only the bare elements can be learned in high school. The idea that rather stupid children used to learn to prattle Latin quite accurately before they were five seems absolutely incredible — yet they did.

Naturally, these Roman five-year olds had never heard of a direct object or an accusative case. They had simply learned by continual exposure that the *-um* form showed that the wolf didn't do anything, but had something happen to him, and that the *-us* form would be used to indicate the actor. They knew these things just as an American child knows the difference between "My father is taller than. *John*" and "My father is taller than *John's*."

Of course these are very simple examples. This is no place to go into detail about Latin grammar. The important point is simply that the basic signalling system of Latin was quite different from that of English. It is useless to argue about which is better. Opinions differ and proof is impossible. Whether they were moved by intelligence or pure laziness our ancestors somehow drifted away from the use of cases to a combination of position and prepositions.

Even the Romans had begun this drift, as you can see by the duplications in the declension of *lupus*. This occasions some difficulty in reading Latin. We have to depend on cases to understand the meaning, and the case-forms are sometimes ambiguous. In Old English the drift had gone much further, and the ambi-

guity was proportionately more serious. To make up for the losses
in distinct inflections we have gradually developed a standard
word-order which indicates meaning by position rather than
cases. We often call this word-order "normal," which has the
unfortunate effect of suggesting that any other order is silly;
ours is normal only in the sense that it has become habitual for
us. The Spanish, for instance, habitually put an adjective after a
noun instead of before it, and get along just as well.

A great deal of unnecessary confusion has been caused by some
grammarians who have shifted the meaning of the term *case*
from the form used to show a certain relation, and use it to indicate the relation itself. Thus many grammars say that whenever
the word *wolf* is used as the subject it is in the "nominative"
case, and whenever it is used as the object it is in the "objective"
case — a combination of the old accusative and dative cases. A
few conservative grammars even talk about separate dative and
accusative cases in Modern English. Thus we have these three
competing declensions of the noun *wolf* in the singular.

Common		*Nominative*		*Nominative*	
case	wolf	*case*	wolf	*case*	wolf
Possessive	wolf's	*Possessive*	wolf's	*Genitive*	wolf's
		Objective	wolf	*Dative*	wolf
				Accusative	wolf

Aside from mere differences in nomenclature we have from two
to four cases postulated. Of course it is obvious that *wolf, wolf,*
and *wolf* look and sound a good deal alike. If you made a mistake
and used a nominative *wolf* where you were supposed to use a
dative one, it would be a little hard to check up on you. The
existence of three or four cases in Modern English nouns is therefore not a fact that can be proved by evidence, but a purely
arbitrary convention which is worth adopting only if it can be
shown to be useful — and which has been dropped as useless by
most contemporary grammarians, though it is still often found in
school texts.

Naturally, the convention is not utterly without foundation. If you will examine the declension of *lupus* you will notice that the dative and ablative cases are shown as identical in the masculine singular and in the plural of both genders. If it were not for the feminine singular (and if all nouns were declined like *lupus*) we could say that the ablative case has disappeared in Latin, as it has in Greek and German. And with the facts as they are we could say that this case has disappeared in the plural of all Latin nouns, and in the singular of a great many. This would be quite as accurate as what we do say, but without some years of experimenting we can't determine whether the new statement would be more or less convenient than the old. It can at least be argued that it is easier to make and apply rules that treat the dative and ablative as different, even though they are often identical, than rules that call for the use of the ablative of some nouns but the dative of others.

But we cannot apply this sort of argument to Modern English without stretching it much too far. There is not a single noun that has preserved more than two cases; and the only reasonable thing to do is to stop talking about those that were dropped six or seven hundred years ago as well as those that were dropped even earlier. Or else we should be really consistent and talk about the vocative, locative, and instrumental cases as well as those already discussed, and attribute them to adjectives as well as nouns.

155. PRONOUNS. The traditional definition of a pronoun is "a word used in place of a noun." Unfortunately, the definition works only if we are careful to consider only such examples as support it. Otherwise it misses badly in both directions.

You and *I*, for instance, are not substitutes for some other words; they are the most natural words to use when referring to *us* — and try to find a good noun for that one. And on the other hand a great many words that *are* used in place of nouns are seldom called pronouns. For instance:

The *poor* are suffering.
The doctors were busy with the *wounded.*
To drive so fast is dangerous.

We may argue about whether *poor* is an adjective used as a noun or one that has actually become a noun, but we never call it a pronoun, any more than we do the participle and infinitive that are used in place of nouns in the next two sentences.

Actually the words that have traditionally been called pronouns in English are simply the words normally used to translate the words called pronouns in Latin; and these Latin pronouns are a group of words used very much like nouns but inflected a little differently. Probably the most nearly reliable definition of a Latin pronoun is "a noun that has a genitive case ending in *-ius.*" By this definition *aliquis,* a Latin word for *anybody,* is a pronoun, since its genitive case is *alicuius.* But the English word *anybody* is obviously a compound form of the noun *body.* It can just as well be called an indefinite noun as an indefinite pronoun.

The personal pronouns *I, he, she, it, we, you,* and *they,* along with *who,* are the only English pronouns which have preserved case-inflections different from those of nouns, and many modern grammarians accordingly consider them to be the only pronouns left in the language. Old English had some other words which can be classified as pronouns because of their inflections, but not nearly so many as Latin.

Much of the confusion about the classification as well as the use of pronouns is the result of a more deep-seated confusion between *antecedents* and *referents.* A referent is the person or thing to which a word refers. An antecedent is a word to which a later word called a pronoun is grammatically related. Suppose you have a cousin, five foot ten, weighing a hundred and sixty-two pounds, named Rick, and you happen to say "Rick asked me to have lunch with him tomorrow." The actual boy, all those inches and pounds of him, is the referent for both *Rick* and *him;* and the word *Rick* is the antecedent for the word *him.* Obviously both nouns and pronouns need referents, unless we want to talk about nothing at all. And pronouns sometimes, but by no means always, need antecedents. Suppose you added to the sentence just quoted: "I told him I was just too busy to get away." Here *I* and *him* both have referents, and *him* has its antecedent in the previous sentence; but *I* neither has nor needs one.

In no language known to me does a pronoun always have an antecedent; but in most highly inflected languages if a pronoun does have one it must agree with it in gender, number, and person. We have seen one example in the French sentence quoted above:

J'ai vu sa majesté, et elle était heureuse.

Since *majesté* is feminine, the pronoun *elle* is required, even if the majesty referred to is a king rather than a queen. In other words, the pronoun disregards the sex of the referent to agree with the gender of the antecedent. This at first seems unreasonable to most speakers of English because, as inflections have become less important, we have tended to use the pronoun most appropriate to the referent, regardless of the antecedent. Thus we may say "I want every one of you to do *your* best," though agreement in person would require *his*. Or "The class decided to invite *their* parents to a party," though agreement in number would require *its*.

156. VERBS. Much the greatest contrast between the Latin and Modern English structures is in the verb systems. In spite of some duplications the Latin *vocō* has over a hundred physically different forms, indicating its *person, number, tense, mood,* and *voice*. The word *vocāvissēmus*, for instance, is first person, plural, pluperfect, subjunctive, active. It cannot possibly be anything else, and it cannot be adequately distinguished from all other possible forms without all five of the terms given above. The complete set of forms is called the *conjugation*, a term which means "yoking together," or showing what verb-forms agree with

what subjects — though, as we have just seen, the forms actually indicate three other things as well as those (person and number) necessary for agreement.

The English *call* has only four forms: *call, calls, called,* and *calling.* Moreover, the use of two of these is a matter of etiquette rather than of communication. We don't need a special third-singular form in the present any more than we do in the past; and the absence of a distinctive past form in such verbs as *put* and *set* does not seem to cause any confusion. Only the two forms *call* and *calling* are consistently useful in our system.

157. PERSON AND NUMBER. There are three grammatical persons, defined as follows: *first,* the person speaking; *second,* the person addressed; *third,* the person or thing spoken of. These are grammatical, not natural, distinctions. Thus if Private Jones says to his captain "I would like your permission to leave the area," *I* is in the first person, *your* in the second, and *permission* and *area* in the third. But if he says (as he is supposed to) "Private Jones requests the captain's permission to leave the area," the third person is used throughout. Except for *am* and the *-s* forms, English verbs have lost all traces of person, but Latin verbs preserve it thoroughout. Latin verbs also show either singular or plural number throughout; but in English number is shown only in the forms that also show person.

158. TENSE. The word *tense* is derived from the Latin word *tempus,* which means *time;* but *tense* is no more a synonym for *time* than *gender* is a synonym for *sex.* Rather, tense is a grammatical device which is one of the possible ways of indicating time, and by no means a completely reliable one. Suppose, for instance, you say "We play them next month." *Play* is in the present tense. It is *next month* that indicates future time. And if you say "If you tried in Phoenix tomorrow you could probably find one" you are quite correctly using the past tense to refer to future time.

Some languages do not have tenses, but always indicate time by words other than verbs. Latin has six tenses, which indicate (roughly) action going on in the past, present, and future, and action already completed in these three divisions of time. Some languages have more. Long before English developed, the Germanic branch of Indo-European lost all but two of its original tenses — the present and the past.

To replace the lost tenses English has developed a number of verb phrases such as *I was calling, I used to call, I have called, I had called, I shall call, I will call, I am going to call,* and so forth. Grammarians disagree as to which, if any, of these combinations constitute tenses. In this book none of them are so called.

159. MOOD. The forms of the *indicative mood* (or *mode*) are used principally for definite statements and direct questions. In four of the six tenses Latin has another set of forms called the *subjunctive mood* which are used to express wishes, fears, contrary to fact conditions, and a few other things. A few modern English expressions, such as "If he were here" and "God bless him" contain verb forms different from those that would be used in statements, and are often said to be in the subjunctive mood; but there is not a form left in the language which is in itself a subjunctive.

Some grammarians speak of infinitive and imperative moods in English. Others add the conditional, the optative, or both. For a reasonable fee I would guarantee to invent nine more, thus putting us on a par with the Cree Indians. But this would, of course, be simply a metaphysical complication. There are no discoverable mood-forms in English.

160. VOICE. Such constructions as *I call* are said to be *active,* and such constructions as *I am called* are said to be *passive.* In Latin there is one set of active inflections called the *active voice,* and an incomplete set of inflections, such as *vocor,* pieced out

with verb phrases such as *vocatus sum,* called the *passive voice.* I have no idea why the term *voice* was chosen, but they had to find some term. English does not have two comparable sets of inflections, but the term *voice* is still used.

161. THE LATIN AND ENGLISH SYSTEMS COMPARED. Since most of our verb-forms no longer indicate person and number, we have developed both a stable word-order and a greater use of pronouns. For instance, we say "you call" where the Latin equivalent is simply, "vocātis." And to make up for the other lost inflections we have developed an extensive system of auxiliary verbs, supplemented by adverbial expressions of time and by such conjunctions as *if* and *though.* But it should be clearly understood that we have not replaced the lost elements by any system of one-for-one substitution. Much of the mystery of traditional grammar is caused by failure to realize this fact.

To anybody who is thoroughly familiar with the organization of a Latin verb, and who has never studied an independent analysis of any other kind, it may seem perfectly natural to assume that a verb is a verb in any language. If he makes this assumption he will look for an active and a passive voice, from two to four moods (depending on whether or not he has been taught to consider the imperative or the infinitive or both as moods in Latin), and exactly six tenses; and he will take it for granted that any finite verb must somehow agree with its subject in person or number, even when there is no physical sign of agreement. Naturally, he will find what he looks for — or, to be more accurate, he will find things that he can, with a little juggling, call by the familiar names. He can then display the four forms of *call,* accompanied by pronouns, auxiliaries, and a few conjunctions, over anything up to ten pages of rather small print, giving each recognized combination an analytical name. Thus *if he had been called* may be described as third person singular, pluperfect, subjunctive, passive — though neither *if* nor *he* is part of the verb-phrase, which in itself has no indication of

person, number, or mood. But *he is to call,* though quite as
legitimate an expression, is usually left unmentioned, since it
has no exact Latin equivalent.

This sort of analysis is of course clear to anybody who knows
Latin, and it may seem easy to a student who does not, if his
mind works in a certain way. It never gave me much trouble, so
that for a long time I had no reason to suspect that it was not
the simple truth. But it eventually dawned on me that a good
many people, not necessarily stupid, instinctively reject it, just
as I reject certain other analyses in other fields. (I don't know
how often I have forced myself to learn enough about astrology
to explain to my students some of Chaucer's references to ascen-
dants, exaltations, and so forth; but I have finally given it up.
There is so much that I want to know and explain about Chaucer that I just can't make my mind bother to retain this.)

There are people who admit that the traditional analysis is
arbitrary, but who believe that it ought to be taught because it
is useful as an approach to Latin or to such other languages as
French or Spanish. These people may be right, but there are at
least three reasons to hesitate before accepting their opinion:

1. Most Americans (regrettably, of course) never learn enough
about any other language to make it worth while to befuddle
them about their own.

2. The idea that it is easier to learn this system in English
before getting entangled with the other difficulties of a foreign
language is decidedly open to question. Students have been saying for generations "I never really understood English grammar
until I studied Latin (or French or Spanish)." What this amounts
to is that the system is reasonably clear when it is used to explain
inflections that are still in existence. When it is applied to the
ghosts of inflections long dead, it strains some minds.

3. There is a good deal of evidence to indicate that students
could learn the other languages more easily if they were told
at the outset that these languages had a radically different structure, instead of being given to understand that they have

basically the same structure with what seem like completely unnecessary complications.

It is my experience that most teachers of foreign languages immediately and haughtily reject these reasons. I can only reply that I have been in their position, and they have probably not been in mine. It happens that I taught French in college for three years before shifting to English. During all these years I made the traditional assumptions, and took a smug pleasure in the statements of students that they were for the first time really beginning to understand English grammar. There I was, just incidentally and by the way, doing a better job than the people who got paid for concentrating on it.

This pleasant illusion disappeared completely during my first semester of trying to teach the English language directly. In the first place my students didn't seem to be learning English grammar any faster under me than under those instructors whom I had previously scorned. In the second, I soon realized that much of what I thought they should learn was of no conceivable value in their handling of English. For instance, I could pretty well boil down my treatment of the subjunctive to the single sentence, "Don't say *he was* when you know he wasn't — and the same goes for *I was.*" If they asked why, I could tell them that such expressions as *If he were here* were idioms — fossil remnants of a time when there really was a discoverable subjunctive mood in English. This not only saved a good deal of time, but reduced their mystification and consequent resentment.

162. ADVERBS. The identifying of adverbs and adverbial elements, and their subclassification as referring to time, manner, degree, concession, and what not is probably at once the most difficult and the most useless practice in the teaching of traditional grammar, since it usually has little to do with either the constructing of sound sentences or the understanding of sentences already written.

The words traditionally called adverbs vary greatly in both

their origins and their uses. The greater number are formed from adjectives by a sort of converter — usually *-iter* in Latin, *-ly* in English. Many of the most common ones, however, are simply prepositions, conjunctions, nouns, pronouns, or adjectives used in new ways. They are most often defined as "words used to modify verbs, adjectives, or other adverbs," and it is easy enough to find sentences in which they clearly do such things. But there are a great many sentences in which this definition does not work very convincingly.

Some grammarians therefore extended it. They point out that adverbs often modify nouns (the man *upstairs*), prepositions (*nearly* in), or whole phrases, clauses, or sentences. Other grammarians disagree, sometimes violently — not usually about the classification of the words, but about what they do. Perhaps the most useful definition would be "an adverb is any word that cannot readily be fitted into any other part of speech."

163. PREPOSITIONS AND CONJUNCTIONS. Prepositions and conjunctions are both uninflected classes of connectives, easier to illustrate by example than to distinguish by precise definition. We are not likely to confuse prepositions such as *at, by, from,* and *under* with conjunctions such as *although, and, because,* and *however;* and the fact that such words as *after, before, but,* and *for* can be assigned to both classes causes little difficulty in constructing sentences, though it bewilders many students in parsing them. In Latin both classes need careful attention because it is necessary to learn which prepositions are followed by the accusative case, which by the ablative; and which conjunctions are followed by the indicative mood, which by the subjunctive — not to mention the fact that some members of each class can be used both ways, but with different meanings. In English most of the trouble is caused by the placid acceptance of two completely inconsistent rules:

1. The part of speech to which a word belongs is determined by its use in the sentence.

2. A word must never be used in a part of speech to which it does not belong.

The first is a reasonable statement of the fact that in English (unlike Latin) words shift their functions very freely — a fact that is usually mentioned with great pride. The second is not a statement of fact, but an expression of determination to keep a very few words from doing this — because somebody once said they shouldn't. Anybody who objects to such sentences as "He is older than me" and "It looks like he will be the next governor" may reasonably correct his students for using them on the grounds that they will be criticized as incorrect by a good many people. But before he complicates his students' approach to the language with a confused and indefensible theory he really should check a few dictionaries — unless, of course, he is a bishop as well as a professor.

164. INTERJECTIONS. An interjection is a word "thrown into" a sentence for its emotional force, rather than structurally connected with the other words. Such words as *oh* and *ouch* are regularly interjections, and many other words may be so used: *Well*, I suppose so; *Now*, John, don't act that way; *Holy cow!*

165. A FEW ROMAN GHOSTS. An educated Frenchman who had studied Latin for years before approaching English might find a grammar embodying all the concepts we have just discussed consistently intelligible and occasionally useful. An American schoolboy who knows no Latin is likely to find it bewildering; and even if he accepts it without protest and masters all the rules, much of what he learns leads only to saying unnecessary things about the language, and is of no value in either understanding sentences or writing sound ones of his own. It does him no good, for instance, to learn that the nominative case is required for direct address, because if he wants to say "John, come here," or even "You, come here," there is no possible alternative; and he can't possibly say "He, come here." In the same way,

he can say "We made him the leader" without thinking about the case of *leader,* and he will never have to choose between "We made the leader *he*" and "We made the leader *him.*"

To the Frenchman the subjunctive mood is a fact of life, and knowledge that it has left only a few traces in English comes as a relief — there is that much less for him to learn. But the simplest way to teach an American child to say "If I were you" is simply to insist on his saying that instead of "If I was you." Call it an idiom, if you like. To insist on an elaborate treatment of the subjunctive mood is to parade our own knowledge rather than to increase his. I remember that when I was fresh from graduate school I used to oppress my classes by explaining that in such expressions as "the more the merrier" the word *the* was not, as they innocently supposed, the definite article, but an interesting survival of the instrumental case of the Old English pronoun ðæt. I do hope the good Lord will forgive me.

The earliest division of Latin words into parts of speech is that of Varro, who found four classes: *nouns* which are inflected to show case; *verbs,* which are inflected to show time; *participles,* which are inflected to show both case and time (Latin participles are much more complicated than English ones); and *particles,* which are not inflected at all. This is an oversimplification which has long since been abandoned, but it is useful in indicating that the parts of speech were once based on observable physical characteristics of words. Donatus later doubled the number of categories, adding *pronouns,* and dividing particles into *prepositions, conjunctions, adverbs, and interjections.* During the eighteenth century this classification was transferred to English with only one change — the substitution of adjectives for participles as a more useful category in English.

In either language each of the eight parts has its own characteristic functions, and in Latin the classification is something like 95 percent reliable. If you cut a Latin paragraph into its individual words, paste these words separately on cards, and then shuffle the cards, you can still classify nineteen out of twenty words confidently and accurately. But if you tried to do the same thing with an English paragraph you would find that only about a third of the words could be assigned to any single class. This is partly because we have lost so many inflectional endings that a good many words that used to be different are now identical; and partly because, since we no longer rely much on endings, we can shift words from one function to another far more readily than the Romans could.

In other words, the relation between form and function was so reliable in Latin that you would get very nearly the same result no matter which you used as a basis for classification. In English the relation is very much looser, and when this fact is not realized absurdities often result. If you tell a class that the part of speech to which a word belongs depends on its use in a sentence, you can justify your statement by one kind of grammar. If you tell them that "He worked good" is wrong because *good* is not an adverb and therefore can't modify a verb, you can justify your statement by another kind. But if you make both statements to the same class, they can be forgiven for being confused. You are.

CHAPTER TEN

Contemporary Developments
in America

166. THE LANGUAGE STILL CHANGING. The world in which we live is changing faster than ever before, and our language is inevitably changing with it. An attempt to evaluate all the forces at work would go beyond the scope of this book, but there has been one great change that deserves our particular attention — the enormous increase in the number of people who continue their education through the high-school and college levels. There are something like ten times as many college students in this country now as there were high-school students sixty years ago — and forty times as many high-school students. The proportion of the population that has had a number of years of formal instruction in English has thus increased from a rather small minority to a considerable majority. There have been similar, though not quite so extensive, developments in other parts of the English speaking world, but I do not know enough about them to discuss them.

If an optimistic schoolteacher of 1905 had been told of the coming expansion she might have expected a sort of linguistic millennium. With practically everybody educated, the use of "good English" would obviously spread; there would be a much smaller problem of combatting semi-illiterate home language; and altogether the prospects looked rosy. Unfortunately, some back-currents which the teacher might not have suspected soon developed. The problem of educating a whole country is quite different from that of educating a privileged or particularly ambitious minority. For one thing, it soon appeared that the only way to get everybody through school was to broaden the curriculum to fit a much wider range of interests and abilities, and to lower or abolish the minimum standards of performance in some areas. These changes may on the whole have been for the better — I am not competent to judge; but one result was that even thoroughly capable and industrious students often got through high school, and perhaps college, with much less change in their original speech-habits than their predecessors would have had to make. It then became much harder to make their successors believe that "all educated people" spoke in a certain way when there were millions, equipped with the necessary diplomas, who obviously did not. A considerable change in the schoolroom attitude toward English was therefore inevitable.

Many of the newly educated people, even if they had resisted schoolroom English with great determination, felt a strong sense of sin about their persistence in old habits; but many others felt that they had earned the right to independence. And the mere fact that a much larger proportion of the population than ever before was exposed to a number of years of instruction in English increased the speed with which developments in academic theory could modify out-of-school use of language. There is no way of deciding just how much effect the developments discussed in the next few sections have had or will have on the language as a whole, but they certainly cannot be dismissed as unimportant.

167. "FUNCTIONAL GRAMMAR." Hardly more than a generation ago the general belief in "good grammar" as one of the indispensable strands in the fabric of public morality seemed to be

unassailable. There had always been individual rebels and heretics, but the American public as a whole — whatever their personal practices — accepted "the authorities" very much as they accepted the Constitution and the Supreme Court. It is true that few of the faithful, even among college professors of English, knew exactly who these authorities were (I used to make a hobby of asking for actual names, and got consistently remarkable answers); but their anonymity strengthened rather than weakened their power. They were literally unquestionable.

However, it did become obvious to certain close observers that the usual way of teaching grammar in the schools had produced remarkably small results for the time and effort invested; and a nation-wide movement arose to throw out "formal grammar" and put "functional grammar" in its place. The reformers were of course denounced as revolutionaries, and the conservatives dug in and prepared to fight to the last diagram. The battle was long and bitter (it is still going on in some areas), and especially confused. The originators of "functional grammar" were radical only about pedagogical method. They did not dispute any of the statements of the traditional grammarians; they simply wanted to teach "correct" practices without any wasteful discussion of theory. Their announced aim was to "eradicate the most common errors" by allotting classroom time in proportion to the frequency with which errors were found to occur. Unfortunately (as they cheerfully admitted), they did not feel up to deciding what usages actually were errors. They therefore accepted the decisions of the very grammars they were discarding as useless, and did not even consider the possibility that when an error is made by the great majority of all speakers of a language it ceases to be an error and becomes standard practice. The natural result was to put a heavy emphasis on dying shibboleths — a rather curious way to be functional.

A good many of the teachers who took up the new battle-cry acted much more intelligently than the originators. They wanted to get away from theoretical complexities and work directly on their students' use of the language; but they did not feel bound to follow the prescribed emphasis. There is no convincing evidence that the results of the functional approach were on the whole either better or worse than those achieved by the formal one; but the withdrawal of grammatical theory from many classrooms probably did something to weaken the superstitious veneration of anonymous authorities.

168. THE DOCTRINE OF USAGE REAPPEARS. Another movement, often confused with the functional approach, but actually quite independent of it, was a revival of the doctrine of usage. Linguistic scholarship had made a good deal of progress since Lowth's time, and the theory of universal grammar had been pretty well abandoned. Some very competent grammars of English, based on observation of actual usage, had been written, and were often referred to with great admiration; but they had not had much effect in the schoolrooms. During the nineteen-twenties a number of scholars felt that the time had come for a change, not merely in methods of instruction, but in the content of what was to be taught.

The American public first became aware of this movement when a study known as *Current English Usage,* begun by professor Sterling A. Leonard, was completed after his death by a committee of the National Council of Teachers of English and published in 1932. A list of 230 expressions "of whose standing there might be some question" was submitted to a group of 229 judges — linguists, teachers of English and speech at all levels, editors, authors, and business men. The expressions ranged all the way from those that might be considered too fussily correct to be fully human ("Each person should of course bear *his or her* share of the expense") to ones like *had of come, that there rooster,* and *they swang their partners. It is I* was up for criticism as well as *It is me,* and both split and carefully preserved infinitives were offered. Each judge was asked to score according to his observation of actual usage, not on his opinion of what it should be; but not all complied. Each expression was to be classified in one of the following categories:

1. *Literary English* — "formally correct English, appropriate chiefly for serious and important occasions."

2. *Colloquial English* — "fully acceptable English for informal conversations, correspondence, and all other writings of well-bred ease; not wholly appropriate for occasions of literary dignity."

3. *Popular or Illiterate* — "not used by persons who wish to pass as cultivated, save to represent uneducated speech, or to be jocose."

The answers were tabulated, carefully studied, and finally classified in three groups. Those expressions which were approved as either literary or colloquial by at least three-fourths of the judges were ranked *established;* those approved by less than one-fourth were ranked *illiterate;* and those in between *disputable.* By these arbitrary standards 121 of the expressions were disputable; but a good many more were actually disputed. In fact there was complete unanimity on only four items, all in the *illiterate category.* There were no defenders of *a orange, hadn't of come, wa'nt* (for *wasn't*), or *he did noble.*

Anybody now reading this report for the first time will wonder how there could have been any question about some of the expressions. Take "I *drove* the car around the block." This was generally approved as standard colloquial English; but 6 percent of the judges condemned it as illiterate, and only 15 percent approved it as literary. How did we use to get cars around a block in our more serious and formal moods? I can't remember. And what could have led to even stronger condemnation of "*Under these circumstances* I will concede the point," and "The New York climate is *healthiest* in the fall"? Oh, yes — the logic of etymology insisted that circumstances were around us, not over us; and I have a vague recollection of having been told that *healthy* applied to people; a climate could only be *healthful.* But .while a few of the issues have dropped out of discussion (to be

succeeded, of course, by others of about the same importance)
it is amazing how many of them persist.

The thing that shocked or delighted the general public was
the recognition as "established" of such expressions as "If it
wasn't for football," "*Who* are you looking for?" and "It is *me*."
All over the country there were outraged protests — in the
schoolrooms, on editorial pages, even from pulpits. "Liberal"
teachers were accused of "letting down the bars," and it was
feared that after our language had become a tasteless and almost
meaningless gibberish, loss of respect for law and decency in all
areas would soon follow. On the other side there was great, but
rather spotty, enthusiasm. A man who had never felt quite comfortable about saying "It is I" was likely to hail with joy any
statement that "It's me" was respectable; but if he had finally
learned to put *whom* in all the places where rules required it,
he didn't want to hear any nonsensical suggestions that his efforts had been wasted. I still treasure a remark made to me years
ago by an extremely well-read and intelligent colleague in the
department of physical education who had just read a "liberal"
article of mine: "Damn you, Myers. The only claim to culture
I ever had was that I could spot a split infinitive as far away
as any man I ever knew — and now you try to tell me that they
don't matter." He still believes that my attitude is a pure pose,
and that I wouldn't dream of splitting an infinitive myself, except perhaps in an attempt to be deliberately naughty in public.

The Leonard report had dealt only with opinions about the
status of various disputed usages. A few years later Albert H.
Marckwardt and Fred Walcott made a second study of the same
expressions, which was published in 1938 as *Facts About Current
English Usage*. Instead of asking for opinions they went directly
to the best available records to find out how and by whom these
expressions had been used in the past. Their principal source was
the *Oxford English Dictionary*, supplemented when appropriate
by the second edition of *Webster's New International Dictionary*
and a few other books based on actual citations. The evidence
they presented indicated that the original judges had been very

conservative. The great majority of the "disputable" items and a third of the "illiterate" ones were actually recorded as occurring in standard English.

These two reports would of course have had little effect if the country had not been ready for them, but they cannot be dismissed as mere symptoms. They were widely discussed in the teaching profession, and gave solid support to teachers and textbook writers of a liberal inclination. The simple division between good and bad English gradually lost ground to the idea that there could be various kinds of satisfactory English, appropriate to different audiences and occasions. Such an expression as "standard colloquial English" was less likely to be dismissed as a contradiction in terms; and regional dialects were treated with increased sympathy and respect. On the whole these new attitudes made more rapid progress in the colleges than in the lower schools; but they gained everywhere. And since the change occurred when a great many more people than ever before were going to high school and college, the effect was much more than academic. The gap between school English and the English of ordinary life is definitely smaller than it used to be. There are critics who think that this is simply because the schools have either rejected or failed in their responsibilities; but there are others who think the schools are now in closer touch with reality.

169. STRUCTURAL LINGUISTICS. The early liberals had questioned both the authority and the accuracy of the usual school grammars, but would on the whole have been satisfied with better books of the same general nature. In the nineteen-thirties, however, a number of linguists began to attack the whole framework of traditional grammar as essentially false, and to devise a radically different approach, basically that referred to in the first chapter of this book as "description-of-practice-theory." Their acknowledged leader was Leonard Bloomfield, whose *Language* appeared in 1933; and their method was to begin by examining the raw data of actual speech, and proceed by purely inductive steps to build up a description of its structure. Since the Bloom-

fieldian approach was almost unchallenged in this country for more than twenty years, it was usually referred to simply as *linguistics* or *linguistic science*. It is now generally called *structural linguistics* to distinguish it from other approaches which depend less on pure induction from the observed phenomena of speech, and attempt rather to analyze the underlying conventions which these phenomena are assumed to reflect. Here are a few of Bloomfield's basic tenets:

1. "Writing is not language, but merely a way of recording language by means of visible marks." (p. 21)

2. All linguistic theories based on philosophical theories should be abandoned: "The only useful generalizations about language are inductive generalizations. Features which we think ought to be universal may be absent from the very next language that becomes accessible. Some features, such as, for instance, the distinction of verb-like and noun-like words as separate parts of speech, are common to many languages, but lacking in others. The fact that some features are, at any rate, widespread, is worthy of notice and calls for an explanation; when we have adequate data about many languages, we shall have to return to the problem of general grammar and to explain these similarities and divergences, but this study, when it comes, will be not speculative but inductive." (p. 20)

3. "The study of language can be conducted without special assumptions only so long as we pay no attention to the meaning of what is spoken." (p. 75)

This statement is likely to strike a non-linguist as ridiculous, and has been frequently and bitterly criticized. But if we consider language as a system of sounds by which meaning is conveyed, there is certainly some justification for the idea that we should first make a physical analysis of the system, and only after this is completed proceed to investigate the ways in which it is used.

4. The duty of a linguist is simply to describe the speech-forms that he encounters, and he has no right to show preference be-

tween them: "An unfortunate outgrowth of the general-grammar idea was the belief that the grammarian or lexicographer, fortified by his powers of reasoning, can ascertain the logical basis of language and prescribe how people ought to speak. In the 18th century, the spread of education led many dialect-speakers to learn the upper-class forms of speech. This gave the authoritarians their chance: they wrote *normative grammars,* in which they often ignored actual usage in favor of speculative notions. Both the belief in 'authority' and some of the fanciful rules (as, for instance, about the use of *shall* and *will*) still prevail in our schools." (pp. 6–7)

Since we are still making an enormous effort to teach the "upper-class language" to millions of students, this *laissez faire* attitude struck many observers as a simple rejection of responsibility on the part of those scholars who should be best qualified for the job. However, some of the linguists explained that it was only *as linguists* that they couldn't prescribe. When they changed their hats and became teachers they could be as prescriptive as anybody else. And all of them believed, with considerable justification, that accurate descriptions were the only sound basis for prescription.

Most of Bloomfield's followers worked with languages other than English, particularly those of the American Indians. The methodology they developed is much too complicated to be described here, but it proved highly effective, and a few linguists attempted to apply it to English. Two books by Fries and one by Trager and Smith were particularly influential in the teaching profession. The work of these men depended partly on that of many others, but in order to keep the picture simple they will be treated here as if they were the sole originators.

170. THREE APPROACHES TO THE PARTS OF SPEECH. It is quite easy for an American to see that our decimal system of coinage is better than the traditional (but soon to be changed) British

system of pounds, shillings, and pence (not to mention half-crowns and guineas), because it is simpler in principle and very much more convenient to handle. But it is not nearly so easy for us to see that the metric system of weights and measures has exactly the same advantage over our curious conglomeration of ounces and pounds, inches, feet, yards, and miles, pints, quarts, and gallons, and so forth. We may admit the advantage in theory, but we are likely to have a deep-seated feeling that our units are somehow real, and the metrical ones merely clever tricks. It is very hard indeed for most of us to think of a hundred meters as simply a hundred meters, or as a tenth of a kilometer. We feel that it is really a hundred and nine-point-something yards, and wonder why the silly foreigners couldn't at least have made it come out an even hundred and ten. And of course the kilometer is too short to be a serious way of measuring long distances. How can anybody be satisfied with anything that isn't quite five-eighths of a mile?

In a very similar way most of us have a strong feeling that the sort of grammar to which we were exposed when young is somehow real, and that any different analysis of our language is tampering with the truth. But there is no more reason to believe that all words fall naturally into eight parts of speech than there is to think that silver comes naturally in either dollars or shillings, or butter in pounds or kilograms. We may have been taught that the sacred eight were permanent realities, no more open to question than the Ten Commandments or the multiplication table. Yet, since the second English grammar was written, there has never been a time when "the authorities" agreed on what or how many the parts were (every number from zero to ten has been advocated), to say nothing of what words belonged in each part; and just now the disagreement is particularly acute.

Obviously we cannot make any statements about groups of words unless we have some terms to designate the groups, and such words as *noun, verb,* and *adjective* will do as well as any others. But when it comes to allotting words to the different groups we must find some arbitrary basis for the classification. Different bases will lead to different results — none of them completely satisfactory for all purposes. The most familiar basis is the *supposed function* of each group; we have all heard that a noun names something, that a verb shows action or being, that an adjective modifies a noun, and so forth. Such definitions work well enough with a good many sentences; but if we push them too far we soon run into borderline cases and outright contradictions, and we can defend our definitions only by some rather remarkable rationalizations. Consequently a good many modern grammarians have not only given them up but attacked them as essentially vicious.

One quite different method, used by Trager and Smith, is to classify words simply by their form-changes or *inflections*. Thus a word is called a noun if, and only if, it has forms comparable to at least two of the following four: *man, man's, men, men's.* *Boy* is of course a noun, since it has at least two forms and maybe four — that depends on whether you take speech or writing as the criterion. So is *sheep,* since it has plain and possessive forms, though none to show difference in number; and *opinion,* since it has singular and plural forms, though none to indicate possession. But *mathematics,* having only one form, is not a noun in this system, no matter how much it resembles a noun in use. Similarly, the invariable *must* is not a verb, and *beautiful* is not an adjective, because it lacks the *-er, -est* inflections which characterize true adjectives such as *pretty.*

Most of us will at first reject this classification as absurd if not immoral. We have known for a long time that *mathematics* just naturally is a noun, *must* a verb, and *beautiful* an adjective, and we don't like to have our intellectual property disturbed. But if we give it a fair trial we shall see that it handles some questions better than the older system, though it runs into some new difficulties of its own.

Fries used still a third method, which is to classify words by the positions they fill in certain patterns assumed to be typical.

Thus any word that fits into the blank space in "The _____ was good" may be called a noun, and any word that fits into the blank space in "He was a very _____ man" may be called an adjective. This method does not usually seem so shocking at first glance, though it brings up some special problems later.

If we really examine them all we find that the three classifications overlap considerably but by no means completely, and that each has its advantages and disadvantages as compared to the others. And each has adherents who firmly believe that it is true and the others either false or trivial. This makes a situation that students, especially those who are teaching or about to teach grammar, find most disconcerting. Their usual reaction is something like: "Why can't these experts get together, thrash the whole matter out, and reach an agreement? Then we'll tackle the results."

An instructor may reasonably answer that English grammar is concerned with the variable reactions of millions of people, and investigators who seek the exclusive truth about it can't agree, any more than can those who study theology or politics or aesthetics. It is too big and too complicated for any one explanation to cover. Just now several quite different approaches are shedding useful light, and anybody with a professional interest in the language should have some understanding of them all. He can then use whichever one suits his temperament and the circumstances, as long as he does it honestly and doesn't confuse his pupils or readers with metaphysics.

171. A NEW VIEW OF STANDARD ENGLISH. Charles Carpenter Fries's *American English Grammar* (New York, 1940) has been superseded by a second and very different book by the same author, discussed below; but it is still interesting for several reasons. The structural method demands that all work be based on the examination of a *corpus* — a specific selection of the actual language. Fries made the first considerable attempt to derive an English Grammar from the unedited language of ordinary citizens rather than from works of literature. He would have liked

to use records of actual speech for his base, but at the time could find no way of obtaining a satisfactory spoken corpus. As a compromise he used about three thousand letters written to various departments of the federal government by people about whom a good deal of information was available. He wanted to study and compare three levels of English; and the only conceivable way he could do this without going around in circles was to classify his writers on *non-linguistic* grounds before examining their language. Thus he defined the standard English of the United States as "that set of language habits in which the most important affairs of our country are carried on, the dialect of the socially acceptable in most communities." Since these terms are vague, he set up specific criteria, such as graduation from a reputable college and a recognized standing in one of the generally respected professions. He did not suggest that many other people did not also speak standard, but assumed that what these people used, at least in such a serious matter as writing to the government, *was* standard, whether or not it conformed to anybody's theories of propriety. This assumption naturally met with some violent opposition, and it will not be debated here. It is a possible one, and the one that he used. Inevitably, it resulted in the recognition as standard of many usages generally condemned in traditional grammars. Fries also examined two other levels — the "vulgar English" of barely literate people, and the "popular English" of a group in between. To avoid borderline cases, he left considerable gaps between the requirements for membership in each group. For instance, a man had to complete college to be included in the standard group, but could not have more than one year of college to be included in the popular group. If he had more than one and less than four years of college, his letters were not used in either corpus.

172. FRIES's *Structure of English*. The book aroused a great deal of interest, but its description of the language did not satisfy anybody, including the author, who was soon at work on an-

other one, *The Structure of English* (New York, 1952). By attaching a recording machine to his home telephone he obtained a corpus of some fifty hours (about 250,000 running words) of conversation by people whom he could identify as belonging to the standard group. He then set out to examine the structure of what they said, starting (as far as humanly possible) absolutely from scratch. He even discarded the idea that a sentence must have a subject and predicate, along with the usual division into declarative, interrogative, imperative, and exclamatory types. His first effort was to find out what kinds of word-groups acted as independent and effective units by arousing the listener to some kind of response, whether oral (the usual response to *greetings, calls,* and *questions*), action (in response to *requests*), or mere signals of continued attention (in response to *statements*).

Since telephone conversations differ somewhat from face-to-face speech, not to mention writing, this classification is not satisfactory for all purposes. The fact that statements, under certain circumstances, "elicit evidence of continued attention" is hardly the most significant thing about them. Nevertheless, the attempt to analyze our sentences into observable patterns of action has some very important advantages. Fries wanted to find out what system of signals we depend on to convey ideas, and to show how the suppression or irregular use of symbols results in ambiguity or distortion of meaning.

Once he had isolated his sentences, Fries was ready to investigate their structure. Instead of assigning words automatically to eight familiar pigeonholes labeled "noun," "preposition," and so forth, he wanted to find out how many different kinds of words he could discover, and he had no preconceptions about either the number or the shape of the pigeonholes into which they could then be distributed. His analysis showed the following results:

1. Our language contains four "open" classes of words, each with an unlimited number of members. Nobody can know them

all, and new ones can be added at any time. These words differ in their specific meanings, but the members of each class can be interchanged without affecting the structure of a sentence. Fries limited the term "parts of speech" to these four classes, and called them simply Classes 1, 2, 3, and 4. They are roughly equivalent to the classes usually called nouns, verbs, adjectives, and adverbs, but there are some important differences. For instance, auxiliary verbs are not members of Class 2, but of one of the groups discussed below. Fries used the numbers rather than the usual names to help his readers avoid shifting unconsciously between conflicting definitions. He fully realized that if his system came to be generally adopted the old names, newly defined, would probably return to use.

2. Our language also contains a very small number of words (154 in the corpus he examined) which are more important as elements in the structure of sentences than for their individual meanings. These he subdivided into fifteen groups, designated by the letters A to O. These groups are closed, and it is necessary to know all the members in order to use the language effectively. They include the auxiliary verbs, prepositions, conjunctions, relative pronouns, and a good many words ordinarily assigned to the four parts of speech which he recognizes, but which function quite differently. The words *yes* and *no*, for instance, are usually called adverbs, but they are used quite differently from words like *happily* and *indescribably*. In Fries's classification Group L consists simply of *yes* and *no*.

Fries's method of assigning words to the various classes and groups is to take a few simple sentences as "test frames." *Frame A* is the sentence "The concert was good (always)." Here *always* is put in parenthesis to indicate that the sentence would be complete without it. The structure of this frame can be indicated as:

Group A	Class 1	Class 2	Class 3	(Class 4)
The	concert	was	good	(always)

Any word that can be substituted for *the* in this frame is also a Group A function word; any word that can be substituted for *concert* is a Class 1 word, and so forth. Nothing is said about meaning, and no definitions are given — the criterion is purely structural. Among the words that occurred in his material which could be substituted for *the* he found *a, one, this, no, your,* and *John's.* Accordingly these words are all, though not necessarily always, members of Group A. (When the "same" word appears in a second class or group, Fries calls it "another word of the same shape." He thus follows the principle that dictionaries use in counting a word as different in each part of speech in which they list it.)

By using various test frames Fries classified every word that appeared in his corpus, and then proceeded to study the signalling devices by which these words are combined into meaningful utterances, giving due attention to word-order, inflections, and function words, and a rather sketchy indication of the importance of intonation. It is not feasible to give a detailed exposition of his system in a few pages, but the following points are particularly important:

1. If we are trying to study how meaning is conveyed, we should not start with a series of definitions that assume that we already know the meaning. Thus instead of saying something like "a noun is the name of a person, place, thing, or idea," we begin simply by looking for recurrent patterns. One such pattern is illustrated in the frame "The concert was good." We can assume that all the words that can be substituted for *concert* in this frame have something in common. Since we do not yet know what this something is, we call them simply "Class 1 words," and prepare to study them further. Then if we encounter a sentence like "The lonet was good" we can see that *lonet* is a Class 1 word, even though we cannot possibly know what it means. If it eventually turns out that all Class 1 words are used to name something, we may say so. We may even decide to call them nouns. This may seem like a very roundabout procedure, but it has its advantages. We have reached a conclusion based on evidence,

and we can support it by an appeal to that evidence. There is no mystery about it, and some of the arguments characteristic of traditional grammar simply disappear.

2. A useful distinction is made between those unlimited groups of freely interchangeable words which make up the four parts of speech, and the function words which are used in forming the framework of our sentences. Moreover, the various types of function words are differentiated more clearly than in most grammars. Our first reaction is likely to be that eight parts of speech are bad enough, and that it would be intolerable to have to learn nineteen different classifications, especially such anonymous ones. But it really isn't very helpful to lump *badly, how, no, very,* and *yesterday* all together as adverbs when they are typically used in entirely different ways. It may be helpful to have more groups and fewer subgroups. However, some difficulties remain; and though most of Fries's followers have accepted his four parts of speech with little or no change, they have more or less modified his classification of the function words.

3. The analysis of sentence structure by the principle of *immediate constituents,* often abbreviated as *IC's.* In a sentence of any length some words are obviously more closely related than others; and some groups of words are used as units in relation to other words or groups. To analyze this complex relationship it is necessary to examine various layers of structure. Conventional school grammars have done this by first dividing a sentence into subject and predicate, then dividing the subject into noun and modifiers, and so forth. We have all seen diagrams analyzing the structure in this way. But though such diagrams may tell us something about the relations of words in a sentence, they completely destroy the word-order which is the most important of the devices by which these relations are actually signalled. An IC diagram, on the other hand, leaves the word-order unchanged, and simply cuts the sentence into smaller and smaller groupings until the individual words are reached. Compare the two following diagrams of the same sentence:

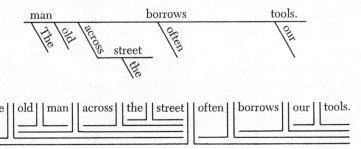

I have no desire to exaggerate the importance of diagramming by any method, or to suggest that the IC approach solves all difficulties. But it can be helpful in analyzing the sentences that actually occur, rather than a partial and distorted transmutation of them.

173. PHONOLOGICAL GRAMMAR. Fries was interested primarily in syntax; and on the reasonable theory that nobody can do everything at once he was willing (for the time being) to take the internal structure of words pretty well for granted. Moreover, he addressed his book to educated laymen (including professors and other teachers of English) with the idea of enlightening them about some of the findings of modern linguistic investigation, and in the hope that some of them would be able to use his work as the basis for texts which might improve the teaching of English in our schools.

George L. Trager and Henry Lee Smith, Jr., working independently at the same time, also attempted to provide a new foundation for future texts, particularly those designed for the teaching of English to foreign students. *An Outline of English Structure* (1951) is a very compact book (91 pages), and is definitely not addressed to laymen. Nobody without a fair knowledge of phonetics and linguistic theory can get much out of it, and even a qualified student will find it heavy going, since the authors use a number of pure abstractions in their analysis, and define many familiar terms in unfamiliar ways. They follow the approved structural method much more closely than Fries does, beginning with what they present as the first complete scientific analysis of the phonemic system; then going on to morphemics, which they divide in theory, but do not separate in treatment, into morphology and syntax. An innocent reader is likely to think of morphology as the study of how phonemes are formed into words, and of syntax as the study of how words are arranged in sentences, but the authors do not consider this division sufficiently precise. Rather, "In English, as in many other languages, it is found to be convenient to dichotomize morphemes into bases and all others (see below), and then to treat morpheme-sequences that involve only one base under one heading — MORPHOLOGY, and those that involve more than one base under another — SYNTAX." Finally there is a short chapter on "metalinguistics," which might be defined roughly as those aspects of language which they do not feel ready to treat with scientific precision.

174. ANOTHER PHONEMIC NOTATION. Trager and Smith found the same consonant and short-vowel phonemes as those listed in Chapter 2 of this book, but used different symbols for some of them. A comparison of the differences between the two alphabets follows.

Myers	*Trager and Smith*
ʃ	š
ʒ	ž
tʃ	č
dʒ	j
j	y
ɑ	a

The remaining symbols are the same in both alphabets. Trager and Smith, whose book was printed by offset from typed pages, obviously chose symbols that can be made with a minor alteration of the standard keyboard, while I have drawn mine from the

IPA because many students are already familiar with them. It cannot be seriously argued that either set is intrinsically better than the other.

A more important difference is in the treatment of long vowels and diphthongs. Trager and Smith hold that in contemporary English there are no long vowels whatever, but that every so-called long vowel is actually composed of a short vowel followed by one of three semi-vowels or off-glides — a front one symbolized by /y/, a back one symbolized by /w/, and a central one symbolized by /h/. Thus they would transcribe *go* as /gow/ rather than /gou/, *day* as /dey/ rather than /dei/, and *idea* as /aydih/ rather than /ɑidiə/. Even such words as *feet* and *boot* are transcribed as /fiyt/ and /buwt/, though it is certainly not uncommon to hear them pronounced with pure long vowels. It seems to me that the use of three symbols with two different values apiece is confusing, even though they are said to be "mirror images of each other." (For instance, if /yes/ is recorded on a tape and then played backward it sounds something like /sey/.) My classroom experience indicates that /h/ used in this way is particularly troublesome, since its relation to the other /h/ — even as a mirror-image — is not at all clear to most students.

175. THE SUPRASEGMENTAL PHONEMES. Much the most significant feature of this book is the emphasis placed, even in the treatment of syntax, on the "suprasegmental phonemes" of pitch, stress, and juncture. A simple word like *pat* may obviously be divided into three successive segments, /p/, /æ/, and /t/. But when it is actually used in speech it has certain audible characteristics which are not limited to the individual segments, but affect the syllable (in this case a complete word) as a whole. It must be pronounced on one musical tone or another (pitch) and with some degree of emphasis (stress). A word may also have a slight pause within it, or be followed by a somewhat longer pause, with or without rising or falling of the pitch (juncture). There is no doubt that these suprasegmental elements are real

and important parts of our signalling system, or that the Trager-Smith analysis of them is an important step forward. Whether they are best classified as phonemes or as something else is another question, on which linguists disagree. However, since they are generally considered phonemes in this country, they will be so called here.

176. PITCH. In some languages, notably Chinese, differences in tone are as consistently significant as differences in vowels or consonants. Several words otherwise identical may have entirely different and unrelated meanings as they are intoned differently. The difference is not simply one of pitch — there are rising and sinking tones as well as high and low even ones. In such languages it is obviously reasonable to regard the characteristic tone as one of the phonemes of which a word is composed. And since Chinese writing is ideographic rather than alphabetical, two words differing only in tone have entirely different written forms.

In English the situation is quite different. We cannot possibly pronounce a word without giving it some kind of intonation; but the particular intonation we give it is determined partly by the environment (verbal or otherwise) in which it occurs, and partly by the habits and feelings of the speaker. Suppose, for instance, that two people are working together to assemble a piece of machinery. One of them picks up a part and, making a bad guess about where it goes, says "Here?" The other, correcting him, says "Here." There will certainly be a rising intonation on the question, and a falling one on the answer; and there may be other differences, particularly in the answer, which may indicate anything from simple information to complete disgust. Both speakers will react to these differences, but they would agree that they are using the same word.

We can therefore accept the fact that intonation is, both in English and Chinese, a part of the signalling system. But it does not function the same way in the two languages; and it is possible to conclude that while differences in intonation are phonemic in Chinese, they are something else in English. Trager and Smith, however, have no doubt that there are four pitch phonemes in English, which they indicate by the superscript numbers 1 to 4 in rising order.

177. STRESS. Differences in stress are much more noticeable in English than in many other languages. Trager and Smith found four significant degrees of stress, which they indicate as ´ (strong), ^ (secondary), ` (tertiary), and ˘ (weak). (The weak stress is usually not indicated in transcriptions.) Relative differences in stress are a more permanent feature of words of more than one syllable than are differences in pitch. Thus we should all recognize (/kánvìkt/) (convict) as a noun, and (/kənvíkt/) as a verb; and we should probably agree that the difference in stress is a more important factor than the difference in the vowels in the first syllables. But we also know that in sentences some words are more heavily stressed than others, so that a particular degree of stress is not a permanent phonemic feature of any syllable. Thus in a sentence like "The dictionary will tell you," we might transcribe *dictionary* as /díkšənèriy/; but in "Try the *new* dictionary," *new* would take the primary stress, and *dictionary* might be transcribed as /dìkšənèriy/. Even syllables which normally bear the weakest stress may be given a stronger one for emphasis.

178. JUNCTURE. Juncture is a term used to indicate the transition between two sounds that do not follow each other in uninter-rupted sequence, or between sound and silence. For instance, the expression *White House* has no internal juncture, and can be transcribed as /hwáythàws/; but the expression *white house* does have what is called plus juncture, and can be transcribed as /hwâyt+háws/. Plus juncture is purely a feature of speech, and does not necessarily correspond to the division between written words. Thus *one of our bookkeepers* might reasonably be pro-nounced and transcribed as /wânəvawr̀+búk+kìypərz/.

There are also three "terminal junctures" which may occur at the end of phrases, clauses, or sentences. These are the level or single-bar juncture, /|/; the rising or double-bar juncture, /||/; and the falling or double-cross juncture /#/. (If you have any trouble keeping these straight, remember that double-crossing is a low way of acting; and that a man might keep on an even keel if he visited only one bar, but would be likely to get high if he went to two.) The single-bar juncture is the kind of transition often, though not always, indicated by a comma. The other two usually occur at places which in writing would be punctuated more heavily, and the double-cross one is much the more common, even in questions. It is quite true, as we have often been told, that questions are pronounced "with a rising inflection"; but the rise does not usually take place at the end. If you pronounce the sentence "Are you going to Chicago next?" in several different ways, with emphasis on different words, you will find that most of the versions go down rather than up at the end, and therefore require the double-cross symbol.

179. THE IMPORTANCE OF INTONATION. The term *intonation* is in general use among linguists to cover patterns of pitch and terminal juncture, and is sometimes stretched (as it will be here for convenience) to cover patterns of stress and internal juncture as well. Our ordinary system of writing indicates the segmental phonemes quite thoroughly, though (because of our curious spelling) very erratically; but it barely suggests the intonation. It is therefore natural for us to think of the elements of intonation as not only less important, but somehow less real than the segmental elements to which our attention is called every time we read or write. To take a very simple example, consider the two sentences:

> You will be there tomorrow.
> You will be there tomorrow?

We may be tempted to say that this is one sentence punctuated in two different ways; but if we pronounce both versions naturally we can hear that they are two different sentences, having the same segmental phonemes in the same order, but differing so much in their suprasegmentals that they convey very different ideas. The change in intonation makes the second one a question just as definitely and just as legitimately as would the reversal of "you will" to "will you."

Of course finer distinctions are possible, such as the difference between "*You* will be there tomorrow?" and "You will be there *tomorrow?*" In fact, the same five words in the same order can convey a remarkable number of different ideas. All of us have been misquoted by people who have repeated our "exact words," but have completely distorted our meaning by setting these words to a different tune. Such distortions are often justified (even in courts of law) on the theory that only the alphabetical sounds are real. This is about as sensible as it would be to evaluate paintings by chemical analysis, with no regard to the impression they convey to a viewer.

The differences in intonation which can only be suggested by such devices as punctuation and italics can be shown specifically by phonemic transcriptions which indicate pitch, stress, and juncture as well as the segmental phonemes. For instance:

You will be *there* tomorrow. /yuw+wìl+biy+ðéhr+təmârow#/

You *will* be there tomorrow? /yuw+wíl+biy+ðèhr+təmârow‖/

It takes a good deal of practice to make and respond readily to such transcriptions, and they are not likely to drive out our familiar conventions for ordinary communication. But they (or their equivalents) are indispensable for studying some important features of structure. For instance, the difference between *came to* (reached) and *came to* (recovered) can be shown as the difference between /kéym+tùw/ and kêym+túw/, which leads to the clearest way that has yet been devised of distinguishing between the prepositional and adverbial uses of a number of words.

Since their treatment of the suprasegmental features was the most original part of their work, Trager and Smith almost inevitably gave these features an emphasis that seems to many other linguists quite out of proportion. Their whole analysis is definitely open to question; but it is just as definitely valuable.

180. THE "NEW GRAMMAR" IN SCHOOLS AND COLLEGES. Very shortly after the publication of the two books just discussed several texts for school and college use were prepared, basing their treatment of phonology on Trager and Smith and their syntax largely on Fries — a development which must have been surprising to the three authors concerned, since their approaches were not entirely compatible. It was announced with some fanfare that the study of English grammar was now, for the first time, on a truly scientific basis, and there was a considerable wave of optimism about the effect that this modernization would have on the teaching of English, and eventually on the national use of the language.

The "new grammars" that appeared in the 1950's certainly had some important advantages over the older ones. They were less beclouded with inappropriate concepts borrowed from the study of Latin; and a competent teacher could answer a student's questions by referring him to observable patterns of speech rather than by calling upon philosophical pronouncements. But they did not, in practice, provide the automatic solution to the problems of teaching English that had been predicted for them; and their principal advocates soon retreated from the claim that "this method will teach you how to write better" to the more modest one that "this is the best description of your language now available, and you ought to know about it." It is too early to determine how much effect the teaching of structural grammar has had on the language habits of those who have been exposed to it. Fortunately or unfortunately, just about the time when it began to look as if the structuralists might succeed in changing the whole direction of English teaching in our schools, another group of linguists began to advocate a very different kind of analysis.

181. GENERATIVE-TRANSFORMATIONAL GRAMMAR. The structuralist approach is based on the examination of a corpus of utterances assumed to be typical of a community, with an attempt to make inductive generalizations. Such an approach can result in a good deal of useful information, but it can never present a complete and consistent picture. In dealing with a language currently spoken by millions of people even the most industrious grammarian can examine only a small fraction of the utterances that actually occur; and whatever conclusions he may reach are subject to revisions as soon as new material is added, since this may very well prove to be inconsistent with his original corpus.

Noam Chomsky's *Syntactic Structures* (1957) introduced an approach which can, at least in theory, produce a complete and fairly compact grammar. It disregards the irregularities in parole (which Chomsky calls *performance*) as no more significant than personal errors in multiplication, which have no effect on the dependable rules of arithmetic. Its aim is to find a set of rules which, if followed, would "generate" all the possible grammatical sentences of a language, and no ungrammatical ones. These rules are not to be considered as directives, but simply as explicit and precise statements of the intuitive knowledge of a language which a community must share in order to be able to communicate. We should all agree, for instance, that "My sister owns that house" is a normal and satisfactory sentence, even if we knew nothing whatever about subjects and predicates. We should also agree that "House my owns sister that" is meaningless gibberish with no perceptible structure. How close we should come to agreeing about all the 118 other possible arrangements of these five words is a question I would rather not go into.

Chomsky assumes that all members of a given speech community know (though perhaps subconsciously) the same rules and therefore have the same "competence" — a return to Saussure's theory that the langue is identical for all members, though its reflection in parole is inevitably distorted. This assumption can be supported by definition — anybody who does not know a given rule, or who knows a different rule from the others, is not quite a member of the community. But in practice it is not possible to find the exact area of agreement among a large number of speakers. It is therefore not always possible to decide whether a particular irregularity in speech is the result of a failure in performance or the normal effect of a difference in competence.

Chomsky and his followers are interested only in competence. The statement above that this cannot be absolutely isolated from performance does not in the least imply that their study is without value. After all, it is extremely useful to know how fast a body would accelerate in falling through a vacuum, even if we can never find a perfect vacuum for it to fall through. The point is simply that their approach, as compared to that of the structuralists, has certain inherent disadvantages as well as undoubted advantages. To a certain extent it involves a return to the aims and methods of traditional grammar, but there are important differences. Chomsky himself gives an illuminating comparison of the aims and possibilities of the three approaches:

> The most careful and compendious traditional grammar may give a full account of exceptions and irregularities, but it provides only examples and "paradigmatic instances" of regular constructions, together with various informal hints and remarks as to how the reader is to generalize from these instances. The basic regular processes of sentence construction remain unexpressed; it is the task of the reader to infer them from the presented material. It turns out that to fill this gap is no small task. In fact, even the best traditional descriptive studies cover only small fragments of a language, and because of their implicit appeal to the reader's intelligence and linguistic abilities, they leave fundamental questions unresolved. In other words, we do not know in any detail what constitutes "the intelligence of the reader" or what is accomplished when it is applied to the data presented in the grammar. Until these questions are answered, our descriptions of language, and of the nature of human linguistic abilities, are incomplete and defective in an essential way.
>
> Modern structural linguistics has reached levels of rigor that often exceed those of traditional grammar, and it has revealed

previously unrecognized aspects of linguistic structure. However, it provides little insight into the processes of formation and interpretation of sentences. Study of these questions has been outside the scope of modern structuralism, which has limited itself, almost completely, to the system of inventories of elements (phonemes, morphemes) and to analytic procedures that may assist in determining these elements. There has been some discussion of syntactic patterns, but it has been fairly primitive as compared with traditional grammar.

It is, therefore, not surprising that there has recently been renewed interest in the formalization and use of techniques and devices that are more characteristic of traditional than of structuralist grammars. In fact, a reader who is acquainted with traditional grammar will find much that appears familiar in this book. Current work in grammar attempts to meet the standards of explicitness characteristic of the best structuralist work without sacrificing scope. It attempts to formulate precisely the processes of sentence formation and interpretation that constitute the linguistic competence of the fluent speaker and that underlie the actual use of language, processes that are only hinted at in traditional grammars and that are quite beyond the scope of structuralist descriptions.[1]

This kind of grammar consists of three parts: *phrase structure* rules which analyze the underlying structure of the most basic or *kernel* sentence-types; *transformational* rules, which show, with mathematical precision, how more complicated sentence-types can be derived from kernel sentences; and *morphophonemic* rules, which are means of converting the abstract form of every possible sentence into a pronounceable utterance. The presentation is in a symbolic form for which most students of English have little preparation. Consequently, they are likely to be either terrified by its apparent difficulty or horrified by what strikes them as a perversion. To explain the system in a manner that is at once brief, clear, and convincing is probably impossible. I can hope only that the following paragraphs suggest some of its possibilities.

[1] Introduction to Paul Roberts, *English Syntax* (Alternate Edition, New York, 1964), pp. x–xi.

182. PHRASE STRUCTURE. The phrase structure rules analyze the components of a kernel sentence in the following manner:

1. Sentence → NP + VP
2. NP → T + N
3. VP → Verb + NP
4. T → the
5. N → man, ball, etc.
6. Verb → hit, took, etc.

Here *NP* stands for *noun phrase,* *VP* for *verb phrase,* *T* for *the,* *N* for *noun,* and *V* for *verb.* Each rule of the form X → Y is to be interpreted as "rewrite X as Y." And each Y is either an analysis of the corresponding X into smaller parts or the substitution of a specific example for the symbol of a type.[2]

A particular sentence can be derived from this set of rules in the following manner:

Sentence	Rule
NP + VP	(1)
T + N + VP	(2)
T +N + Verb + NP	(3)
the + N + Verb + NP	(4)
the + man + Verb + NP	(5)
the + man + hit + NP	(6)
the + man + hit + T + N	(2)
the + man + hit + the + N	(4)
the + man + hit + the + ball	(5)

In one way this may strike us as childishly simple, since each rule involves a change in only one element. On the other hand, we may be disturbed by the new definitions implied, such as that in which a verb phrase contains a noun phrase. The justification is that this sort of analysis makes possible an orderly and regular manipulation of the elements, and avoids the confusion that

---

[2] These and the following examples are taken from *Syntactic Structures.* In later works rules like 4, 5, and 6 above are separated from the phrase structure component and called "lexical rules."

sometimes results from definitions based on meaning. (For instance, the familiar definition of the subject as the performer of an action runs into immediate trouble when we encounter such sentences as "Slattery took a hard right to the jaw," or "The book taught him something." The latter is equivalent in meaning to "He learned something from the book," but has a quite different grammatical construction. In both versions *he,* not *the book* performed the action.)

183. TRANSFORMATIONS. It would of course be possible to give phrase structure rules for generating all the recognized types of English sentences; but this would involve a great deal of duplication, and would run to inordinate length. A very great economy can be effected by making a phrase structure analysis of only the simplest types, and then specifying the transformations by which these can be converted to more complicated types — negatives from positives, passives from actives, questions from statements, and so forth. Such a process has often been followed rather sketchily and informally in traditional grammars; but the systematic and rigorous use of transformations is new and has already been amazingly productive. Economy of description is not the only, or even the most important, result. A number of apparently irregular features of our sentence structure are proved to be systematically derived from an underlying regularity not previously suspected, so that the whole system becomes more coherent.

The transformational rules may involve the addition, deletion, or rearrangement of such elements as are found in the phrase structure rules. No examples will be given here, because even the simplest would involve a more detailed analysis of the phrase structure rules than would be intelligible to most beginners.

184. MORPHOPHONEMICS. As rules of the form "N → man, ball, etc." suggest, a grammar of this sort should theoretically include a complete lexicon of the language. The combined phrase structure and transformational rules would then make possible the

generation of every possible grammatical sentence in the form
of a sequence of morphemes. To convert these sequences into
pronounceable utterances we need a set of morphophonemic rules
such as *"walk* → /wɔk/," *"take* + past → /tuk/," "hit + *past* →
/hit/." Notice that this is not simply a matter of phonemic transcription, but a set of directions for converting morphemes into
phonemes. The morpheme indicating past tense is a very definite
element in our grammatical structure, but it is not in itself pronounceable. It may occur as a suffix, as a vowel change, or even
as a zero element.

The analysis of *hit* as composed of two elements — *hit* + zero —
may at first seem an unnecessary complication; but it makes it
possible to treat all our verbs under the same rule. The gain in
simplicity for the whole system is much greater than the loss in a
few cases. In fact, a great many of the rules involving phrase
structure and transformations, as well as morphophonemics,
would have to be expressed in a much more complicated way if
we could not make use of zero elements.

185. SOME GUESSES ABOUT FUTURE DEVELOPMENTS. The English
language will inevitably continue to change, and the direction of
the change can neither be accurately predicted nor completely
controlled. But it can obviously be affected to some extent by the
kind of instruction that is given in our schools and colleges. If
we make the reasonable assumption that comparative uniformity
of speech is a good thing, it follows that we need some kind of
agreement among teachers about how the language can be most
effectively analyzed for the purpose of explaining it to students
with the idea of helping them to make better use of it. We cannot
expect the solution to be perfect or the agreement to be absolute,
but we can hope for something better than the present chaotic
competition among three incompatible systems or a return to the
Lowthian effort to impose a miscellaneous set of dogmas and
prejudices. Some sort of compromise seems to be inevitable; but
just what sort is open to guesses.

Ten years ago there was reason to believe that the structuralist approach — at that time usually called simply the "linguistic" or "scientific" approach — would gradually drive out the "pre-scientific" approach which we had inherited from the muddled past. The very influential National Council of Teachers of English was definitely swinging in that direction, and *scientific* is a magic word. Possibly the swing will continue, but it now has to face not only the inertia of the conservatives but the scorn of the transformationalists, many of whom (less generous than Chomsky himself) denounce it as trivial. At any rate, it has brought about some important advances. Our future grammars will certainly have to recognize the reality and importance of those previously neglected elements of the language that do not appear in writing, and will be hesitant to make pronouncements that cannot be supported by definite evidence.

It is much harder to guess how much the generative-transformational approach will contribute to the school grammars of the future. Some textbooks based on this approach have already been constructed — prematurely, I think — and have apparently proved quite successful in pilot experiments. But almost any experiment in teaching, conducted by an enthusiastic pioneer in an atmosphere of exciting discovery, is likely to be successful at its introduction. Whether the success will continue when the experimental stage has been passed, and the same material is taught in a routine way by less zealous thousands, is a question that cannot be answered until the evidence accumulates.

In his introduction to one of these texts Albert R. Kitzhaber says:

> Whereas grammar is now justified in the schools on the dubious ground that it will teach students to speak and write better, Miss Rogovin makes no such claim for the kind of grammar that she presents here. Rather, this book invites the student to study the nature of his own language, simply because, as a human being, he should be expected to be curious about that invention which, in large measure, makes him human. The study of grammar,

then, is justified in this book on the grounds that it will offer knowledge that is intrinsically interesting and worthwhile — knowledge for the sake of knowledge.[3]

I am, of course, all for offering knowledge — and particularly my own subject — for its own sake. But unless we can present some evidence that the study of grammar does have some tendency to teach students to speak and write better, I doubt that we can justify continuing the emphasis that our schools have placed on it for the last two centuries. Moreover, the generative-transformational analysis of language has not yet reached the point where it can fairly be offered simply as "knowledge." It is a theory, still in the early stages of development, based on certain arbitrary assumptions, by no means universally accepted by the best qualified students.

It seems to me that Kitzhaber is on much sounder ground when he goes on to say:

> Schoolbook grammar usually manages to evade most of the difficulties of normal language by blaming such difficulties on "idioms," which by definition lie outside the "rules," and are therefore unexplainable. Transformational grammar, by contrast, faces such problems squarely and, when it finds a grammatical English construction that falls outside its rules, assumes that the fault is not with the language but with the rules and sets about at once modifying the rules to take account of the construction and fit it into the general syntactic scheme of English.[4]

This seems to me a fair statement. Generative-transformational grammar is intrinsically more coherent than either of the other approaches. It has already demonstrated that certain apparent irregularities are actually regular developments of deeper layers of linguistic structure not previously investigated; and it may go much further. We cannot yet say whether its basic theories, or merely certain conclusions to be drawn from them, will be appropriate for teaching to the general public; but the contribution in

[3] Syrell Rogovin, *Modern English Sentence Structure* (New York, 1965), p. iv.
[4] *Ibid.*, p. v.

either case will be important. There is of course the possibility
that the assumption of uniform competence can lead to a prescriptive attitude. For all the rigor within the system, the basic
term "grammatical" is still defined simply as "acceptable to a
native speaker." And since native speakers sometimes disagree,
and we don't have time to ask them all, the reactions of a few
may be given more weight than they deserve. But it is still rather
early to worry about that.

It is also still rather early to assume that traditional grammar
is completely dead, or even certainly doomed. Some of its assumptions have definitely been exploded, and if it is to be taught
in the future by anybody but entrenched reactionaries it must be
considerably reformed. But it is still a possible approach, and it
has the enormous advantage of being at least vaguely familiar
to millions of people who regard it as sacred. We must therefore
consider the possibility that it will swallow its invaders and, thus
fortified, continue its course. My own guess is that this is the
likeliest outcome for at least the next generation. Beyond that
I can not even guess. Our recent advances in knowledge of the
language are so important that they must eventually be used in
the schools. It is as indecent to teach demonstrably erroneous
theories in grammar as it would be in medicine. And it is admirable for scholars to be exploring in all directions. But until we
have had time to test out competing theories and reach at least
a temporary consensus, any prediction about a future curriculum
would be ridiculous.

Select Bibliography

This bibliography is limited to two kinds of books: first, those of which considerable direct use has been made in the preparation of this text; second, those likely to be particularly useful to students beginning to explore various areas of the language. Many of the books listed contain much more detailed bibliographies.

The American College Dictionary. New York, 1947.

Bach, Emmon. *An Introduction to Transformational Grammars.* New York, 1964.

Baugh, Albert C. *A History of the English Language.* 2nd ed. New York, 1957.

Bloomfield, Leonard. *Language.* New York, 1933.

Brook, G. L. *A History of the English Language.* London, 1958.

Bryant, Margaret M. *Current American Usage.* New York, 1962.

———. *Modern English and Its Heritage.* 2nd ed. New York, 1962.

Chomsky, Noam. *Syntactic Structures.* The Hague, 1957.

———. *Aspects of the Theory of Syntax.* Cambridge, Mass., 1965.

Curme, George O. *A Grammar of the English Language,* Vols. II and III. Boston, 1931, 1935.

———. *Principles and Practice of English Grammar.* New York, 1947.

Emerson, Oliver Farrar. *A Middle English Reader.* New and rev. ed. New York, 1948.

Francis, W. Nelson. *The Structure of American English.* With a chapter on American English dialects by Raven I. McDavid, Jr. New York, 1958.

Fries, Charles Carpenter. *American English Grammar.* New York, 1940.

———. *The Structure of English.* New York, 1952.

Gleason, H. A., Jr. *An Introduction to Descriptive Linguistics.* Rev. ed. New York, 1961.

———. *Linguistics and English Grammar.* New York, 1965.

Jespersen, Otto. *Essentials of English Grammar.* New York, 1933.

————. *Growth and Structure of the English Language.* 9th ed. Oxford, 1954. (Originally pub. 1905.)

————. *Language: Its Nature, Development and Origin.* New York, 1922.

Jones, Daniel. *The Pronunciation of English.* 4th ed. Cambridge, Eng., 1958.

Kaiser, Rolf. *Medieval English.* Berlin, 1961.

Krapp, George Philip. *The English Language in America.* 2 vols. New York, 1925.

Laird, Charlton. *The Miracle of Language.* New York, 1957.

Leonard, Sterling A. *Current English Usage.* NCTE Monograph, No. 1. Chicago, 1932.

————. *The Doctrine of Correctness in English Usage, 1700–1800.* University of Wisconsin Studies in Language and Literature, No. 25. Madison, Wis., 1929.

Long, Ralph B. *The Sentence and Its Parts.* Chicago, 1961.

Lowth, Robert. *A Short Introduction to English Grammar.* London, 1775. (First ed. 1762.)

Marckwardt, Albert H. *American English.* New York, 1958.

————. *Introduction to the English Language.* New York, 1942.

————, and Fred G. Walcott. *Facts About Current English Usage.* New York, 1938.

McAdam, E. L., Jr., and George Milne. *Johnson's Dictionary, A Modern Selection.* New York, 1963.

Mencken, H. L. *The American Language: The Fourth Edition and the Two Supplements.* Abridged and ed. Raven I. McDavid, Jr. New York, 1963.

Moore, J. L. *Tudor-Stuart Views on the Growth, Status, and Destiny of the English Language.* Halle, 1910.

Ogg, Oscar. *The 26 Letters.* New York, 1948.

The Oxford English Dictionary. 13 vols. Oxford, 1933. (Originally pub. 1884–1928 as *A New English Dictionary on Historical Principles,* reissued with Supplement in 1933.)

Potter, Simeon. *Our Language.* London, 1950.

Pyles, Thomas. *Words and Ways of American English.* New York, 1952; London, 1954.

————. *The Origins and Development of the English Language.* New York, 1964.

Roberts, Paul. *Understanding English.* New York, 1958.

————. *English Syntax.* Alternate ed., New York, 1964.

Robertson, Stuart. *The Development of Modern English.* 2nd ed., rev. Frederic G. Cassidy. New York, 1954.

Robinson, F. N. *The Complete Works of Geoffrey Chaucer.* 2nd ed. Boston, 1957.

Rogovin, Syrell. *Modern English Sentence Structure.* New York, 1965.

Sapir, Edward. *Language: An Introduction to the Study of Speech.* New York, 1921.

Saussure, Ferdinand de. *Course in General Linguistics,* ed. Charles Bally and Albert Sechehaye in collaboration with Albert Reidlinger, trans. Wade Baskin. New York, 1959.

Starnes, DeWitt T., and Gertrude E. Noyes. *The English Dictionary from Cawdrey to Johnson, 1604–1755.* Chapel Hill, N.C., 1946.

Trager, George L., and Henry Lee Smith, Jr. *An Outline of English Structure.* Studies in Linguistics: Occasional Papers, 3. Norman, Okla., 1951.

Webster's New World Dictionary of the American Language. College ed. Cleveland, Ohio, 1953.

Webster's Seventh New Collegiate Dictionary. Springfield, Mass., 1963.

Webster's Third New International Dictionary. Springfield, Mass., 1961.

Index

Ablaut, 84
Abstract and concrete terms, 197
Academy:
　an English, 211–212
　the French, 211
Acronyms, 238
Ælfric, 96, 101, 103
Affricates, 32
Alfred the Great, 68, 69, 107, 114
Algonquian languages, 46
Allophones, 23
Alphabet:
　history, 24–25
　Modern English, 25–26
　Old English, 25
Alveolar stops, 31
Alysoun, 139–140
America, language developments in, 282–315
American English Grammar (Fries), 293
Analytical language structure, 71–72
Angles, 62
Anglian, 59, 68
Anglo-Saxon Chronicle, 69, 119
Anne, Queen, 212
"Antecedent" and "referent," difference between, 271
Apostrophe, possessive, 152, 171
Arabic, 46
Arte of Rhetorique (Wilson), 184
Aspirated consonants, 23

Bailey, Nathan, 215
Bede, 62, 67, 68
Bloomfield, Leonard, 14, 288–290
　on "universal grammar," 211
Blount, Thomas, 214

Boethius, 68
Borrowing, word, 41–42, 198–201
Bow-wow theory, 3
Britons, early, 61, 62
"Broad" transcriptions, 26, 27
Bullokar, William, 177–178, 221, 257

Canterbury Tales, The, 142–143, 182
Carew, Richard, 191
Cases, loss of, 75
Castle of Love, The, 204
Cawdrey, Robert, 214
Caxton, William, 8–9, 175, 182, 210
Celtic, 50, 61
　English words from, 63
Chaucer, 125
　adjectives, 152
　Chesterton on, 181
　grammatical structure, 151
　homonyms, 148–149
　impersonal constructions, 155–156
　negatives, 154–155
　nouns, 151–152
　pronouns, 152
　pronunciation, 143–147
　text, 141–142
　verbs, 153–154
　vocabulary, 147–150
Cheke, Sir John, 189, 190
Chesterfield, Earl of, 220
Chesterton, G. K., 181
Chomsky, Noam, 307–309, 313
Christianity:
　conversion to, 63, 67, 105
　influence, 103
Classical words in English, 179, 192–195
Cnut, King, 113, 114

Compounding, 236–238
Concrete and abstract terms, 197
Conjugation of verbs, 272
Consolation of Philosophy (Orosius and Boethius), 68
Consonants, 20
Cornish, 63
Current English Usage (Leonard), 285, 287
Cursor Mundi, 137–138

Daniel, Samuel, 189
Danish conquest of England, 63
Danish invasions and temporary rule, 68, 69
Declension of nouns, 263
Defence of Ryme, A (Daniel), 189
Dentals, 31
Derivational suffixes, 88
Diagramming, 253, 298–299
Dialects:
  language, 9
  local, 205
Dictionaries:
  early, 208, 212–221
  Johnson's, 216–221, 232
  Oxford, 217, 242, 287
  Webster's, 216, 219, 232, 239, 241, 242, 249, 287
Digraphs, 35
Ding-dong theory, 3
Donatus, 280
Double comparatives and superlatives, 172
Double negatives, 227
Double pronunciation, 126
Doublets, 107
Dryden, John, 208–210, 226
  and an English academy, 211–212
Dual number, 76–77

Ecclesiastical History of the English People (Bede), 67, 68
Eden, Richard, 195
Edward the Confessor, 114
Elementarie (Mulcaster), 178
Ellsmere MS, 141
Elyot, Sir Thomas, 194–196
Emphatic constructions, 229–230
England, pre-Christian, 63–65
English:
  American, 233–236
  genealogy, 59–60

English (Cont.):
  Middle (*see* Middle English)
  Modern (*see* Modern English)
  Old (*see* Old English)
  periods, division into, 65–66
  pre-history, 40–60
  spread of, 231–254
  stress in, 303
  submergence, 119–120
Ethandum, battle of, 107
Euphemisms, 248–249

Facts About Current English Usage (Marckwardt and Walcott), 287
Feudalism, 115–117
Fifteenth century vowel shift, 168
Finnish, 58
Flat adverbs, 88
French conquest of England, 63, 69, 113–115
French language in England, 118, 119
Fricatives, 21, 31
Fries, Charles C., 290, 292–299, 306
Frisian, 59
Function words, 4

George I, King, 212
German:
  High and Low, 58–59
  second sound shift, 59
Germanic:
  branches, 58–59
  heavy stress, 57–58
  influence on English, 50
Germanic languages, 45, 46
Gildas, 66
Glossaries (*see* Dictionaries)
Gothic, 58
Gove, Philip B., 232, 241
Grammar:
  definition, 255–258
  "formal," 284
  "functional," 283–285
  generative-transformational, 307–309
  Renaissance neglect of, 201–202
  traditional, 255–281
    adjectives, 261–264
    adverbs, 277–278
    case, 267–270
    conjunctions, 278–279

Grammar (Cont.):
  traditional (Cont.):
    gender, 265–266
    interjections, 279
    mood, 274
    nouns, 261–264
    number, 264–265, 273
    person, 273
    prepositions, 278–279
    pronouns, 270–272
    tense, 273–274
    verbs, 272–273
    voice, 274–275
  universal, 211
Great vowel shift, 168
Greek influence on English, 50
Greek words in English, 179, 192–195
Gregory the Great, Pope, 67, 68
Grimm, Jacob, 53
Grimm's Law, 52–57, 104
Group genitive, 170

Harold of Wessex, 114
Hastings, Battle of, 114
Hebrew, 46
Hellenic (Greek) influence on English, 50
Henry III, 119, 131
Higden's *Polychronicon*, 121

Idiolects, 9
Indo-European, 46
  modern discovery of, 50–52
Indo-European languages:
  branches, 48–50
  origin, 46–48
Inflection, 4
Inkhorn terms, 183, 188, 192–195
Instrumental case, 79
International Phonetic Alphabet, 26–28, 301
  Jones's modification of, 28
Intonation, 304–306
IPA (*see* International Phonetic Alphabet)
Ireland (Eire), 63
Italic influence on English, 50

Johnson, Samuel:
  dictionary, 216–221, 232
  grammar, 221–222
Jones, Daniel, 27–28

Jones, Sir William, 50
Juncture, 27, 303–304
Jutes, 62
Jutish, 59

Keltic (*see* Celtic)
Kernel sentence types, 309
Kersey, John, 215
Kitzhaber, Albert R., 313–314
Knowledge That Maketh a Wise Man, The (Elyot), 194

Labials, 31
Language(s):
  Algonquian, 46
  Germanic, 45, 46
  Indo-European, 46
  origin, 3–4
  reconstructing, 40
  Romance, 40–44
  Semitic, 46
  stability in time, 9
  structural levels, 4–5
  and thought, 2
  written and spoken, 5–6
Language (Bloomfield), 288
Langue, 10–11, 307
Latin:
  medieval, 180
  in schools, 120, 174
Latin words in English, 179, 192–195
Leonard, Sterling A., 285
Lexicography (*see* Dictionaries)
Linguistics, structural, 288–290
L'Isle, William, 206
London as the center of printing, 176
London dialect of Middle English, 140–141
Lowth, Robert, 212, 222–228, 253

McDavid, Raven I., Jr., 233
Malory, Sir Thomas, 125, 159–165
Marckwardt, Albert H., 287
Meaning, changes in, 245–249
Mencken, H. L., 233
Metalinguistics, 300
Metaphors, frozen, 247
Metathesis, 99
Middle English, 69, 113–165
  consonants, 126–127
  diphthongs, 126
  diversity, 120–122

Middle English (Cont.):
  French words, 128–130
  impersonal constructions, 155–156
  London dialect, 140–141
  loss of inflections, 127–128
  manuscripts, 122–125
  negatives, 154–155
  sound changes, 125–126
  spelling, 133–135
  vocabulary, 128–133
    learned and popular, 130–131
    Norman, 130
Modern English:
  consonant phonemes, 29–33
  early, 166–167
  education, effects of, 173–174
  inflectional changes:
    adjectives, 172
    nouns, 170–171
    pronouns, 171
    verbs, 172–173
  printing in, 175–177
  pronunciation, 168–170
  vowel phonemes, 33
Morphemes, 4
Morphophonemics and morphopho-
    nemic rules, 309, 311–312
Morte Darthur (Malory), 159–165
Mulcaster, Richard, 178
Murray, Lindley, 223
Mythology, Germanic and classical,
    64–65

"Narrow" transcriptions, 26
Nash, Thomas, 188
National Council of Teachers of En-
    glish, 285, 313
New World of English Words, The
    (Phillips), 199
Norman Conquest, 63, 69, 113–115
Norman words, characteristics of,
    130
Normative grammars, 257

Oblique cases, 263
OED (*see* Oxford English Diction-
    ary)
Old English, 61–112
  adjectives, 80–81
  adverbs, 87–88
  alphabet and pronunciation, 25
  conjunctions, 88

Old English (Cont.):
  history, 65–68
  interjections, 88
  Latin elements, 104–107
  nouns, 73–76
  prepositions, 88
  pronouns, 76–79
    demonstrative and interrogative,
      78–79
    personal, 76–78
  Scandinavian elements, 107–112
  sounds, 69–71
  structure, 71–73
  verbs, 81–87
    strong and weak, 82
Old Norse, 110
Open parts of speech, 109
Orosius, 68
Orrm, 124, 135
Orrmulum, 135–137
Outline of English Structure, An
    (Trager and Smith), 299
Oxford English Dictionary, 217, 242,
    287

Palatal sounds, 31
Parole, 10–11, 307
Particles, 280
Parts of speech, 290–293
Pastoral Care (Pope Gregory), 68
Petrified datives, 151
Pettie, George, 200
Phillips, Edward, 199, 200, 215
Phonemes, 4, 22, 27, 28
  suprasegmental, 301–302
Phonetics, student prejudice against,
    20
Phrase structure rules, 309–311
Picts, 61, 63
Pitch and tone, 302–303
Place-names, Scandinavian, 108
Plattdeutsch, 59
Pléiade, 184
Plosives, 21
Polychronicon, 121
Pooh-pooh theory, 3
Pope, Alexander, 228, 229
Preposition at end, 209, 226
Prescriptionism, 207–230
Prescriptive grammars, 257
Priestley, Joseph, 222
Printing, introduction of, 175–177
Progressive constructions, 229–230

"Properties" of nouns and adjectives, 264

Raleigh, Sir Walter, 205
Rask, Rasmus, 53
Reduplicating verbs, 85
"Referent" and "antecedent," difference between, 271
Religion in early England, 64
Renaissance, English, 166–206
Richelieu, Cardinal, 211
Romans in Britain, 61
Runic alphabet, 66

St. Augustine, 67
Sanskrit, 50–53
Saussure, de, Ferdinand, 10–11, 307
Saxon, 59
Saxons, 62
Scandinavian invasions, 68
Scotland occupied by Picts, 61
Scots, 61, 63
Scottish dialects, 205
Semantic shift (*see* Meaning, changes in)
Semitic languages, 46
Sentence structure, development of, 202–205
Shakespeare, verbs in, 172, 173
Short Introduction to English Grammar (Lowth), 212
Shortened words, 238
Sidney, Sir Philip, 201–202, 208
Smith, Henry Lee, Jr., 28, 36, 290, 292, 299–303, 306
Smith, Thomas, 177
Sound change:
    eighteenth century, 228–229
    mechanics of, 43–44
Speech:
    anatomy, 20–22
    and writing, 5–6
Spelling:
    conventionalization, 177–179
    fixed, 167
Spelling reform, 135
    systems of, 177–178
Spenser, Edmund, 189
Stops, 21
    alveolar, 31
    voiced and voiceless, 30
Stress, 303
    heavy Germanic, 57–58

Structure of English, The (Fries), 294
Subjunctive mood, 274
Suprasegmental phonemes, 301–302
Swift, Jonathan, 212
Syntactic Structures (Chomsky), 307
Syntax, 4
Synthetic language structure, 71–72

Thought as affected by language, 2
Tone and pitch, 302–303
Trager, George L., 28, 36, 290, 292, 299–303, 306
Transformations and transformational rules, 309, 311
Trevisa, 121

Ulfilas, Bishop, 58
Umlaut, 105–106
Unaspirated consonants, 23
"Universal grammar," 210–211
Unvoiced consonants, 23
Usage, doctrine of, 285–288

Varro, 280
Velar sounds, 31
Verb-adverb combinations, 254
Verbs, changes in, 253–254
Verstegan, Richard, 191, 205
Vocabulary:
    disadvantages of a large, 243–245
    increase in, 183–184, 232
    size of, 239–241
Voiced consonants, 23
    stops, 30
Voiceless stops, 30
Vowels, 20

Walcott, Fred, 287
Webster's dictionary, 216, 219, 232, 239, 241, 242, 249, 287
West Saxon manuscripts, 68
William, Duke of Normandy, 114, 116–118
Wilson, Thomas, 184–189
"Word," definition, 239–241
Word-order, 4
Writing and speech, 5–6
Wulfila, Bishop (*see* Ulfilas)

Yiddish, 59
Yo-he-ho theory, 3–4